GALLANT FOURTEENTH

John R. McClure   *James H. Simpson*

GALLANT FOURTEENTH

The Story of an Indiana Civil War Regiment

by

Nancy Niblack Baxter

Guild Press of Indiana, Inc.
Carmel, Indiana

GUILD PRESS OF INDIANA, INC.
435 Gradle Drive
Carmel, Indiana 46032
317-848-6421

ISBN 0-9617367-8-X
Library of Congress
Control Number 81137972

OTHER BOOKS BY NANCY NIBLACK BAXTER:

The Movers: A Saga of the Scotch Irish
 The story of the McClure family, 1735–1813, as they move from Northern
 Ireland to Indiana.

Lords of the Rivers
 The McClure family, 1818–1861.
 First-place winner of the National Federation of Presswomen
 Award, Historical Novel.

The Dream Divided
 The McClures in the Civil War

All the Bright Sons of Morning
 The Midwest in the time of the mound-building culture in 1100 A.D.

Charmed Circle: Indianapolis, 1895—A Mystery
 The McClures in Indianapolis near the turn of the century.

CONTENTS

This book is dedicated to two of the last and best of the Victorian gentlemen:

To my father, John Lewis Niblack, raised by one of the veterans of the Fourteenth Indiana Regiment,

and to Bruce Catton, without whom this book would not have been completed

PREFACE

This book relies heavily on original documents from family collections and historical libraries in Indiana. I wish to thank Mary Nash of Carlisle for use of the Colton letters, descendants of the Harbison family for use of the Harbison letter, Ann Ackerman, my cousin, for her help in historical research in Martin County, Alice Reed of the Indiana State Museum for continual help and encouragement, Tom Krasean of the Indiana State Historical Society, Indiana military historian Harry Grube, Donald Gonzales of Colonial Williamsburg and Howard and Nancy Baetzhold of Butler University for specific editorial suggestions, and Mrs. Joyce Orahood of Owensboro, Kentucky for information on E Company. Of invaluable help in researching the book were the Indiana Historical Society Library, the State Library of Indiana and its archive and periodical and newspaper divisions, Robert Stevens of the Byron Lewis Historical Library of Vincennes University, the Lilly Library of Indiana University of Bloomington, and the Indiana Civil War Roundtable. Appreciation is also due to the Vassar College and Brown University libraries for aid in researching Eastern regimental history. Finally, I wish to thank the Pioneer Study Center.

In the citations from letters, diaries, and journals I have in all cases retained original spellings and phrasings.

KIMBALL AND HIS MEN

By Henry Hitchcock

All hail! the gallant Fourteenth brave,
Who'd rather fill a soldier's grave
    Than act the coward's part.
They're Indiana's glory, pride —
    Their name is echoed far and wide
And cherished in each heart.

"Our Banner" floating o'er them, bright
With gorgeous hues of morning light,
    Makes each one brave and strong
And hearts aglow. "On, onward, on!"
They go, and think of WASHINGTON,
    And join in Freedom's song.

With eyes upon the good old flag
That traitors in the dust would drag,
    Their souls become inspired;
And keeping step to martial strain,
The battlefield they quick would gain,
    To strike till life expired.

Tho' leaden death around them fly
Like hail, in storm, from yonder sky —
    They heed not, neither pause.
But strike for God — their native land —
The loved ones left — the household band —
    And Freedom's holy cause.

With Colonel Kimball in the van —
Than whom there ne'er was braver man —
    His voice they all obey;
And tho' to certain death he'd lead,
They'd still press on with quickened speed
Each eager for the fray.

They hear, as from the clouds afar,
A voice that discords never mar —
As coming down from Heaven:
"None nobler are those who fight
For God, and 'Country, wrong or right' —
    The 'Crown' to them is given."

Wher'er the Fourteenth shall be found,
No more the foe shall taint the ground
    And slimy treason crawl:
For theirs shall be a fate most dire
Before our heroes' "steady fire"
As scores and scores shall fall. . . .

Terre Haute, Indiana
October 21, 1861

INTRODUCTION

In the summer of 1949 six old men rode in convertibles around the Monument Circle in Indianapolis, Indiana. The sun shone on their bald heads, where a few strands of hair covered pink scalps; all were more than 100 years old. With thin wrists protruding from blue uniform sleeves, they waved at the crowd cheering from office windows around them. Then they were taken to the Claypool Hotel, where they gathered around a microphone to sing "Tenting Tonight on the Old Camp Ground." It was the last encampment of the Grand Army of the Republic, and these six ancient survivors and the other nine veterans who could not come to this eighty-third and final meeting[1] were all that was left of one of the greatest fighting machines the world ever produced.

The Grand Army of the Republic, which Lee had never been able to destroy, was at last dying, falling victim to those unbeatable and determined foes — time and age. In its youth it had been magnificent, marching down Pennsylvania Avenue in Washington, D.C. 200,000[2] strong to signal a dramatic close to the Northern Army's action in the Civil War. It had stormed the heights at Vicksburg, charged into the hellish furnaces at Shiloh and Antietam, manned the trenches at Petersburg; but that had been eighty years ago. Now it was all these incredibly old survivors could do to get through the formalities of the program without falling asleep, even when they were helped by their sons or grandsons.

All of us watching (even I, an unwilling fourteen year old brought to "watch history being made") had a sense of something profound ending. When the moment came to declare the encampments officially ended, it was almost anticlimatic; we had the feeling that these men were already the property of history. It would be only a few short years before Albert Woolson, the last Union survivor, would die.[3]

It was fitting that the last encampment of that remarkable army be held in Indianapolis, Indiana, because it was the Middle or Old West that finally won the War Between the States for Lincoln and the North. The arsenals of Mid-America delivered guns, its rapidly growing cities were the supply depots, and its soldiers became the guts of Lincoln's army. The Midwestern soldier was quite a man; not enough has been said about him in all the reams of material on the great conflict. Marching through the mud and clouds of mosquitoes to victory on the Mississippi while his counterpart in the East brazenly seized the flags of Southern regiments at Gettysburg, spitting his "chaws terbaccy" in the roads at Perryville, the Midwestern soldier displayed a strength of arm and spirit that enfused practical vitality into a war effort that otherwise might have split on the shoals of Eastern political intrigue and public indifference. The Midwestern soldier had learned his lessons on the frontier, and on the frontier people did not give up until a job was done. It is a paradox that an attitude as simple as that could be decisive in the infinitely complex Civil War.

This book is about a Midwestern first-call regiment of Lincoln's army, the Fourteenth Indiana Regiment. It had the reputation of being one of the finest regiments in the Northern Army, not only because of its spectacular battle record in the East and the length of its service, but also because of its regimental spirit. In the Fourteenth, as in many other crack regiments, the fervor of the earliest days, when the men, full of *McGuffey Reader* idealism, marched off to save the nation, evolved into something deeply good; it sustained the men through the disillusionments of camp life and the battlefield horrors of one of the most soul-wrenching wars in history, and it became one of the dominant forces in the veterans' lives and in the new America to which they returned.

This, then, is not only the story of some of these best Midwestern soldiers of the Grand Army. It is also the story of the Spirit of 1861-65: of its roots in pioneer history and society, and of the impact it had both on the combat action of the unit and on the lives of the regiment's soldiers. Although the story is told through the eyes of the Fourteenth and the Gibraltar Brigade of which it was a part, in another way it is the story of all the Western regiments, who did not give a damn for protocol, who wore beards and mud-spattered uniforms, but whose practical moral courage was sound as a stone.

And, as any spirit reflects its times, this is also the story of the area which sent the boys to war — the Old West of the pioneer period, when the ideals and traditions of the people were as fresh and green as the corn on an Indiana hillside in July, and when the first encampment of the Grand Army was as yet many years in the future.

CHAPTER ONE

SOUTHERN INDIANA SENDS THE BOYS TO WAR

Mt. Pleasant, Indiana does not exist today, even though it is still listed on the map of Indiana. To call it a ghost town, however, would not be accurate. There are no dilapidated, gray shells of buildings, no weeds in abandoned streets. In fact, a small subdivision has started up on the sites of stores and homes abandoned over 130 years ago. All that is now left, however, of the town's original structures are two brick houses. One was built in 1832 by Lewis Brooks and later inhabited by his brother Thomas Jefferson Brooks when the town itself was established as a better, healthier replacement for the pioneer settlement of Hindostan Falls nearby on the White River. (Hindostan Falls had been decimated by a fever in the early 1820's.) The other, a Mt. Vernon among Indiana cornfields, is the federal plantation house built by mill owner Aaron Houghton down by the river. These houses are all that remains of a community that for over thirty years was a prosperous village of 200 people, the stagecoach stop on the road from New Albany to Vincennes — unless one counts the two cemeteries up the road from the Brooks house, where creeper and bent grass are cut back from tombstones bearing many Houghton, Brooks, Reilly, and Gibson names.

In 1861, when Martin County young men went to the Civil War, Mt. Pleasant had already run out its life as a thriving

1

town. Just as it had replaced an earlier settlement, in the 1850's it was replaced by a new town — Loogootee, three miles northwest on the Ohio and Mississippi Railroad. By 1850 the stagecoach line was obsolete and Lewis Brooks, nephew of the original pioneer of the same name, moved one of Mt. Pleasant's log cabins (which had itself been earlier moved from Hindostan Falls) to Loogootee so that he and his bride Amanda Crooks would have a home to "go to housekeeping in."[4]

When the Martin County boys in the war thought of home, they did not visualize the new frame houses and the raw-cut streets of Loogootee. Instead they remembered rural, sleepy Mt. Pleasant. Lewis Brooks and Will Houghton (a nephew of the mill owner) and Charlie Gibson and George Reilly remembered the schoolhouse where Lewis's aunt had taught school, and its grapevine swing so right for running and leaping high into the air. And they remembered

> Gibson & Brooks' store where they could sell you a silk dress pattern or a fish hook, quinine, or a Webster spelling book, sugar or cream of tartar, sole or side leather or a pair of sewed high heeled boots. . .fat hogs, dressed or alive, wheat, corn, furs, hides or whiskey by the barrel[5]

and the church and the graveyard in the meadow, where their grandparents were buried. It was in Mt. Pleasant that they left behind their childhood.

It was from Loogootee, however, the newer town with the large industrial brick kiln,[6] that they joined the Union Army. On April 15, 1861, Fort Sumter had been fired on, and soon the town was on fire with speculation, anxiety, and enthusiasm. Wagons rumbled into town bringing country people to hear the news and ask questions. Was all the compromising on slavery over? Had the secessionists finally made good their promise that electing Lincoln would mean war? Would they immediatey try to seize Washington? Small clusters of men gathered for information near the telegraph office, holding the latest copies of the *Martin County Tribune*. Women whispered to each other gravely; their sons were talking about forming a company of soldiers. The President had called for 75,000 troops and Martin County wanted to be among the first to respond. Prominent among those calling for action to help defend the nation was Nathan Kimball, a Loogootee physician who had been an officer in the Posey Guards during the Mexican War. After speaking to several leading citizens, he called for an outdoor recruitment meeting to organize a company of volunteers.

Kimball made a speech which the men from Martin County never forgot, although it could have been the speech of many small-town patriots in mid-century America. He denounced the Southerners as traitors and called for the defense of the American flag, and by the time he had finished more than 100 men were ready to sign the rolls of the "Martin County Guards." Two of the first to sign were Lewis Brooks and his first cousin William Houghton. With Houghton came his boyhood friend Charlie Gibson and Isaac Crim, a nineteen-year-old farmboy who had walked eight miles to join the army.[7]

Brooks was then in his early twenties, a dashing, handsome man of high ability. He had adventured in Minnesota Territory when he was not running his father's general store. The father, Thomas Jefferson Brooks, was one of the early pioneers of Martin County. A descendant of Massachusetts Puritans, he had come to Indiana to homestead in the woods. On the side of Brooks' mother were even more impressive pioneer credentials: Susan Poor Brooks was the daughter of Hannah Chute Poor, who had flatboated down the Ohio and White rivers to become one of the original Hindostan Falls pioneers in the days when there were plans to make that settlement rival Louisville. Widowed almost as soon as she arived, she brought up nine children in a literally howling wilderness.[8]

Houghton, also the grandson of Grandmother Poor, was another natural-born patriot. He was a direct descendant on his father's side from the first New Jersey volunteer of the Revolution. William Houghton with his shock of blond hair and a courtly, reserved manner, was what was known as a

southern Indiana gentleman. He had taught school for a while
and yearned for a classical education. The best he had been
able to do in Mt. Pleasant was reading *Plutarch's Lives* in
translation.[9]

Martin County was not the only place in southern Indiana to
respond to the first vibration of war in these April days of
1861. In Greene County nearby, leading citizens were also
taking up the colors. E. H. C. Cavins, a local attorney, recruited
a company at Bloomfield and then found himself, as the most
prominent citizen in the town, elected captain. Cavins' father,
Judge Samuel Cavins, had served under Andrew Jackson at
the Battle of New Orleans. The judge's son Elijah (who always
went by his initials) had been well educated — at Asbury (now
DePauw), and at Indiana University. He was not the only
officer of whom the family could boast — his brother Aden
Cavins recruited a regiment under a later call and eventually
became a lieutenant colonel in the Ninety-seventh Indiana.
E. H. C. Cavins was married with two small children when the
war broke out.[10]

Others were rapidly acting to form our cast of characters.
David Beem became the first man in Owen County to volunteer for the war on April 19, 1861. Fired to enlist a company on
his own, he strode into the blacksmith shop of his friend Jesse
S. Harrold. Harrold was in the middle of a carriage job. When
Beem told him about Lincoln's call, Harrold threw his ham-
mer into the corner of the shop and took down an old gun
from the wall and began to oil it carefully.[11] Harrold, Beem,
and a third friend planned an Owen County enlistment meeting and what would be Company H of the Fourteenth Indiana
Volunteers came into being that very night. Beem was always
proud of the haste of the company organization and the patriotism which inspired that haste; he pointed out that Owen
County men were on their way to the war on "the same day the
famous Sixth Massachusetts Regiment was assailed by a secession mob in the Streets of Baltimore on its way to
Washington."[12]

Beem, a lean-faced, slight man, was an attorney whose family was from the pioneer elite. His grandfather Daniel Beem had built the first cabin on the site of Spencer about 1817. From this home his son Neely and Neely's wife Leah Beem had welcomed scores of other Beems and settlers from Jackson County, Indiana. Their experience was typical of southern Indiana pioneers; they were a large clan who had survived Indian wars in Jackson County before the Battle of Tippecanoe. Then, restless, they had moved onward as the Harrison Land Purchase opened up new frontier territory. They moved to virgin territory in Owen County and began to plant in peace, girdling trees on the site of an earlier Indian maize field.[13] David Beem, writing the history of his family, said:

> Sometimes they felled several small trees so as to lodge against a large tree, to save the labor of cutting the trees into logs and burning, at the same time making an opening for the sun to reach the ground. This was thirty years before Spencer became a town and was an era of good feeling and neighborliness among the settlers. The little settlement in the forest was bound together by natural hardships and necessities and animated by common hopes and prospects, helping each other as occasion required and their lives, though seemingly hard, were not without joys.[14]

Beem understood what community action could do and he was determined that his neighborhood would go to war together.

Unlike hilly Owen County, Vigo County was one of the richest of southern Indiana's sections, nestling comfortably in the abundant valley of the Wabash. Its flat prairies ripened some of the tallest corn in the state, and its queen city was Terre Haute. Not too far from Terre Haute's village limits lived bachelor George Washington Lambert. Although his family did not have the pioneering credentials of some of our military cast of characters, his life bears examination. It was like that of many of the young village swains who would soon be enlisting in the new southern Indiana regiment.

George Washington Lambert had completed school near Clinton and had bought a grocery store to set himself up in business in 1858. A very sociable young man in his early twenties, he was a member of a group of young people who were products of the peaceful years of plenty in Indiana in the 1850's — when the stockading days were long past and there was ample time for temperance-society meetings, schoolhouse spelling bees, and "sparking till four a.m."

Lambert as a member of the Good Templars Lodge had committed himself to abstinence from hard liquor. His diary gives an interesting picture of a happy young man dividing his business hours between tending the grocery store, teaching school, and helping relatives on the farm with hog killing and corn shucking.[15] In the evenings he danced, went to Philomathian Society meetings where political debates were held and listened to preaching (a Universalist preacher was a sensation on the eve of the Civil War).

He was courting Mattie Shepherd, a neighbor girl whom he had evidently known since they were children. He was accepted by her family and came to play the parlor piano and sing ballads of the day. Carefully he copied "Darling Nelly Gray" in the back of his diary:

> There's a long green valley on the Old Kentucky shore
> Where I've whiled many happy hours away
> Sitting and singing by the little cabin door
> Where lived my darling Nellie Gray
> Oh my darling Nellie Gray, They have taken you away
> And I'll never see my darling anymore
> I'm sitting by the river and I'm weeping all the day
> Farewell to the Old Kentucky shore.

He and Mattie would sit on the parlor sofa hugging "till the old man got up to make a fire," and he once fought another young man over her until he got a black eye. On April 20, 1861, infused with war fever, he "took a notion to volunteer" and walked to Terre Haute because he believed that the Clinton

Company, containing many of his friends, would already be full.

When Lambert and his friends wanted to go "to town" they journeyed to Terre Haute. Terre Haute thought of itself as a real town in the 1850's — with opera houses and bookstalls and restaurants "uptown" and muddy, impassible streets. But Vincennes was the city — the big town — unmatched in its cosmopolitan tone (such as it was) since founded as a French village in 1732.[16] It was also unmatched in its history, having been the site of the only Indiana battle of the Revolution, when the troops of George Rogers Clark captured Fort Sackville and created legends told around Knox County firesides even up to the time of the Civil War. It was appropriate that many of the troops would assemble to go to the Civil War from the place that called itself "Mother of southern Indiana cities."

Vincennes in 1861 was a town of many churches and saloons and even mansions. A foundry, brewery, mills, dry-goods stores, tailors, agricultural-implement sales, livery stables, and wagoners stimulated the town's business.[17] Attorneys, judges, and physicians patronized artistic and cultural efforts. In spite of its genteel pretensions, however, Vincennes was still really just an overgrown Hoosier village. On summer evenings the lawyers and merchants put strawberries and heavy cream into freezers and invited friends down to their front porches for parties. One of those most often invited was Augustus Van Dyke. Van Dyke was a smooth, young Victorian townsman: charming, dark complexioned, and somewhat cynical. He had left the Ohio farm of his father, a debt-ridden tailor, when the boredom of life in the country became too much for him. He was working in the law firm of James C. Denny in 1861.

Like Lambert, Van Dyke spent a good deal of his time at parties and socials. He played the violin and sang tolerably well; his sense of humor flowered when there were ladies around to appreciate it. Some of these ladies were whispering that he was engaged to be married; in a style that was typical of the times he debated this large and looming question with a friend, Angie Kent:

What do I want to be making an engagement for marriage when I have set down my time of marriage nearly six years hence? She is a fine, not pretty lady, but what she lacks in beauty, she makes up for in size and above all she is good and knows how to prepare a good dinner and is not ashamed to sweep the pavement. The man that gets her gets a fortune within herself and it is said a fortune beside herself.[18]

VanDyke was as ambitious as he was realistic. When it became obvious in April that an infantry volunteer unit was forming in Vincennes itself, Van Dyke decided to go[19] simply to get advancement and to help his family pay its debts.

And out in historic Palmyra Township of Knox County, two cousins, John McClure and Henderson Simpson, both the descendants of Revolutionary War veterans of Fort Sackville, told their relatives that they were going to "see the elephant" — to pack their satchels and go into Vincennes to go to the wars. McClure was an orphan who had little to lose — he had been expelled from school after the fifth grade for having set a hog loose to trample up the schoolhouse, and he was bored with the farm chores and kinfolk gatherings at his Uncle Archibald Simpson's house.[20] Eight miles, the distance into Vincennes, would mean the distance between the bee-buzzing boredom of the Wabash Valley and the bold and daring (albeit unknown) future promised by those organizing the Knox County Invincibles.

Recruiting was also going on right near Rebel territory, in Evansville on the Ohio. Here Charles Myerhof, the son of German immigrants, became the first citizen of Vanderburg County to enlist in the war.[21] Presumably he did it at a large patriotic meeting in the Crescent City:

> On the morning of April 17, a call, signed by leading citizens, was issued for a public meeting at the court house in the evening of the same day. . . . Warren's Crescent City Band paraded the streets playing inspiring airs. It being ascertained that hundreds desirous of participating were in the streets unable to get into the house, an adjournment was had to the street about the Washington House, from the balcony of which the band continued to discourse enlivening music.[22]

But the crowd was still too large for the area, and they moved to the biggest building in town, the market house. There they listened to several speeches, including one of future governor Conrad Baker, who did not seem to be distracted by hoots and howls of two secession sympathizers who seemed bent on overturning the meeting.[23]

Baker's speech was predictably patriotic and moved the crowd

> to the wildest demonstrations of approval, and in the midst of the enthusiastic outburst Judge Baker administered to most of those present an extemporized oath to support the Constitution and the Union. . . the meeting adjourned with three cheers for the Union, the Constitution, and the enforcement of the laws of the Stars and Stripes.[24]

A full contingent had signed into Company E by April 20. Myerhof, a serious but unpredictable man with a mustache, and others of foreign ancestry like himself (Evansville had the second-largest immigrant population in the state), men named Eberhardt and Reichert and Bergmann, began drilling far into the evening to be ready to go whenever the government called them. They sent their captain, Noah S. Thomson, to Indianapolis to arrange for their immediate mustering into United States service.[25]

So the first steps had been taken, the first commitments made, motivated by youthful enthusiasm and real patriotism, but reckless enough for all that, given how little real knowledge the southern Indiana boys had about what was going to happen. Within a week the ten companies which would be the Fourteenth Indiana had named their officers in that most democratic process of the Civil War — a vote of neighbor for neighbor. In the Martin Guards (C Company) Kimball was, predictably, named captain, Brooks was first lieutenant (soon in a shift of personnel Brooks would become captain and Houghton would be named lieutenant).[26] Van Dyke, in Vincennes, began the long climb to "advancement" in a bitterly contested election and had finally settled for first sergeant.

The higher positions went to men he did not respect — John Coons, whom Van Dyke considered to be incompetent, and William Patterson, a fellow lawyer, whom he thought a buffoon and a coward.[27] Beem was lieutenant of the Owen County Company and Cavins was, as has been said, captain of D. George Washington Lambert went into Terre Haute's Company F as a corporal; McClure and Simpson of G and Crim of C were privates.

But now these local units had to be accepted by the governor for service. By May 10 most of the Martin County and Knox County youth were assembling at Vincennes, which seemed a logical starting point. They spent the night sleeping on the floor of a Vincennes eating house and in the morning walked to the Wabash River to wash. Here they happily splashed near the spot where some of their ancestors had waded the icy waters at flood tide to surprise Sir Henry Hamilton on February 23, 1779.[28] After breakfast they stood at attention in the main street of the town to receive a battle flag which had been hastily stitched by the women of Vincennes. Mrs. Carrie L. Stallard presented the flag (how many flags were being presented that very day at how many county seats from Baton Rouge to Milwaukee?), saying:

> With mingled feelings of pain and pleasure we look upon your noble company; pain, when we look upon the distracted condition of our once happy country, pleasure when we remember that we have such a gallant band willing to leave home and friends and go forth at their country's call. . . .
>
> We believe the bravest and best blood would be poured out in defense of the flag under which our fathers, with George Washington as their leader, fought and won such glorious victories. Our heavenly Father was with them; he will be with you. Death to the traitors that would dare to trail that flag through the dust of shame.[29]

The new soldiers gave three-times-three cheers for the ladies, and their leader Captain William Harrow delivered a fittingly eloquent response on behalf of the group. Then they were herded to the train for a trip to Terre Haute, which was to be rendezvous point for the formation of the regiment. The real war was about to begin. They knew that camps were springing up all around Washington and they wished to be a part of the swelling ranks of the ninety-day wonders who would have the honor of saving the capital—or whatever needed doing to end the war quickly. What they did not know was that it would be many months before they would see the capital, that their ninety days would stretch to three years (if they were not unlucky enough to have time stop forever in the whiz of a bullet or the flash of a shell's explosion). These farmboys were only the unformed fragments of a military unit, the iron filings which would have to be brought together through the magnet of discipline into a solid, cohesive whole before they could even use the term regiment.

Fragments they were, and yet they shared even then much more than just having been Hoosiers who were going to "see the elephant." They were the products of a strongly unified society, one which had grown up in a particular region, shared the same history, and developed the same basic set of ideals. If we can freeze the boys at the train stations en route to regimental organization, we can examine the traditions and the background which were so important in shaping both the spirit and performance of the regiment as a fighting unit in the Civil War.

Of prime importance was the fact that the regiment was from southern Indiana, a region that prided itself on being pioneer through and through. It is true that the region was not raw frontier, unlike sections in northern Michigan and Wisconsin. But the frontier experience and generation were fresh in the minds of the men from the nine counties because of the stories of their own parents and grandparents. Here in southern Indiana, the frontier had had a chance to settle in after careful testing, like a dog settling into prairie grassland. Southern Indiana's frontier period began with the Revolutionary land grants and was virtually ended by 1835. The Civil War generation, then, although definitely still a frontier genera-

tion, was what might be called a "high-frontier" society. Its
villages and rural areas had gone through that mellowing and
consolidating process that occurred in America everywhere
when the immediate threats and difficulties of pioneer life
were finally over. High frontier, of course, occurred in different regions at different times; in northern Michigan log-
ging towns the late-frontier phase of social development did
not occur until 1885-1905 when, during one remarkable five-
year burst in Traverse City, for instance, over 500 frame
houses were built to replace earlier shanties and cabins.[30]
High-frontier society is one of the most attractive and produc-
tive phases of American social development. It is a time when
prosperity is ripening the land, when the Indians and bobcats
and deer have retreated forever, and the mantel in every
parlor becomes loaded with geegaws from not one but several
general stores in town. High frontier is Loogootee instead of
Mt. Pleasant, *Tom Sawyer* instead of *The Last of the Mohicans,* a
time of good, hot dinners and mellow, staunch ideals; and if
we have tended to idealize it, it is because it is the era of the
grandparents we loved, when issues were much more black
and white and much less confusing gray than they are today.

The young Western men from Ohio and Indiana were high
frontier; soon they would join the backwoodsmen from the
newer frontier areas to form a tough and competent corps of
soldiers with the same background of experience and geo-
graphic unity: the Western soldiers in the Civil War.

That background of frontier experience was part of the
character of the young men who were joining the local companies to go to war. The frontier values were exactly the ones
needed for the shattering conflict that was to come. They
were:

(1) Keep a few simple virtues. When survival in a hostile
wilderness is the work of day-to-day living, there is not much
time left for sophisticated sinning. Just as the pioneers
brought into southern Indiana strawberry and grape-
hyacinth plants from Massachusetts, they brought religious
training and belief in strong family life and love of country.

(2) Know your friends and if you must die, die together. Groups of settlers traveled into the forests together establishing villages and blockhouses for mutual defense. The necessary loyalty and interdependency of both the frontier settlement and the Civil War regiment is well known, and their relationship is not accidental. Beem had grown up with stories of the Owen County stick-together-or-die settlement; it is not odd that as a commander in the war he would expect the men to depend on each other for survival.

(3) When you discover who the enemy is, do not stop until you have wiped him out. In Sullivan and Knox counties from 1810 to 1820, settlers lived in stockades, only logs away from Delawares and Shawnees made restless by the great push of settlers into the hunting lands. Heads were split on both sides and "the only good Indian is a dead Indian" became a cry for survival on the parts of hundreds of isolated pioneer families until Harrison's treaties and wars against Tecumseh ended in the Indians' defeat in 1815. When southern Indiana soldiers met the Rebel enemy, they hated and fought with such determination that they transformed their ancestors' cry into "the only good Rebel is a dead Rebel." Private John McClure conceded a vicious fighting spirit to the Rebels also:

> Sis, I don't know what you think about the war but I will tell you what I think and that is the north will never whip the south as long as there is a man in the south. They fight like wild devils. Every man seems determined to lose the last drop of blood before they give up. . .[31]

(4) Use your wits and be wary and cunning when necessary. Settlers in the clearing cabins in Indiana are said (and this is only one of the theories about it) to have acquired the nicknames "Hoosiers" from the night cry of frontiersmen suspicious of strangers: "Who's there?" Backwoods people often saved themselves by their wits as much as by their rifles, bartering hogs and whiskey for their freedom. This almost animal acumen would be helpful in the thickets of Cheat Mountain or the Wilderness.

(5) Know when to laugh. Frontier humor was a lens on a harsh and otherwise unexplainable world. As those who knew Abraham Lincoln said, the spinning of tall stories and the telling of jokes often put difficult situations into perspective, cutting through pompous motivations and baring the real issues. Midwestern regiments were scorned by those from Eastern areas for their eve-of-battle antics and practical jokes, but the release-valve effect of country humor on the soldiers' morale was important.

That the members of the new regiment appreciated their ancestors' practical wisdom in an instinctive way is obvious; what is unusual is that, unlike many other generations, the Civil War generation of young people consciously revered the pioneers who had been their parents and grandparents, unabashedly and without a trace of youthful know-it-allism. Beem, writing after the Civil War about Owen County pioneers, said:

> The people who built their cabins were pressed by many wants which were not easy to supply. Food and clothing had to be provided for their families. Every necessity had to come from the soil. Before a crop of grain or other product could be obtained trees had to be felled, brush piled and burned and the ground had to be made ready for the plow. It required an infinite amount of labor and required the united efforts of every member of the family.[32]

Beem believed his generation owed these sturdy pioneers a debt of thanks for the perseverance that built the state. What that perseverance had shaped was a *culture*, and sense of history, with distinctive economic and social views and political outlooks.

Their economy was a strongly agrarian one. Most of the would-be soldiers were farmers. Beem's and Van Dyke's fathers lived on farms, and McClure and Simpson and Brooks would be farmers for the rest of their days. Most of the southern Indiana farmers still used old-fashioned methods for raising corn, wheat, and hogs on their plots, which ranged from

125 to 250 acres. The improved farming methods which were just beginning to revolutionize Midwestern farming had had little effect on the basically conservative society in southern Indiana by 1860.[33] Farmers still broadcast seed by hand, plowed by team or by hand, and, like Brooks, flatboated down the Mississippi to New Orleans with crops. The politics of the men from nine counties reflect the conservatism of the area and also show the shift from pioneer to the more settled high-frontier phase which was in its final stages just before the war. Many of the men had been Democrats (if they were old enough to vote) in the fifties, with only a few mentioning Whig or Know-Nothing as early political preferences when they discussed their politics in later years. But all counties that sent men to the Fourteenth Indiana Regiment went for Abraham Lincoln in 1860[34] and of course in the 1880's the veterans were strongly Republican.

Clearly a complicating factor in the political picture of the men of the new regiment at the time they were preparing for war, a factor not typical of most of the Midwestern regiments, was the streak of Southern sympathy which ran through this part of Indiana during the wartime era. Almost on the Ohio River and with many of its pioneers having come from the South, southern Indiana had continual troubles with disloyalty. Not a one of the Fourteenth's home counties was free of it. Martin County, which produced some of the most independent and reliable soldiers Indiana sent to the war, was particularly torn by Copperhead conflicts. In 1864, a recruiter for the Twenty-first Indiana was set upon by the Knights of the Golden Circle, shot six times, and buried in an unmarked grave.[35] The trial of his assailant rent Martin County society at a time when it was already severely strained by war.

This streak of Southern sympathy, running like a vein of fool's gold through village and countryside, accounts for a certain ambiguity in the view of the men; among these intensely loyal to Union volunteers Lincoln was not always trusted. His Emancipation Proclamation was roundly con-

demned in the letters home, and the question of Negro slavery
was a constant irritant in the soldiers' minds.

The men of the Fourteenth, in fact, wished it clearly understood as they joined the cause that they were going to war for
one reason: to save the Union. Their area was for the most
part resoundingly anti-abolitionist. A Greene County description of sentiment on the eve of the war states:

> No interference with slavery as to its abolishment was first con-
> sidered. The question which engrossed the public mind was
> whether the States had the right under the Constitution to
> peaceably leave the Union. . . . Some thought the North right,
> others the South, and still others were in doubt. . . .men did not
> fully know their own minds. . .but when the blow at last fell
> upon Fort Sumter. . .the mask of peace was thrown aside and
> the call of arms sent a thrill of joy and hope to thousands of loyal
> hearts. . . .[36]

Beem as an abolitionist was an exception; more common was
the view of McClure, who wrote home on the eve of
Emancipation:

> I am thinking if old Abe makes his words true, you folks will
> have an awful bad smell amonxt you by the time we get home,
> get all the niggers on an equality with you. But Old Abe has got
> to whip the South first and that is a thing he will not do very
> soon.[37]

If the volunteers did not understand the complexities of the
slavery issue early in the war, neither did they have a very clear
picture of exactly how long and dreary that war would become. A private in Company A wrote during the first year of
the war that within six weeks the early victories of the North
would cause "terror and panic to overtake the rebels and drive
'Jeff' from his seat." He said the North would soon see "the
Southern Confederacy reduced to its birthplace in the District
of South Carolina."[38] McClure wrote that he was going immediately "after Jeff Davis's Scalp" and that he would be home
in one year.[39] Beem wrote to his anxious fiancée that he

would return to marry her at the end of the war, in three months.[40]

The political views of the soldiers-to-be, naive but loyal, did not have a direct bearing on their behavior on the battlefield. Their common social and cultural background, however, did. It was an important force in stimulating that spirit and unity which were praised by the military leaders of the time as a mark of the Fourteenth and other regiments. The Fourteenth Indiana was chosen for heavy responsibilities, from the charge on Marye's Heights at Fredericksburg to the draft riots in New York.

Men of Company A or G had a communal vision of home. While camped at Paw Paw Tunnel or Chancellorsville, they could indulge their memories and talk about dining-room tables loaded with fried chicken and "hot bread" (biscuits, rarely light bread), butter churned at home, and sunshine-cherry preserves. They dreamed at night, on cold rubber blankets, of hot slices of ham with fresh eggs by the dozen and of homemade custard. They spoke often of food, of seasonal customs: of firecrackers shot off at Christmas, of weddings and long night watches in the parlor when some relative died, of church socials and ghost stories told at night, of the harvest, and lard rendering and fruit "caning" and the many comfortable things sold in the village store.

Another factor which undoubtedly contributed to the homogeneity of outlook of this regiment was their close family ties. It is possible that more than one-fourth of the soldiers in some companies of the Fourteenth were relatives through birth or marriage. Because southern Indiana had been settled by pioneers extending their settlements along its river valleys, with settlers from the lower counties moving northward to mingle with newcomers from the South and East, families spread out further with each settlement push. In Knox County, for instance, so many families had descended from the original Vincennes-donation freeholders and other early arrivals that many of the men in G Company were first, second, or third cousins.[41] And the relationships extended across county lines: Martin County people were closely related to the Knox County boys by blood and marriage; young men who came from Sullivan County to join H Company were descendants of Knox County settlers and therefore distant cousins of men in B and G companies.

Although the strong ties of blood and neighborhood provided an immediate unity not always possible in newer frontier regiments, it would also provoke some of the most difficult moments in actual warfare. Two brothers from Carlisle, John and Ed Colton, joined the Fourteenth together and were separated briefly when Ed was transferred to the brigade band, where he died of fever. John's correspondence speaks of the deep and terrible sufferings he experienced when he learned of the death of his brother.[42] Men in C Company went through the agonies of the damned trying to dig up the decomposing body of a friend they had grown up with. Old friendships were strained by the disappointments of army life, and men experienced the ultimate horror of helplessly watching those they loved, with whom perhaps had fished or hunted in the Hoosier countryside, die of awful wounds in battle.

The group's kinship and similarity of background, in spite of their sometimes tragic effects, were in general rivets, strengthening the regiment's unity and guaranteeing that it would act with one will when it needed to — as at Antietam's Bloody Lane, where General French, seeing it and sister regiments standing like a wall, christened them with a name they carried all through the war — Gibraltar Brigade.

*   *   *

The men in the regiment were also unified by the educational patterns of the times. Houghton later wrote: "It would seem as if Indiana had schooled her boys for the field." And truly, as the twig was bent through the educative agencies of the forties and fifties, so the regiment performed in the war.

One of the great transmitters of the traditional ideas of the frontier was the church — the Protestant "church in the valley

by the wildwood, no lovelier spot in the dale." Indiana's high-
frontier society was outwardly quite religious, as a visitor from
England noticed in 1856.[43] The correspondence of the regiment is full of all the varieties of religious experience, from the
dashed-off "attended Divine service today" in a list of other
routine duties to the conventional "Remember me in your
prayers" to the passionate convictions of the new, on-the-eve-
of-battle convert like the one who wrote:

> For if we should fall in battle, we must bow to the mandates of
> the King, for we know that if this earthly tabernacle should
> fail. . . .[44]

Beem's letters are full of spiritual soul searching; he set to with
a will to "work out his own salvation with fear and trembling."
    The would-be soldiers had grown up with the Bible; they
quote it freely and accurately in their letters. But it was not the
only religious book they had read in their lives; *The Pilgrim's
Progress,* the book that came west with the pioneers, gave
constant meaning to the many sloughs of despair and vanity
fairs that they were meeting as young men and would continue
to meet in the war. In addition, many young men in southern
Indiana often chose for their "closet reading" books of a
religious nature. The library of Lewis Brooks' family has been
preserved and some of the books in it show what typically
pious young men spent their hours with: *Cumberland Presbyterian Hymns; Wedge of Gold,* a book of sermons by W. A. Scott, D.
D.; *The Angel Visitant,* practical applications of the Christian
religion; and *The Right Way: Practical Lectures on the Decalogue,*
with thirty pages for *each* of the ten commandments. *The Right
Way* is aimed at solving one problem: what is the nature of
Christian virtue. The first ten pages alone are concerned with
one subject which the author of the book must have found
burningly relevant and which the readers would also have
believed interesting: "Wherein consists the holiness of God?"
    This question, which today would confound all but the most
abstract of theologians and bore the average reader pro-

foundly, would have been understood by most of the officers and men of the Fourteenth. Religious conviction was a part of the idealism which sent them to war and inspired their bravery. Although the men in the companies of the Fourteenth would not have fully agreed with the more radical abolitionists that the Lord had loosed the "fateful lightning of His terrible swift sword" because of slavery alone, they believed their cause was right in the eyes of God.

Their religious ideals had been specifically cultivated in the small Methodist, Presbyterian, Disciples of Christ, and Lutheran churches they attended. More were Methodists than anything else, at least when the veterans listed their denominations in the 1880's,[45] and this proportion followed a state pattern.[46] Some members of B and C companies worshiped at the Indiana Presbyterian Church, the first Presbyterian church in Indiana, founded in 1806 by Mrs. William Henry Harrison and others, among them the great-grandfathers of McClure and Simpson.[47] The present Upper Indiana Church stands today in a meadow on a country road near Vincennes, on the same site donated by McClure's ancestor, the Revolutionary War soldier. In its grassy churchyard are buried veterans of the Revolution, of the War of 1812, and of the Fourteenth and other Civil War regiments, sometimes together in family plots.

The Martin County boys worshiped in a variety of places. There were at least two churches in Mt. Pleasant—the Catholic church of St. Rose and a Baptist church.[48] Cavins attended the Presbyterian church at Bloomfield. The Houghtons attended services in the little Christian church three miles outside of Loogootee. Martin County had been washed with the religious enthusiasm of the Campbellites in the 1830's and 1840's, and there were many Disciples across southern Indiana. Religious observance was a family matter in most of the boys' homes. When the soldier of the Fourteenth wrote "Pray for me," he had visions of his family sitting around a table or hearthside with an open Bible and the sad "empty chair" everyone sang about testifying to his absence in the service of his country.

Faith was not accepted blindly and some, of course, did not accept it at all. There was always plenty of healthy scepticism about hypocrisy, poor preaching, and denominationalism. Van Dyke shopped around for the church of his choice and sometimes he chose nothing at all:

> I don't go to church in the daytime for the reason that I can employ my time better by staying at home. I don't like the Methodists—there is too much outward show of religion. They groan in the flesh and not in the spirit. . . . The Episcopal is the church of the aristocracy. . . as for the Presbyterians they have a "cambric" man for a preacher. . . a perfect fop with less sense than common people.[49]

Just as important as the church as an educative agency in southern Indiana was the family home. The men of the regiment appreciated their homes more than any other thing (except perhaps the good cooking) that they had left behind. "I never knew how much home was worth until deprived of it," Houghton wrote and later added, "We find that same reverence paid the word 'home' in every company of the regiment. There is something magical in the word."

At the center of the home was Mother. Put on a marble pilaster, she was the symbol of all that was pure in nineteenth-century society. Women seem generally to have welcomed being viewed as pure, holy, and exemplary. A book which belonged to Susan Brooks, the sister of Lewis, contains the admonition to young women to remember who they were:

> Nothing has softened or purified the intercourse of social life, more than the *self respect* of females. By respecting themselves, for the sake of their sex, they have won respect and homage. Their moral influence has kept pace with their moral tasks and intellectual character. . . . You do not and cannot forget what is expected of you on the single ground of your sex.

The letters of the Fourteenth are full of reverence for women in general and Mother in particular. At Christmas of his first year in the army Houghton would write of the "free and

happy days of boyhood" and the "home that sheltered me. . .
and especially the Mother who soothed each pain."[50]

In the home religion and virtue were consciously taught for
their own sake, and so was patriotism. A vital pioneer love of
country infused the thinking of the Civil War generation.
Children in southern Indiana were named America Smith or
George Washington Lambert or Winfield Scott Purcell. The
friends of the teenaged soldiers of G Company called their
own group the "Young Americans" as if that were the highest
possible peer identification they could make. It was extremely
popular to be patriotic as well as a matter of deeply felt conviction. Stories of Clark, Tecumseh, and the Battle of Tippecanoe were popular folklore and history lessons in Knox and
Vigo counties. And since none (or almost none) of their ancestors had fought in the unpopular (in Indiana) Mexican
War, the men of the Fourteenth were not troubled by direct
knowledge of what guns and shrapnel could do to human
limbs and lives. But their love of the new country their own
grandfathers had had a part in shaping was sincere, and their
admiration of "George Washington and the patriots" almost
worshipful.

The central object of veneration in the cult of patriotism of
the high frontier was the flag. As the Evansville guards prepared to go to war, they were told:

> in every battlefield, when the din and storm of strife is loudest,
> as the soldier through the thick smoke of battle catches sight of
> his country's flag, his heart beats quicker and his arm grows
> stronger to think that bright colors were put on by the bright
> eyes, and its pure white by the still white hands of his countrywo-
> men. . . . This flag was born at Bunker Hill and baptized at
> Saratoga. . . . So do not be afraid of soiling that noble flag, if it be
> blackened by the smoke of battle, the same fair hands will make
> the folds white again on your return.

Neither a virtuous woman, nor the flag, which both seem to
have sprung from the same rich sources of idealism, could be
dishonored:

As [the flag's] long and graceful folds bend and wave in the
breeze, the red stripes look like so many veins or arteries filled
with the healthful life blood, drawn from the wounds of the old
revolutionary sires. . . .There is magic in that flag which makes
brave soldiers and you will find it.[51]

The flag, then, the boys were told, symbolized their cause, and
to rally round it was to rally round the goodness of their home
society and the nation itself. One of the most memorable
flag-centered incidents on the part of the Fourteenth occurred
on the battlefield of Fredericksburg, when, after the color
bearer of the regiment was killed, the flag was snatched up by a
corporal who refused to drop it even when he was wounded in
the neck. "This is what we are fighting for," he told company
officers; he finally had to be ordered off the field by the
division commander.[52] Seeing the flagstaff shot in two on
Cemetery Hill helped rally the men of the Fourteenth to
complete the charge that saved the Union batteries at
Gettysburg.

The shaping of the social, patriotic, and religious ideals of
the men in the regiment was, as we have seen, the result of
family, church, and neighborhood influences. It was also, and
perhaps most importantly, a product of the schools in southern Indiana. In early frontier days Indiana had the highest
illiteracy rate of any Northern state, but by the 1850's free
education was taking hold, and most of the men in the regiment had access to at least an eighth-grade education. In
addition to free public schools, excellent subscription schools
still provided opportunities for some of the men in the regiment to achieve "the equivalent of an academy education."
David Beem of H Company described an early subscription
school in Owen County:

There were as many methods of teaching as there were teachers.
In some schools the lessons were studied aloud. In others the
utmost silence was required. The scholar who arrived first to the
school house was the first to recite. . . each scholar was in a class
by himself. There was a dearth of school books. Nearly every
scholar, however, could afford Noah Webster's Elementary

Spelling. It was a good while before Goodrich's History or McGuffey's Readers came into use. In their stead, each scholar used almost any book he could procure. Bunyan's Pilgrim's Progress and Robinson Crusoe answered the purpose very well.

He characterized his first teacher in an Owen County subscription school as "an accomplished scholar and in every way qualified to teach."

Another good subscription school whose alumni became officers and enlisted men in Company C was the Mt. Pleasant School in Martin County, established and subsidized at least partially by Thomas Jefferson Brooks. The elder Brooks sent to his home in Massachusetts for a suitable teacher to establish the educational standards he believed in. His sister Becky Trask traveled one season five hundred miles to teach reading, spelling (with the Roosevelt spelling method), and basic math in the schoolhouse her brother built.[53]

At a reunion in 1906 an old man who had attended the Mt. Pleasant school described several of the men of C Company in the days when they were his fellow students, studying and engaging in pranks, such as placing a board on top of the flue in the schoolhouse to smoke it out, burning the birch and switches, throwing away the dipper, and cutting the grapevine swing so it would break down with the big girls.[54] The schools were small and were wonderful socializers for the children who attended them.

The greatest influence in these country schools in passing on the ideals of post-pioneer culture was the McGuffey and other school readers, which distilled the values of their society for the children of the 1850's. First published in 1851, when the Free School movement was taking hold in southern Indiana, the *McGuffey Reader* was widely adopted for schoolroom use. It became the state textbook in Indiana and was published as the *Indiana Reader*.

William McGuffey was an Ohio schoolmaster who believed that the cultural habits and moral attitudes of the rapidly growing Midwest should be shaped by interesting books of an elevated nature.[55] Through what was really a rather radical educational concept for the time, he published "eclectic" readers which included poetry, bits of famous literature, excerpts from the Bible, and even illustrations of labored humor. The purpose of the series was twofold: to foster cultural appreciation in the West and to reinforce traditional conservative views of government, religion, and property rights.[56] The process was remarkably successful; to read the *Indiana Reader* or the *McGuffey's New High School Reader* is to find the ideas and ideals of the Civil War soldier almost intact, as if they had passed from the book into the collective mind of an entire generation. It was one of the most remarkable examples of educative osmosis in the history of learning.

Here the young reader could find, in a palatable form, the value system of his pioneer home and community. Many are the references to the most fondly regarded place on earth — the Victorian man's home.

> There is a spot of earth supremely blest,
> A dearer, sweeter spot than all the rest
> Where man, creation's tyrant, casts aside
> His sword, and scepter, pageantry and pride,
> While in his soften'd looks benignly blend
> The sire, the son, the husband, and the friend.
>
> Here woman reigns: the mother, daughter, wife
> Strew with fresh flowers the narrow way of life:
> In the clear heaven of her delightful eye,
> An angel guard of love and graces lie
> Around her knees domestic duties meet
> And fire-side pleasures gambol at her feet.[57]

In *McGuffey* also is religion — "The Prodigal Son," "Moral Courage of the Savior," "Song of Moses," "The Widow of Nain," "Adam and Eve" — and a hatred of traitors ("Breathes there a man with soul so dead/Who never to himself hath said/This is my own, my native land. . ."). Much of this is in a style prized by the letter writers of the Fourteenth (and indeed by a large majority of amateur and professional writers from

1840 on)—the soulful and saccharine sentimentalism which hung like a dripping pall over everything from *Graham's Magazine* to the *Report of the Adjutant General.*

But here also is the *McGuffey* view of America, fresh and young and full of promise, almost mythic in its visionary tone, that was so influential on the mind of the future soldier of the land. Even today it is stirring. The *McGuffey* portrait of George Washington is the exalted one of Parson Weems, which every American home came to know because of Washington on his knees at Valley Forge, or as a youth (in a tale which no boy in the fifties could fail to recognize as an example) gone a-surveying in the Blue Ridge Mountains, exposing himself to the rigors of the forest "with nary a murmur" to earn his living the hard way:

> If there is an individual in the morning of life who has not yet made his choice between the flowery path of indulgence and rough ascent of honest industry, if there is one who is ashamed to get his living by any branch of honest labor, let him reflect that the youth who was carrying the theodolite and surveyor's chain through the mountain passes of the Alleghenies in the month of March, sleeping on a bundle of hay before the fire in a settler's log cabin. . .is GEORGE WASHINGTON.[58]

Washington was the soldier's greatest hero. It is difficult in our day to appreciate how closely he was identified with the ideals of the country's founding — soldiers passing on steamboats by Mt. Vernon on their way to the James River peninsula were awe-struck to have been in the territory of the great patriot. Drawn up in full review in February of 1862 at Falmouth, they fired cannons and made speeches to pay Washington homage.

Washington is not the only manly leader exalted by *McGuffey*. An 1856 *High School Reader* from the Carlisle Public Library has articles on Christopher Columbus ("a mind enflamed by noble ambition"), Sir Walter Raleigh (who in his farewell letter to his wife wrote, "Know it, my dear wife, your child is the child of a true man, who in his own respect despiseth death"), and the Pious Polycarp ("A voice from heaven said to Polycarp as he entered the stadium, "Be strong, Polycarp, and behave yourself like a man'"). In this important company are other unlikely but highly moral heroes: the Dutch boy who put his hand in the bursting dike, and Major Andre of Benedict Arnold's plot, who,

> upon being told the final moment was at hand, and asked if he had anything to say, . . .answered, "Nothing but to request you will witness to the world that I die like a brave man."

McGuffey taught an entire generation of young men that bravery and glory are the highest goals men can aspire to (just as it taught a generation of young women that submission and purity are the highest female goals). Occasionally one finds sincere anti-war sentiments in *McGuffey,* but they are rare in the midst of the idealistic hero worship and glory questing that crowd its pages. Day after day the young men in Indiana had studied McGuffey's lessons on personal bravery; they could not help but be tremendously influenced by him when they found their own courage put to the test.

If William McGuffey had had the ability to see the Civil War coming and had consciously decided to create a mystique of military honor, he could not have succeeded more brilliantly than he did. He and other writers of the period wrote scores of biographies of Napoleon, discussions of Washington's military strategy, and American histories extolling sacrifice in the noble cause of freedom. All of them found ready response in the frontier mind. The lusty patriotism of a young nation exalted by these books combined with the high idealism, the reverence for home, and the natural religious bent of the frontier and were transmuted in a matter of weeks, and in a time of authentic need, into one of the finest military spirits the world had seen: the esprit de corps of the Midwestern regiments.

The men of the companies from southern Indiana were aware of the development of spirit among them early in their experience as a group. "We are still as patriotic as we were in

Loogootee," Houghton wrote of the Martin County Guards
when they reached Terre Haute. "We are all one now and
there is more harmony and less wickedness than I expected to
find," he added.[59] The embryonic regimental spirit just then
beginning to develop would become just as important in sustaining morale through the difficulties of camp and field life as
the song "Tenting Tonight" or the Hoosier yell.

Every man attempted consciously to be a soldier in a tradition stretching back at least to Napoleon. Privates from Bedford or Rockville longed to be experts on tactics, inspired by
the constant discussion of the success or failure of Lincoln's
generals, frustration over McClellan's ineptness, and bitterness over the "unpardonable blunders" of the Peninsular
Campaign. The judgments of these men, without the benefit
of distance, were incisive and accurate, and they did not easily
tolerate fools as their military commanders. Every general or
colonel in the Civil War had to submit himself to the scrutiny of
a democratic army, where soldiers often from his own area
were tolerably well equipped to judge both his ability as a
"Christian commander" and his horse sense.

All of the training and instincts of these young men from the
Hoosier state told them that their manhood was at stake as
they joined the combat units for the conflict to come. It was
probably wrong for society to heap such a burden on them, but
that was the way the times and social conditions had determined it. They were ready. The Evansville guard was "impatient to reach the seat of war and gain distinction,"[60] distinction
which had been lost for Indiana when at Buena Vista in the
Mexican War Hoosier troops had turned and run under fire.[61]
It did not seem ironic to them that almost none of them had
had any military experience. The rather surprising fact, however, is that even among Midwestern regiments, where
amateur soldiering was common, the Fourteenth Indiana's
men were truly inexperienced. Among the final forty colonels,
lieutenant colonels, and majors of the ten companies, only
Nathan Kimball of Loogootee had seen military action. The
Iron Brigade's five regiments, in contrast, contained a

graduate of West Point, veteran soldiers of Garibaldi's staff in Europe, graduates of Virginia Military Academy, and an officer of the Hungarian army.[62] Most of the southern Indiana men who were to become officers and enlisted men had never held a gun except to shoot squirrels or rabbits in the Indiana hills. They were going to war as if it were a county fair (indeed, they were mustered at a reconverted fairground) and taking with them the toy-soldier dreams of the books of their youth. And they weren't the only ones. Hundreds of thousands of men in hamlets and cities all over the North and South were rushing to the colors in a festive, exultant mood.

Counteracting all of the sentimental idealism and the influence of Victorian society in the men from southern Indiana was a strong strain of Yankee practicality and high-spiritedness which was founded on the lessons of the frontier. The roughness of the dying pioneer era, tempered a good bit by time and "fine manners," insisted on manifesting itself from time to time in the wartime actions of the men, sometimes as a truly saving grace. It could be seen in the wryness of the correspondents' reports home, in the stoic acceptance of the trials of bivouac and battlefield life, and in the horseplay which seemed almost to keep the men sane at times of excruciating boredom or tension. In the middle of the Battle of the Wilderness the men dared each other to retrieve a hugh coffee maker near the enemy lines, and Myerhof, then a first lieutenant, flippantly decided to take the dare and dragged the urn back to the Northern lines with bullets flying about his head.[63]

Occasionally, during the grimmest days of the war, the pragmatism of the frontier went too far and became ruthlessness which allowed men to drink themselves into insensibility, to fight and stab each other to death in camp, to forage and pillage and break the bonds of Victorian morality, as when they stole furniture and smashed historic homes in the embattled city of Fredericksburg. They were, of course, the children of a pioneering generation who had occasionally reverted to senseless butchery of Indians and who had experienced murder and insanity in the isolation of the settlement villages in the woods. The pioneer spirit had two faces.

But this darker side was not at all evident at the bright beginning of the war, when the expectant men stood at train stations waiting to go to battle. Confident and courageous, they knew what they were fighting for.

Mrs. Stallard, speaking at the Vincennes send-off, had stated the reasons, in a type of battle code that all the ladies and all the other recruits in train stations across the Midwest would have understood. As a matter of fact, so would the rest of the Northern Army, for her code was theirs too. *Fight to the death for our country; on, in the name of Washington and the patriots; God is on our side and the flag is the symbol of our American way of life. Death to the traitor who would dare to trail the flag in the dust of shame.*

The distilled idealism of half a century of pioneering experience was ready to be tried by young men who were not only willing, but eager to leave their comfortable villages and Greek Revival farmhouses to put it to the test. In them, as in the members of other Midwestern regiments, the frontier was making its finest offering on the only altar the times provided: the Civil War. From Rich Mountain to Cold Harbor the American experiment which had come to fruition on the frontier would receive bitter trial and the men from southern Indiana hoped not to be found wanting.

But in May, 1861, the bitter realities lay, thankfully, far ahead. The boys from Vincennes and Dugger kissed relatives goodbye and to the strains of "Hail Columbia" boarded their trains. They were off to war.

1. Articles on the last encampment are in the *Indianapolis Star*, the *Indianapolis News*, and the *Indianapolis Times*, August 30 and September 1, 1949.

2. Richard Bates, *The Union*, Columbia Records commemorative album, 10.

3. There is a front-page obituary on Albert Woolson in the *New York Times*, August 3, 1956.

4. Lewis Brooks, *Some Recollections of a Busy Life*, privately printed memorial booklet (1913), hereafter cited as *Brooks Memorial Booklet*.

5. Ibid., p. 5.

6. One of the few articles on this historic area in Martin County is Pamela Nolan, "A Hike Through Scenic Martin County," *Outdoor Indiana*, 42, no. 7 (September, 1977), 15-18.

7. Letter of Isaac Crim to one of the sons of Lewis Brooks (circa 1930), hereafter cited as Crim, Memoirs.

8. Thomas Jefferson Brooks, ed., *The Brooks and Houghton Families Descended from Hannah Chute Poor*, privately printed (1909), hereafter cited as *The Brooks and Houghton Families*.

9. *In Memoriam Major William Houghton*, privately printed (Loogootee, Indiana: Loogootee Tribune Printing Company, 1918), hereafter cited as *Houghton Memorial Booklet*.

10. *History of Greene and Sullivan Counties* (Chicago: 1884), pp. 120, 337-39.

11. "The Soldier Shot to Pieces," an article based on interviews with David Beem and Jess Harrold, *Indianapolis Sunday Star*, March 19, 1911, in the Beem Papers, Indiana Historical Society Library.

12. David Beem, in *Counties of Clay and Owen* (Chicago: F. A. Battery & Company, 1884), p. 627.

13. David Beem, "History of Owen County" (unfinished), in the Beem Papers, Indiana Historical Society Library.

14. Ibid.

15. Journal of George Washington Lambert, entries 1858-1860, in the Indiana Historical Society Library, hereafter cited as Lambert, Journal.

16. John D. Barnhardt and Dorothy L. Riker, *Indiana to 1816: The Colonial Period* (Indianapolis: Indiana Historical Bureau and Indiana Historical Society, 1971), p. 80, hereafter cited as *Indiana to 1816*.

17. *History of Knox and Daviess Counties, Indiana* (Chicago: Goodspeed Publishing Company, 1886), pp. 250-51.

18. Letter of Augustus Van Dyke to Angie Kent, February 3, 1861, in the Van Dyke Papers, Indiana Historical Society Library, hereafter cited as Letter of Van Dyke to his wife-to-be..

19. Letter of Van Dyke to "the Folks," April 28, 1861.

20. Nancy Niblack Baxter, ed., *Hoosier Farmboy in Lincoln's Army: The Civil War Letters of John R. McClure* (privately printed, 1969), pp. 8-9, hereafter cited as Letter of McClure to his sister in *Hoosier Farmboy*. The description of McClure's early life is also in the McClure Papers.

21. Joseph P. Elliott, ed., *A History of Evansville and Vanderburg County, Indiana*, (Evansville: Keller Printing Company, 1897), p. 338.

22. *History of Vanderburg County* (Brant & Fuller, 1889), p. 474.

23. Ibid., p. 475.

24. Ibid.

25. Ibid., p. 478.

26. W. H. H. Terrell, *Indiana in the War of the Rebellion*, 2, 115 (1960, reprint ed. of *Report of the Adjutant General*, vols. 1–8 [1869], Indiana Historical Society). Hereafter the reprint will be cited as *Indiana in the War of the Rebellion* and the original as *Report of the Adjutant General*.

27. Letter of Van Dyke to "the Folks," April 28, 1861.

28. *Indiana to 1816*, p. 207.

29. *History of Knox and Daviess Counties, Indiana*, p. 215; Letter of William Houghton to his parents William Hileary and Harriet Poor Houghton (hereafter cited as Letter of Houghton to his parents), May 19, 1861, in the Houghton Papers, Indiana Historical Society Library.

30. The statistics are given in a promotional booklet published by the Traverse City Board of Trade in 1903.

31. Letter of McClure to his sister, December 19, 1862, in *Hoosier Farmboy*.

32. Unfinished "History of Owen County," in the Beem Papers.

33. Emma Lou Thornbrough, *Indiana in the Civil War Era* (Indianapolis: Indiana Historical Bureau and Indiana Historical Society, 1965), pp. 375-78.

34. A good discussion of the changing political patterns in Indiana on the eve of the Civil War is in *Indiana in the Civil War Era*, pp. 85-103.

35. Harry O. Holt, *History of Martin County, Indiana* (Paoli, Indiana: Stout's Print Shop, 1953).

36. *History of Greene and Sullivan Counties*, pp. 118-19.

37. Letter of McClure to his sister, January 2, 1863, in *Hoosier Farmboy*.

38. Letter of Dickson T. Harbison to "Kind relatives," February 26, 1862.

39. Letter of McClure to his sister, May 7, 1861, in *Hoosier Farmboy*.

40. Letter of David Beem to Mahala Joslin, May, 1861, in the Beem Papers, Indiana Historical Society Library, hereafter cited as Letter of Beem to his wife-to-be.

41. "Knox County Marriages 1807–March 1832," *Hoosier Genealogist*, 14, no. 3 (July–September, 1974), 50-64.

42. Letter of John Colton to Araminta Colton Starner, July 9, 1862, in the Collection of Mary Nash, Carlisle, Indiana.

43. *Indiana in the Civil War Era*, p. 597.

44. Letter of Houghton to his parents, May 9, 1861.

45. County histories *(History of Knox and Daviess*, etc.) published in the 1880's are sources of information on the veterans. They often paid to have biographical information included and frequently wrote the article themselves.

46. *Indiana in the Civil War Era*, p. 599.

47. History of the Indiana Presbyterian Church in the Indiana Historical Society, Indiana Historical Society Library.

48. Kevin W. Biggs mentions these places of worship in his *Forum* article, *Indianapolis Star Magazine*.

49. Letter of Van Dyke to "Family and Friends," June 23, 1860.

50. Letter of Houghton to his mother, December 29, 1861.

51. *Evansville Journal*, May 11, 1861, reprinted in *History of Vanderburg County*.

52. David Beem, "History of the Fourteenth Indiana Volunteers" in the Beem Papers, Indiana Historical Society Library, hereafter cited as Beem, "History of the Fourteenth Indiana."

53. *The Brooks and Houghton Families*.

54. Ibid.

55. Richard D. Moiser, *Making the American Mind: Social and Moral Ideas in the "McGuffey Readers"* (New York: Russell and Russell, 1965), pp. 1-25.

56. Ibid.

57. *McGuffey New High School Reader* (Cincinnati and New York: 1857), now in the Carlisle Public Library, "Home," pp. 445-46.

58. Ibid., p. 119.

59. Letter of Houghton to his parents, May 19, 1861.

60. *History of Vanderburg County*, p. 484.

61. As the men from Parke County of Lew Wallace's Eleventh Indiana left the Rockville train station they were told, "Remember Buena Vista!" (*History of Vigo and Parke Counties*, p. 468).

62. Alan Nolan, *The Iron Brigade* (New York: MacMillan Company, 1961), pp. 5-18.

63. Myerhof tells the Wilderness story in a pamphlet, *Nathan Kimball and Later of Gen. S. S. Carroll Brigade*, in the Indiana State Library.

CHAPTER TWO

RENDEZVOUS CAMP

Beem's Owen County company, without waiting to hear where rendezvous camp would be, had secured wagons to go from Spencer to Gosport on May 8 and had then boarded the train for Indianapolis. It arrived too late.[1] Indiana's capable and dynamic governor Oliver Morton had promised Lincoln 10,000 troops even before the first call had come. Ten thousand men and more had poured into Indianapolis and in less than a week the quota of six three-months regiments had been filled.[2]

Beem, and other representatives of units which would make up the Fourteenth Indiana, awaited word in a state of frustrated anticlimax. Captain Thompson of the Evansville company almost went home and disbanded the group of new German soldiers; they didn't seem to be wanted.[3] It was all very disheartening; on that very day, May 8, Lew Wallace's Eleventh Indiana Zouaves were being presented with their battle flag preparatory to heading immediately toward Evansville to defend the border.

Soon word came. Morton had not stopped with arming the three-months regiments. On his own authority (soon seconded by the legislature) he had organized from the leftover troops in Indianapolis five regiments of one-year men to be held in waiting until Lincoln should issue (as they knew he would) additional calls for troops.

Terre Haute was to be the assembling point for what would become the southern Indiana regiment. The Martin and Knox County boys had received that word before they left, thus sparing themselves the unnecessary trip to the capital. Beem and his men were transferred by train from Indianapolis to Terre Haute. The Rockville Guards, the first full company from Parke County, altered plans for the trip to Indianapolis and headed for Camp Vigo in Terre Haute with their company still tallying a few vacancies. Captain Foote returned home to Rockville to recruit and returned quickly with more of the men needed so that the Rockville guard could become Company A of the Fourteenth Indiana Volunteers, as it was now being called.[4]

The men from Martin and Knox counties — C, B, and G companies — made a smooth, effortless, two and one-half hour trip from Vincennes to Terre Haute, exhilarated by the patriotic send-off at the railway station, euphoric about military service. Will Houghton, newly elected lieutenant of Company C, described his feelings on the trip in his first letter home:

> Dear Mother and Father,
>   According to promise I take the present opportunity to speak to you through the medium of pen & paper. It is the first letter that I ever addressed to you, and a deep feeling of sadness comes over me when I reflect upon the happy home that's left behind and the prospect of a long interlude of toil and separation. . . .We left Vincennes at 2:10. . . our company shouted and waved their hats at every man, woman, child, horse or dog that they could see.
>   The country from Vincennes to Crawfordsville [sic] is very uninviting. It is either very swampy at places, while at others it is but a narrow pass between the hills on one side and the Wabash on the other. . . still when you come towards this place the view improves. . . notwithstanding it looks so well, I did not see a single field of wheat so good as that by Grandmothers . . . but with all the change of scene & life that old familiar picture of home and friends is ever before me and that vow that I made before God and angels & men to take his word for my guide is still the Grand Idea of my soul.[5]

The promise he made "before God and angels" referred to his own baptism the day before he had departed with the Martin Guards. He had been briefly immersed in the White River by the minister of the local Christian church. When he had emerged from the water, he had been clasped by his mother, who had said, "My son, you have given yourself to the service of the Lord; now, I give you to the service of your country. Go and do your whole duty to both."[6]

Houghton was to become one of the finest officers of the regiment. He was ambitious and intelligent, with a courteous quality which endeared him to all he came in contact with. The strong strain of traditionalism and duty which animated the characters of many of the Fourteenth's officers was evident in him even in these days at rendezvous camp.

Terre Haute found itself even less ready for the influx of men going to war than Indianapolis had been, and it began to make whatever preparations it could for them. The fairgrounds had been designated Camp Vigo in honor of the patriot-trader Francis Vigo, who also gave his name to the county. Its mechanical-arts and other fair buildings were to be used as barracks and its display fields as parade grounds, but it could not be readied for at least a week from the time of its designation by the legislature. Men arriving for the new regiment had to be housed at the firehouse in downtown Terre Haute.

The main streets of the city were congested as local folk watched the men from neighboring counties, and many stragglers who had not joined local units, arrive to be mustered. The men marched in the streets, ate their meals at the hotel, and enjoyed the local hospitality churches and homes offered them.

After three days at the fire station, the companies were marched to the new camp, which was two and one-half miles from Terre Haute. Houghton described this fairgrounds area as

an enclosure 4 to 5 acres, high ground in the middle and grove
to the west, with our quarters running along each end of the
ground north and south. They consist of houses and stalls used
in the fair grounds.[7]

Officers' quarters were comfortable, but equipment was
Spartan at best. The men all complained of the cold. They had
brought little bedding and then discovered that none was to be
provided at the camp. Beds were simple affairs with mattresses
of straw. Each mess was given its own cooking equipment: one
stew pot, one frying pan, one dish pan, one wash pan, six cups,
six tin plates, six knives, six forks, and six spoons. Food rations,
which the men were to cook themselves, included light bread,
cold shoulder, ham, coffee, sugar, vinegar, hominy, and rice.[8]
The officers, on the other hand, had a cook to handle chores
from onion slicing to doing the tin dishes.

The men soon settled into life in their first camp. Brooks,
Beem, Houghton, and Van Dyke had duties daily, one of
which, from the first, involved keeping the men under control
and out of trouble, especially in town. Beem wrote home:

> I know you would laugh to see how many and different amuse-
> ments the men get up in order to pass away the leisure time.
> From five o'clock in the morning until nine at night there are the
> eternal rattling of drums and blowing of fifes. . . all kinds of
> musical instruments, fiddles, banjos, tamborines. . . dancing
> parties. . . all kinds of singing and sometimes very good
> singing. . .They are nearly all without money and want to bor-
> row it and when they get it they generally buy whiskey and just
> about ½ of the men get drunk.[9]

On the first Sunday night in camp, Beem had to go to Terre
Haute to bring back some of the twenty men in H Company
who had overimbibed. He was impatient for the group to be
properly organized as a military unit.

Joseph J. Reynolds, who had been in command of Camp
Morton and was now brigadier general of the new regiments,
arrived to supervise regimental organization.[10] His assistant

Commandant Hager reviewed the original muster rolls (which were all differently decorated and subscribed) and accepted the soldiers to be mustered into United States service. A physical examination was one of the first requirements. John Campbell of Parke County had been regaling the people at home in Annapolis, Indiana with "spicy letters... sketching the humor of camp life"; but when examination day came, John was rejected for having no upper teeth. He came home in a rage but in a few days recovered enough to begin recruiting a company of his own, which later became Company H of the Twenty-first Indiana.[11] Not only Campbell complained that medical standards for all of the first-call regiments were ridiculously high. One soldier, listing the names of the first men to volunteer from his county, stated:

> They left the next day for Indianapolis and there, we learn with surprise, several of them were rejected on examination—men who did good service later in the war. But along in 1863-4 the government wasn't so particular about a lost tooth or a strabismical eye. What it wanted was *men*.[12]

A different view was expressed by a reporter for the *Terre Haute Telegraphic News* who had visited the camp for a day. He found that "while the inspection was rather rigid, few were found unfit for service." Two men, he noted, were rejected while he watched and one of them "wept bitterly," having failed his preliminary test of bravery long before the unit even reached the battlefield.[13]

Men returned home for other reasons than failing the physical examination during this time. Some had joined expecting to be gone only three months, but late in May it became obvious that the regiment would be organized for what the men were at first told would be a one-year stint, which resolved itself finally into a three-year term. Van Dyke described the stir in camp:

> Last Thursday was a great day in camp. Pursuant to the call of the President for three regiments to offer their services for

three years, the proposition was submitted to a vote of this regiment. Many of them are displeased at the way in which the matter was managed. Those of the companies who do not choose to offer themselves for that time will be transferred to other companies among strangers and will be under the control of officers they do not know.[14]

Most of the three-year recruits expected to be home as soon as the one-year transfers; this hope, coupled with a $100 bounty and excellent possibilities for promotion, confirmed Van Dyke in his decision to go for three years. Eventually, only a few men resigned. Twenty-seven wishing shorter service were sent to Richmond to be distributed among the companies forming there. The entire company from Putnam County also left, and it was at this point that the Greene County unit took its place as Company D.

Thus the Fourteenth Indiana Regiment came into being. It was the first Indiana regiment to volunteer for three-year service, and that fact was always its proudest claim, placing it among the most eager of even the "first callers." Men from Martin, Owen, Parke, Vermillion, Vigo, Greene, Monroe, Vanderburg, and Knox counties, 1134 of them, made up the regiment (Knox sent two companies, B and G).

Some of the original "home-guard" officers also returned home at this time, complicating the process of confirming the regiment's officers. The units filled resignations with new officers, and it was at this time that Houghton was named second lieutenant. All nominations went through the hands of Governor Morton for final approval. For colonel of the regiment, Morton wanted R. W. Thompson of Terre Haute, but Thompson declined and suggested Kimball of Company C, whom Morton confirmed. Kimball, who had commanded the Washington County Posey Guards during the Mexican War, was a fine choice, as later events were to prove; his character combined strength and insight with the psychological sensitivity of a good physician, qualities which encouraged the confidence and respect of the men. He seems, however, to have been good rather than brilliant. Aiding Kimball in the formation of the regiment were William Harrow, already a major, and Adjutant Thomas Blinn. The entire regiment was mustered into service about sunset on June 7. There could be no more going home now — at least not with honor.

Although the unit now could call itself a regiment, it had only the beginnings of military discipline. The atmosphere at Vigo was more that of a picnic than a camp. Constant visiting went on; the ladies from Spencer called on Beem and the other boys, and the Parke County women came to prepare a big dinner for their boys. The men spent much time in these first days wisecracking and playing pranks; the rendezvous camp was like a gigantic boys-gang hideout, with everybody swearing to be true to the death to the gang code and having a whale of a time doing it meanwhile. The men were swaggering about imagining themselves the heroes of a great untold romantic adventure. They even had their resident chroniclers to take down the fine points to send to the adoring mothers and aunts back home, and of course, to preserve for posterity.

J. T. Pool was a journalist who traveled with the Terre Haute boys in F Company. He wrote back dispatches to the *Terre Haute Express* and later that year published them in a book of recollections, *Under Canvass,* "containing incidents" (it said on the title page) "of scouting parties, skirmishes, battle anecdotes of the war, life around the campfire, etc."

Soon W. D. F. Landon, a sergeant in G Company, would begin writing dispatches to the *Western Sun* in Vincennes under the pen name of "Prock."

On June 18 the regiment was marched into Terre Haute to receive their arms. Houghton commented, "There was some disappointment that they were nothing but muskets and as for uniforms [they] are among the things not mentioned." Pay was evidently also among the things not mentioned — Kimball had departed from camp two days before "to see the paymaster and have him pay us off." Indiana, like every other state, was having difficulty getting its lumbering military machine rolling.

The citizens of Terre Haute, however, were impressed by army life:

> The passage of the troops through the streets attracted an immense multitude to the city walks and windows, it being the first armed regiment probably which ever marched through the streets of Terre Haute. The fine athletic forms of the soldiers was the theme of universal admiration and the bristling of over 800 bayonets gave to our citizens a comparative idea of the strength of an army fully equipped in the field.[15]

Life at Camp Vigo was not uncomfortable. The soldiers' health was generally good, but lack of blankets at night seemed to cause colds and several cases of measles. The women of the city organized a hospital and supplied it with donations of blankets, pillows, and comforters from local homes.[16] The patients were soon being cared for, having their pillows fluffed and soup brought to them by volunteer nurses not unlike their own mothers. George Washington Lambert, assigned to the hospital because of his red spots, rebelled against the female ministrations and slipped away to the house of his uncle. His measles turned out to be a serious case and he was delirious for several days.[17]

Morale was high and patriotic sentiments abounded — "I am going to get Jeff Davis' scalp!" and "Death to the Rebs!" — as well as homesickness. Houghton wrote, "As I lay down to sleep I see the family group and tears will come as I petition the heavenly king in their behalf."[18] Private Amory Allen of C Company sent his wife a lock of his hair for her to keep. "Take good care of my dear little children and I will not forget you," he promised.[19]

David Beem was in the middle of a personal crisis. He had joined the army with the belief that he would be home in three months — to be married. His fiancée, Mahala Joslin, a Spencer girl, did not seem to have much of Beem's confidence and stoic self-control. In each letter she begged him to return, to marry her, to give up the soldier's life. Patiently he wrote to explain why he would remain for the three years:

If I was to turn back now, many would say I was a coward. I would rather be shot at once than to have such a stigma rest on me. War is a cruel thing, but I feel that this one will not last long.[20]

Whatever its length, the war for the moment was beginning to fall into a routine of military drill at the rendezvous camp. The schedule was "bound up pretty tight here. . . .we have to toe the mark," Houghton reported. The day included reveille, 5 a.m.; drill call, 5:30; recall, 6:30; sick call, 7:00; police call, 7:30; guard mounting, 8:00; drill, 8:30; recall, 9:30; drill, 10:30; recall, 11:15; dinner, noon; drill, 2 p.m.; recall, 3:00; drill, 4:00; recall, 5:00; regimental-dress parade, 5:30; dismissal until 9 p.m. tattoo and then to bed.[21]

Not everyone could stomach this type of stringent discipline. During the first week of June, a man was discharged from the army long before he ever saw the enemy. As Amory Allen described the event:

there was one man drummed out of the service for misbehavior, getting drunk, fighting and abusing the officers. He was made to march along the line of dress parade on Sunday evening with a chain around his leg with a big chunck of wood.[22]

It was the first of many times that the regiment would hear the "Rogues March" played for someone who could not live up to the code.

Kimball showed more mercy for three men in Company C who attempted to desert after being sworn in. Urging that the disgrace of returning to their homes as deserters would be enough punishment, he forbade the drumming ceremony;[23] he gave them passes to their home county.

Speculation, an intellectual exercise that would become a stock-in-trade of the regiment in later months, now occupied much of the time not spent in drilling. Where would they be sent, and when? Rumors filtered up from southern Indiana constantly that secessionists were preparing to invade the Ohio Valley, and the troops thought they might be sent there.

Kimball believed there would be action in Manassas Junction; others mentioned such places as St. Louis, Missouri, or Cairo, Illinois. Houghton said that the war, now two months old, had seen no real land battles, and the men were aware that the stinging hoard of Rebel bees might light anywhere from Washington to the Mississippi Valley.

Uniforms arrived, provided by the city of Terre Haute. Early photos probably taken at Vigo show McClure and Simpson posing jauntily in light-colored uniforms with felt hats. Van Dyke described the new soldier suits:

> They are grey satinette 'round abouts' and pants with a black cloth, strip, very good clothes, but not handsome. They will be merely a fatigue dress. The dress uniform if it ever comes will be the same material.[24]

They were too large, and the men altered them wherever necessary. Two pairs of drawers, two flannel shirts, and a pair of army brogans were also provided.[25]

By this time most of the new soldiers realized that Virginia was to be the stage for the first act of the drama. They were chafing to get into action. "I expect we will start for Virginia in a week or so," McClure wrote to his sister. Later Pool remembered, "Where we were going, none of us knew, but all turned their eyes to the South East hoping that Western Virginia would be our destination." They would have reason to curse that hope before long.

By the middle of June, when men furloughed for a few days had returned with a few new recruits, the organization of the regiment was complete. The 1000 and more men, from an area over one hundred miles in length, had been formed into a working if unpredictably new military machine. Pool described the development of pure, raw esprit de corps:

> Here was the broad shouldered six footer from the backwoods swearing that he was a ring tailored roarer and ready to chaw up any amount of rebels. . . here were found the lawyer, the doctor, the mechanic from his shop, the ploughman from his field, the

clerk from the dry goods store who, tired of measuring tape, was anxious to measure his strength with the foemen of his country. All these [heretofore] scattered fragments had to be consolidated by the commandant and brought to act as one man.[26]

It was a real cross section of late-frontier life.

On June 25 the regiment left Camp Vigo for Indianapolis. They encamped in a special addition to Camp Morton reserved for them and designated as Camp Kimball, after the commander. There they drilled, raised new tents, and watched other first-call regiments preparing to go East, where conflict was gathering like a squall line of an approaching thunderstorm. Independence Day came; the citizens of Indianapolis gave a gigantic Fourth-of-July celebration for the soldiers. It was conducted in an almost sacrificial spirit; on that very day the Thirteenth Indiana was to leave for Virginia, and the next day the Fourteenth would follow.

The regiment left disappointed over the weapons they were to take with them. They had expected Enfield rifles, the new .577-calibre muzzleloaders which fired a small cone known as the minié ball. But only the "sharpshooters" (the flank companies and five men of each company in addition) were to have Enfields, at least for the present. The rest had to content themselves with muskets — "latest pattern."[27]

The order to strike tents came at sunrise, or as Pool, with the somewhat overwrought sense of the dramatic which was a part of his writing style, wrote to the Terre Haute paper:

> The sun rose bright and clear over the Capital of Indiana on the morning of the 5th of July, 1861, and as its first rays kissed the white tents of the Fourteenth Regiment, which lay spread out in all its untried strength. . . the order was given to "strike" and in ten minutes the white tents. . . disappeared as if by magic.[28]

The "sending-off-to-battle" rites followed a rather fixed pattern common to all sections of the country. In these early days of the war, crowds invariably cheered lustily and ladies wept and kissed the departing soldiers. So the Fourteenth was sent off, and each time their train stopped in eastern Indiana well-wishers brought doughnuts and cried, "Godspeed!" Years later, Beem recalled the reception at Muncie, which was particularly heartwarming and included a "sumptuous dinner."[29]

Crossing the Ohio River at Bellaire, they disembarked at Clarksburg in what is now West Virginia, ready to start by forced march to join General George McClellan's command. The war was beginning in western Virginia. The northwestern counties which were strongly loyalist had been encouraged by federal authorities to secede from the state of Virginia and to organize a state which would join the Union. This proposal was bitterly opposed by the southern counties of Virginia. Robert E. Lee was assigned by Jefferson Davis to command in this sector, and he at once dispatched a large force under Colonel John Pegram to positions around Beverly. McClellan was readying troops to challenge the Rebels and to protect the important supply lines and railroads in the area. The Fourteenth was to join him as rapidly as possible.

First, however, wagons and horses to carry the supplies of the vastly overburdened regiment had to be supplied by the quartermaster's office at Clarksburg. Brooks of C and Captain Kelly of K were directed to equip and load ten two-horse wagons, all that were available at the post, which was suffering from short supplies like every other unit in Lincoln's army. According to Brooks, after selecting thirty men to act as teamsters and helpers, he and Kelly "appropriated" necessary collars and then equipped and loaded seventeen teams and wagons. But it was obvious that they would have to leave much equipment behind until, Brooks related:

> We found ten wagons loaded with crackers for the front in charge of citizen teamsters. Remembering that in olden times the teamster signs a receipt for his load, I told them to go round the corner to the office and sign their papers and we would look after the teams.[30]

In five minutes the wagons were unloaded and on the way to

the regiment, where they were quickly loaded with camp furniture. When word reached the quartermaster, so much hue and cry was raised that the regiment departed as soon as it could to avoid further trouble and reclamation of the needed wagons.It was the first of many incidents of "impounding," "borrowing for the military," "appropriating," and "foraging" that would mark the career of the Fourteenth.

Pegram was at Rich Mountain and W. S. Rosecrans, McClellan's subordinate in command of the Northern forces, was preparing to attack. The Fourteenth headed cross country in the line of march to reinforce Rosecrans. What was looming was the first important land battle of the Civil War. Pre-battle tensions began to build in the raw recruits of the regiment as they imagined secessionists, traitorous and bloodthirsty, lurking silently behind every laurel bush they marched past.[31] On the night of July 9, when the regiment was sleeping briefly at Middle Fork Bridge after a long day of forced marching, pickets began firing in the dark. The regiment hastily aroused themselves and began to form apprehensively in battle line — they had viewed the new graves of the victims of some guerilla Rebels who attacked by night. But the alarm was false. Beem reported that the cause of the ruckus was a large Rebel hog, unarmed. There was little sleep that night.

Breakfast on the march was what it would be all through the war: sheet-iron crackers and scalding coffee. The men now were marching lighter. At Buckhannon they had been ordered to cast all superfluous articles away, and so, reluctantly, they threw kettles, blankets, boxes of canned blackberries, and other parting gifts into a heap for the hill people to sort through. What they *were* carrying, Pool reported, was two blankets, canteen, knife and fork, plate, tin cups, haversack and one day's rations, musket, cartouche box with forty rounds, one shirt, one pair of socks, and one pair of drawers.[32]

Finally, about ten o'clock on the morning of July 10, the advance guard rounded a small mountain and looked over the valley of Rich Mountain, where the "white tents of 10,000 soldiers"[33] awaited a confrontation with the Confederacy.

When the main body of the regiment arrived at the campsite, there was time to pitch tents and eat a meal. The battle plans had already been drawn and the Fourteenth, along with the Fifteenth, was to be held in a reserve position for the present. They slept on their arms and then at daybreak resumed a position close enough to the battlefield on the mountain to let them see smoke rising through the trees and hear cannon and musket fire. The smaller Rebel force could not hold, and about eight o'clock a white flag was seen over their entrenchments. They had abandoned their camp and weapons and were retreating toward Beverly. Pool wrote:

> "Up tents and after them" was the order, and as if by magic, our canvas fell to the ground, the wagons drove round and were loaded, the men with all their accoutrements upon them, fell into line, and away we went, the Fourteenth leading the van, to hunt down the fratricidal host.[34]

As the Fourteenth led the pursuit onto the road to Beverly, a distance of seven miles from Rich Mountain, they met the victorious soldiers of the Eighth, Tenth, and Thirteenth Indiana Volunteers trailing the Confederate flag in the dust as they floated the Stars and Stripes. It was the first time any of the Fourteenth's men had seen the "Bonnie Blue Flag."

The men in the Fourteenth noted the brevity of this, their army's first engagement, and praised the men in the other Hoosier regiments for their crack "Hoosier aim." They crossed the battlefield and saw for the first time men killed in battle, sprawled in contorted positions or shot through the head. "This made us sick at heart," Pool said. Van Dyke told his friends back home:

> I stopped to look into the trench prepared to bring the dead out in which there were at the time about thirty. I never saw so horrid a sight or imagined it. They lay promiscuously, some naked, others partly so, blackened with smoke. . . .[35]

A little further on, when they asked a question about a dead man left behind by the Confederates, someone in one of the victorious regiments told them that during the last part of the battle, after a series of misses on the part of a group of Indiana sharpshooters, one Rebel turned his back to the Hoosiers, stooped over and "offered our squad a glaring insult." The "tearing mad Hoosier" fired, and his bullet went all the way through the body and came out at the throat.[36]

The Fourteenth entered Beverly, McClellan's command post and the seat of Randolph County, in the evening, and here 600 Rebels surrendered. Pegram had found his escape route cut off by mountain ranges and decided that his part of the campaign was over. His was only a small part of western Virginia's Rebel force; Lee with almost 10,000 men settled into the mountains near the Greenbrier River. The Fourteenth marched to Huttonsville at the foot of Cheat Mountain and then encamped on the summit, fifteen miles from the Confederates.

The regiment had had a taste of battle. They had been innoculated but had avoided the disease. They had smelled the smoke, hissed the Rebel flag, and seen the glazed eyes and stiff limbs on the field at Rich Mountain. They had been "sick at heart" for a minute or two and had the next moment passed on to make rude jokes about the deaths. They did not know how to react. Hearing the bands play "Yankee Doodle" as the victorious sister regiments emerged with their flags flying from the battle, the Fourteenth "pushed on with a determination as of winning a name [for the regiment] that should vie with the proudest in the land."[37] It was all heart stirring and dangerously deceptive.

The *McGuffey* ideals had yet to be tested. Only the surface of the regimental ethos had been scratched — the superficial quest for glory of men who had never shot a gun at a fellow human. The brass-band militarism would have to be transmuted into finer, more serviceable qualities in the experiences of real war.

1. *Counties of Clay and Owen*, p. 627.
2. *Indiana in the Civil War Era*, pp. 124-25.
3. *History of Evansville and Vanderburg County, Indiana*, p. 477.
4. *History of Vigo and Parke Counties*, p. 469.
5. Letter of Houghton to his parents, May 12, 1861.
6. *Houghton Memorial Booklet*.
7. Letter of Houghton to his parents, May 12, 1861.
8. Ibid. Indiana military historian Harry Grube believes that the disorganization and unsanitary cooking and eating arrangements helped to spread disease in rendezvous camps in the state.
9. Letter of Beem to his wife-to-be, May 15, 1861.
10. *Indiana in the War of the Rebellion*, p. 16.
11. *History of Vigo and Parke Counties*, p. 470. Campbell became captain of Company H.
12. Ibid., p. 468.
13. *Terre Haute Telegraphic News*.
14. Letter of Van Dyke to "Folks at Home," May 26, 1861.
15. *Terre Haute Daily Express*, May 20, 1861.
16. Ibid., June 1, 1861.
17. Lambert, Journal, June 11, 1861.
18. Letter of Houghton to his parents, May 19, 1861.
19. Letter of Amory K. Allen to his wife, June 18, 1861, in *Indiana Magazine of History*, 1, no. 4 (December, 1935), hereafter cited as Letter of Allen to his wife.
20. Letter of Beem to his wife-to-be, May 31, 1861.
21. May 19, 1861.
22. Letter of Allen to his wife, June 9, 1861.
23. Letter of Houghton to his parents, May 19, 1861.
24. Letter of Van Dyke to "Folks at home," June 16, 1861.
25. J. T. Pool, *Under Canvass; or, Recollections of the Fall and Summer Campaign of the 14th Regiment, Indiana Volunteers*, p. 6, hereafter cited as *Under Canvass*.
26. Ibid., p. 7.
27. *Indianapolis Journal*, July 5, 1861.
28. *Under Canvass*, p. 6.
29. *Counties of Clay and Owen*, p. 627.
30. *Brooks Memorial Booklet*.
31. *Under Canvass*, p. 10.
32. Ibid., p. 11.
33. Ibid., p. 12.
34. Ibid., p. 13.
35. Letter of Van Dyke, July 17, 1861.
36. *Under Canvass*, p. 15.
37. Ibid., p. 14.

CHAPTER THREE

"CHEAT MOUNTAIN IS A CHEAT"

A Hoosier "saw" began to go around the "Grapeshot Grape-vine" after the Fourteenth had been on Cheat Mountain for a time. George Washington Lambert, the Vigo County bachelor (who was now fully recovered from camp measles), recorded it in his diary to express his distaste for the region:

> The name of this mountain certainly could not have been more appropriate nor more applicable to our situation. For we have been cheated in various ways and at various times since our arrival here. . . .We have to be obligated to live on half rations . . .we are cheated in the weather that is. . . cold, colder, coldest and rainy, rainier, rainiest. The next cheat is our clothing. It is actually a fact that some of the boys have to wrap their blankets round them when they appear outside to hide their nakedness.[1]

Cavins, the officer from Greene County who later became lieutenant colonel and who lived through Antietam, Fredericksburg, and many other battles of the Army of the Potomac, believed Cheat Mountain to be

> the severest campaign of this company. Its severity consisted in the cold and rain of this dreary and uninhabited country, the lack of sufficient rations and clothing. In the usually mild September, horses chilled to death in that camp.[2]

49

To these reasons he might have added another: boredom and frustration at being on "outpost duty" far from the real scenes of action. For the men of the Fourteenth, psychologically ready for battle and chafing to be in action, Cheat Mountain was an exercise in endurance.

Lee's army was encamped a few miles away, among many Southern sympathizers whom he could count on to help him control western Virginia for the Confederacy. The Fourteenth, leaving four of its companies to guard the Elkwater Pass through the mountains, encamped at the summit of Cheat Mountain on July 16.[3] Within a week they were joined by other units—the Twenty-fourth, Twenty-fifth, and Thirty-second Ohio, and a (West) Virginia battery.[4] They were all under the command of General Joseph J. Reynolds in the Cheat Mountain division. Reynolds, of course, was the Hoosier who had helped to organize the regiment.

The Cheat Mountain unit was the outpost of the Union army in the area and, as his commanders reminded Kimball, the regiment was guarding the very strategic Staunton Road which led eastward into the Shenandoah Valley. The Rebel force was large and at first the Fourteenth held Cheat Mountain with only 600 men. The sense of isolation, therefore, was strong; the men were fifty miles from the railroad and the local people in the sparsely settled hills hostile. The men could laugh off the problems of living among Rebel sympathizers (the daughter of the owner of a nearby tavern, whom they named the "maid of the mist," when asked what she would take for her favors always replied, "Lincoln's scalp"), but the treachery and hatred of the local people kept the men in a constant state of uncertainty. Cavins wrote his wife that he kept a pistol and an Enfield with him at all times even though captains were not supposed to carry guns. And there was always the knowledge that while events around Washington lurched on (as it turned out, toward disgrace at Manassas), the Fourteenth was not on the cutting edge of the war.

The Fourteenth dug in on the mountain. Kimball decided to erect breastworks of logs, stone, and earth and to fell trees

Precious is the memory of our dead and dear to our hearts are the living heros who are never defeated in battle

Nathan Kimball

14TH INDIANA RE-UNION,
SEPTEMBER 17.

Antietam, 1862.   Bedford, 1897.

Finley,   PAOLI. IND.

Colonel Nathan Kimball, who organized the Martin County volunteers in response to Lincoln's first call for troops and later was the surveyor general of Utah Territory.

William Houghton, the regiment's philosopher who when promoted to major became the youngest field officer in the Army of the Potomac.

George Reilly of Martin County, a boyhood friend of many men in Company C.

The grave of Colonel Lewis Brooks in Brooks Cemetery, Mt. Pleasant, Indiana.

Col. Lewis Brooks, whose portrait appears today in the Civil War dioroma of the Battle of Perryville leading his troops.

Bourgholtzer · GROUND FLOOR B STUDIO · WASHINGTON, IND:

Hannah Chute Poor, Lewis Brooks' and William Houghton's grandmother, at 75. This courageous widow reared nine children in the wilderness around Hindostan Falls, Indiana and lived to be 95.

Brother Thomas Webb of Vigo County, who accompanied his southern Indiana neighbors as Methodist chaplain.

Captain Charles H. Myerhof of Vandenburg County, one of the numerous German immigrants who joined Indiana volunteer units.

The old Presbyterian church in Bloomfield, Indiana, which E. H. C. Cavins attended. Indiana's Protestant churches transmitted frontier ideals to the boys who grew up to be Union soldiers.

Major Augustus Van Dyke of G Company, a Vincennes
volunteer with hopes of advancement.

and underbrush so that the approach to the camp was impassable except for one road, and communications between the
bushwackers and Rebels rendered difficult.[5] He left Captain
Foote of Company A to guard the bridge over Cheat River, a
roaring mountain stream; picket lines were set up above and
below the bridge.

The camp, spread out over the summit, was a sprinkling of
white tents surrounded by wagons, with an unenviable view of
stumps and felled trees on its eastern approach. The area was
desolate and rugged, with rocks strewn about, rushing waters,
and impenetrable laurel thickets. One man commented that
Cheat Mountain must have been where the Devil's apron
string broke as he was on his way to build a bridge over the
Wabash.[6] Morale, however, was strong in those first weeks of
the real war. Brooks reported, "The boys are in fine spirits."[7]
The weather was fine and sunny.

Beem was content with life as a soldier, all things considered.
His eye was on his duty; he had been advanced to first lieutenant; using his usual stiff-upper-lip strategies to keep cheerful,
he went about his daily routine. No furlough seemed in view,
and the marrying he had promised Mahala would have to be
postponed. Letters flew almost daily, with all the difficulties of
long-distance courtship obvious. Mahala seemed not to have
understood the beast of war very well; he sought to soothe her:

> I would feel like I had violated my most solemn duty and that I
> could no longer call myself a patriot. Every person, at such a
> time as this, must make some sacrifice for the good of our
> distracted country, and although you and I sacrifice a great deal
> of pleasure and some happiness in being separated, yet
> remember that the reward for doing one's duty will be certain
> and I hope the greater will be our reward in the end.

> And Mrs. Browning thinks the best thing you could have done
> would have been to have married Dave Beem the morning he
> left! Ah well, she's a very wise woman and she ought to have
> given us her advice before hand. But I know what you can do

that will be better than that. . .and that is to marry Dave Beem as
soon as he gets back. Don't you think that will do?[8]

She really didn't.

Beem and all the men were keeping busy in camp at picket
duty. Rosecrans' strategy called for Reynold's brigade to take
the offensive to put forth a show of force and generally harass
the enemy. The four companies that had been guarding the
road to Huttonsville came into camp; and with the regiment at
full strength, scouting parties began to be organized daily to
cut up the Rebel scouts, kill and drive in the pickets, and
capture men and horses.

There was always confusion in the woods on these scouting
raids. Brooks wrote:

> Our men have been in five skirmish fights, killed four and taken
> seven prisoners, captured thirty-five guns. On last Thursday a
> party under Captain Woods, Company K, was sent after cattle
> and our scouts said 20 rebels were on the road to Stanton. On
> return of a small body of our men driving in the cattle in
> advance of the main body they were fired on from the roadside,
> wounding a private in Co B (who has since died) Tom Drafus,
> seriously. The scouts pursued the party some 12 miles up the
> mountain, captured several guns, accountirees, canteens, etc.[9]

Captain Edward Williams of Terre Haute, with part of
Lambert's Company F, attempted to break up a nest of bush-
whackers in a local farmhouse which served as a guerilla headquarters. Pool reported:

> By some means the rebels got wind of our boys before they could
> succeed in surrounding the house, and a part of them broke
> cover and started for the nearest mountain jungles, having their
> retreat covered by women and children.

The men from the Fourteenth doubled back and pounced on
the Rebels from behind to avoid hitting the hostages. They
poured verbal abuse at the cowards for using women and
children to cover their flight.

Regimental headquarters were established at the house of a

taciturn old Rebel farmer named White. Pool, sending his weekly dispatches to the *Terre Haute Express*, described White's "farm of 20 acres on which was about 10 rocks to one blade of grass, on an average." Scouts had found tools and bowie blades in White's cellar and put him under arrest. They turned his house into a hospital and his barn into a quartermaster's commissary. He seemed to the supercilious Pool a fair sample of the mountaineer, a "gaunt, lean half-starved devil" who marveled at the telegraph connecting the camp to his house:

> He could understand very well how a paper with a communication written upon it could be strung upon the wire and shoved along, but how to get the paper past the pole without tearing the paper to pieces was a puzzler.[10]

John McClure seemed to have more sympathy for White. He told his sister that White was a brother to a hired man the McClures used to have and added that the timber clearing the regiment was doing would soon "have a big farm cleared for old Mr. White."[11]

McClure and the other farm boys were faring better than their city messmates on Cheat Mountain. In mid-August, when the rains set in, G Company built log houses. McClure described their situation:

> Our houses are built of spruce fir logs and covered with spruce bark. It is a very good covering and keeps everything dry. We sit by a bright fire in a dry house (shantys we call them) and cook our meals.[12]

While many of the small-town aristocrats were holding up their coat tails and complaining about the rain's making the roads impassable, McClure, Simpson, and others in G Company hauled rocks to pave the streets. Van Dyke made himself a cot from a burlap bag to keep himself off the damp ground. The only problem with the cot was that it was likely to fall down unexpectedly, tumbling Van Dyke out.[13]

Pool, himself one of the more citified types and strongly aware of the differences between villagers and farmers, was surprised to see those differences lessening daily:

> At first it was a matter of astonishment to the author how men could so readily accommodate themselves to circumstances, and appear to be as cheerful as those engaged in some cheerful pastime. It is true that a large portion of the Fourteenth was composed of men inured to hardships by incessant toil in opening up the rich resources of the fertile lands in the Wabash valley and cared very little for a wet jacket or a night on the damp ground. . . .There were many men, however, in the Regiment who, until now had never passed a night in the woods, or had never slept from under a good roof, or out of a comfortable bed. To see these men taking their four hours relief from guard duty, laying on the wet ground, rolled up in a blanket, the cold drizzling rain of the mountains saturating their scanty covering. . . at the same time sleeping as soundly as if at home. . .we were astonished.[14]

Clearly, toughening influences were at work, and men were having to tap inner resources for defenses against the weather, the fear of surprise attacks, and the inactivity. Beem had "taken up housekeeping" with Second Lieutenant Porter B. Lunday from Gosport. Lunday was a moral man, and Beem wrote Mahala that they shared many ideas: he didn't mind at all if Beem read the Bible.[15]

Other men were making themselves as comfortable as they could, but against the subtle challenges of boredom, defenses were all but useless. Kimball's scouting parties had not as yet bearded the lion, and Lee refused to be forced into action. As August wore on, the men tried different means of passing the long hours in camp between scouting expeditions, falling back on their own back-home pastimes. They played cards, took "chaws terbacky," and organized debating societies. At night they gathered in knots around the campfire singing "Yankee Doodle," "Dixie," and other favorites. And there were prayer meetings; but these seemed only to increase their homesickness by carrying the hearer back in imagination to old familiar scenes until he could almost fancy he was once more at his home in the beautiful Western village, sitting in the old meeting house, surrounded by family and friends.[16]

As the rains continued, fewer scouting parties went out; they found in turn fewer Rebel scouting parties on the road. It was as if both sides had grown tired of the game of scout and ambush and each had pulled back to see what the other would do. The parties which went out at the end of August reacted brazenly to the uneasy tension in the air, foraging for want of better amusement and securing dinners of beef, boiled potatoes, and maple sugar at gun point. They attacked wagons and questioned mountain men and their children, and played reckless games of hide-and-seek too near the Rebel camp.

The correspondents to the hometown papers referred to these sallies as "devil-may-care contempt of danger." In truth they were nothing more than recklessness and poor judgment stemming directly from boredom. The Fourteenth's attitude toward foraging, and the people whose lands were going to be foraged — the "enemy" — was beginning to emerge clearly by this time anyway. Foraging, as they looked at it, was one of the "necessities of war." (You could excuse a vast amount of repulsive human behavior under the term "necessities of war.") Quite simply, the Rebels deserved it. They had started the war, hadn't they? There was a choice to be made in these mountains; you could support the flag of your fathers or the fratricides, just as there would be choices for the people of Frederick, Maryland and Fredericksburg. If you made your choice for the wrong side, you should be prepared to pay the price which, presumably, was helplessly watching your food supply for the winter be destroyed, your livestock slaughtered, and your homestead ruined. Though they might not have admitted it, under this philosophy of warring the Fourteenth had no right to complain about anything that Morgan the Raider might do in the Hoosier hills.

And so, with devil-may-care contempt of danger urging them on, the youth of southern Indiana dashed down roads of western Virginia in search of swashbuckling escapades among the hogs and hill people because they had nothing better to do. Sometimes they encountered real, honest-to-goodness Rebels. Two of Cavins' lieutenants with a group of men from D who were on guard near the deadwood about three miles from camp came around a bend in the road to encounter some 400 of the enemy about fifty yards away. Retreat would have been wise, but instead the men of the Fourteenth gave the Hoosier yell and charged with bayonets fixed. The Rebels, astonished at the sight of a few men firing pointblank at their far superior force, could not organize themselves to return fire before the men had turned and safely made their retreat up the road.[17]

More serious, or more exciting (depending on whether one considered the experience on Cheat Mountain a war or a skylark), was another episode. On August 31 Coons was ordered forward with about 100 men from G Company. After a twenty-mile march on limited rations, Coons ordered camp made at a deserted farmhouse near a mill, where tempting food supplies had been left in the hurried flight of the occupants. He posted advance guards.

Most of the men slept on their arms; Coons evidently shut his eyes while the remainder slaughtered and dressed a young calf and "requisitioned" new potatoes from the garden. Pool wrote:

> All things appeared to be going off smoothly and nice, the beef and potatoes sizzled in the pot as loving as a newly married couple on the honeymoon.

Then pickets came charging into camp, followed by the vanguard of about 400 secessionist cavalry. The men, surprised at their cooking, managed to form on the double quick anyway and retreated without loss.[18] Most of the men treated the skirmish as a great rollicking adventure, but Houghton recorded another view in his diary:

> Our scouts were attacked by secesh cavalry and three companies of infantry. Came near to being cut off through the carelessness of Captain Coons.[19]

Houghton was beginning to feel an ominous decline of morale. The dreams of recruitment times were melting away like cotton candy in the drizzling rains of Cheat Mountain. So this was war: extreme personal discomfort, petty bickering, and second-hand battles far away over the Shenandoah Mountains near Washington. The men grew taciturn and irritable, and many summer soldiers decided to fold their dreams of glory, pack them among the cotton batting, and look out for the first opportunity to get out. Company H had its share of difficulties. Beem wrote Hala:

> Yesterday we had quite an interesting time, and it is rather serious too. Perhaps you are aware that Captain Martin is exceedingly unpopular in the company; so much so that nearly every one is anxious that he should resign and go home. He has several times said that he would go home if a majority of the company wanted him to. Well they yesterday morning got up a paper which read that they were willing for him to go home and thought that his health was so poor that he ought to do so. . . . Martin went to the Colonel and told him that these boys were trying to get him to resign. The Colonel considered it an act of insubordination and reduced all the non-commissioned officers to the ranks who signed it.[20]

Beem was trying not to give in to "the blues." He admitted that he hadn't been to "preaching" for quite a while but insisted to Hala that he would "never prove unfaithful to a kind and merciful Savior." The irritations of camp life were distracting him, he said, and a visit from the camp chaplain did not help. It was difficult to be a Christian in camp on Cheat Mountain.

> This evening I was called upon by our very worthy Chaplain Bro Webb. He frequently calls in to see me and ask how I am getting along religiously. What do you suppose I told him this evening? [I told him] I do not know if I have made any permanent spiritual advancement. I shall try to keep my spiritual strength renewed.[21]

Mahala had received reports that he had been swearing;

these Beem denied. But certainly many others in the regiment must have been cursing, at the cold, dreary drizzle, the picket duty, and, most of all, the ragged and embarrassing uniforms. Van Dyke believed the tattered uniforms were a detriment to morale: "Some men more modest than the rest wear their blankets to hide their sitting down places."[22] Coons was so infuriated at his own torn breeches and the state of his men's clothing that he wrote Governor Morton. It was also a way to get noticed: Coons had nothing but his own grim determination and bravado as an officer to advance him.

> Camp Cheat Mountain
> September 2, 1861
>
> Gov. O. P. Morton
> Sir. You may deem it presumptuous in me to address you upon a subject over which you may perhaps directly have no control but may indirectly have a great influence as the executor of our State, and if I did not conceive that the service absolutely required it I would not now trouble you with any complaints. . . . Our boys have had no clothing of any kind since they left Camp Vigo, and the condition of their uniforms is absolutely disgraceful. . . this state of things should not be permitted to exist in a government like ours. . . . There is nothing that creates dissatisfaction among the men so much as the apparent neglect of the proper authorities to furnish them with those articles which they so much need for their comfort. I am proud to say that the gallant men of the 14th have never failed to do their duty when called upon. . . .
>
> Yours respectfully
> John Coons, Captain Co G[23]

The request for overcoats which Coons sent to Oliver Perry Morton had far reaching effects. Somehow it appealed to Morton's paternalism. His boys were out in the field, freezing, and it was a real indignity in a war which hadn't yet got off the ground. He determined to make an issue of it and personally supervised the acquiring of decent coats for the men on the mountain, raising cane in Indiana and in Washington, D.C. itself, where he went to directly superintend the delivery of the

coats. But Coons got more than just a coat on his back from the
furor he caused; he had successfully brought himself to the
notice of Morton, and this was an age and a war in which the
notice of the governor of the state went a long way for a poor,
undistinguished military man with high aspirations.[24] Coons
had quite neatly started himself down a long road toward the
colonelship of the Fourteenth Indiana, just as his governor
had put his feet on the long, tough path of political service in
an incendiary time.

Requests from half-naked officers for breeches were only
one of the things Morton had to hear about as governor of
Indiana. A gifted and conscientious administrator, he kept a
tight rein on military as well as political affairs in the state. He
had many odd requests during this early part of the war; some
were from the Fourteenth and reveal the minor inconveni-
ences of camp life, which appeared large to those involved.
Kimball asked for tubas, cornets, and cymbals which had been
promised to the band to "sustain the credit of the regiment
and state"; citizens of Bowling Green, Indiana wrote bemoan-
ing that their sons joined the Fourteenth as band members
with the promise of new instruments; not only had they not
arrived, but Kimball was making the boys "do menial things
properly belonging to privates." He had sent them out as
pickets and scouts and "they must act as servants and or-
derlies." Louis Lamby, an assistant surgeon, was passed over
for advancement and wrote, "I am not surprised that I should
be overlooked for the simple reason that I am a German."
Adjutant Thomas Blinn had everyone he could find write to
urge his appointment as a field officer; Coon had everyone he
could find write against Blinn, claiming that he would not
serve under such a "puppy." Several wrote about Harrow's
"bad habits." Harrow wrote asking for a transfer from this
undistinguished situation so he could make his fortune
elsewhere.

Political intriguing in general was growing as thick as the fog
on a Cheat Mountain morning. Van Dyke wrote home on
August 12:

> You will see that we are still stationed on the summit of this
> infernal mountain which is the meanest campground that I have
> ever seen. The mud is not less than shoe leather top deep. . . .
> We have not had three hours of dry weather for more than a
> week by actual count. . .the men have become dissatisfied with
> the field officers and in many instances with their company
> officers. . . .I know that there is not a man in our company but
> what would be pleased to get rid of our Captain Coons and many
> are the curses, not loud but deep he gets.

Van Dyke, who had joined the company for advancement, was
trying to get out when he could not find it. He had written
Ohio Representative John Gurley to aid him; he wished to
organize a company of his own.

Dissatisfaction grew until it broke into the open August 24
with what was described by some as a "mutiny." The trouble
arose ostensibly over Congress' legalization of President
Lincoln's call for three-year troops. As Van Dyke put it, "A
great many think we cannot be held longer than three months
and swear that they will go home the Seventh of next month."[25]
What was really behind the mutiny was intense irritation over
life on Cheat Mountain. Both officers and men met in protest,
with the day ending in the resignation of several officers:
Lieutenants Dudley Rogers and Wiley E. Dittemore of H;
Lieutenant Taylor and Captain Noah S. Thompson of E
(Thompson had helped organize the Crescent City Guards);
and Lieutenants William D. Lewis and Lynch M. Terrell of B.
The matter was far from settled. E Company refused to elect
new officers and finally General Reynolds came down from
brigade headquarters to force the issue on September 2. By
September 3 all vacancies were filled and all noncommissioned
officers and privates with a few exceptions were in the guard
house for the mutiny. Houghton hoped, "The excitement will
pass away without disgrace to our regiment," and the matter
was hushed up, with orders evidently given that the men not
write home about the matter.[26]

Reynolds realized that the regiment needed more rigorous
discipline and a better organized permanent encampment.

The camp had been set up on the summit in a haphazard way, "each company having pitched their tents wherever they chose." But now a great flurry of ditching, paving of streets, and orderly pitching of tents set the post in order to suit the army engineers' plans. The men, including Van Dyke, decided that they were in the war to stay and settled into the acceptance of whatever military life might bring.

What it brought was battle — the first real engagement of the Fourteenth.

The western Virginia campaign intensified as Lee determined in the middle of September to test the strength of the Northern Army. On September 12, he ordered an encircling movement: 3000 Arkansas, Tennessee, and Georgia infantrymen were to undertake a flank movement by night and join forces with troops in the rear to surprise the sleeping regiments on Cheat Mountain.[27] Kimball was aware that there was movement; he ordered a scout toward the camp of the Fifteenth Indiana and Van Dyke detailed sixty good men from G Company to form a scouting party.[28]

Coons was to lead the men. He started them off toward headquarters and after finding nothing began to return to camp. His party encountered Rebel troops, and an Indian-style battle began. The surprised Southerners, probably believing that the entire west Virginia command had come upon them, suddenly bolted. Meanwhile, in camp, the men waited for an attack that would now never come. John Kuppenheim, a private of F Company, evidently writing in his diary from moment to moment, described the tension as the waiting men listened to the firing of Company G nearby in the woods:

> We expect every minute Seceschs coming out of the woods. We will defend our post to the last drop of blood. The men are all silent as death. Liet. Brasher just told us in a whisper to cock gun and hold ourself in readyness. They seen them passing through an opening no further than ½ of a mile. This is the only moment in my life that a certain feeling of that I, like so many others, is about to pass from this world. The moment ended is very holy. Nothing has occurred yet. Cannoniers are ready for

action, they are ready to aim. One piece is not further than 50
yards from my post. It is now ten o'clock. The col just came up
the road again saying, "Now boys give them hell." He is brave
and sure I love him like a father. It is now near noon. The sun
shines bright. Captain Martin just came up the road. He says the
rebels left their position. . da. .m . n. . cowarts are afraid to fight
a fair fight.[29]

Coons came into camp almost exhausted, with his tattered
breeches half gone. Kimball supplied him with his own pants.
Three men of the Fourteenth were killed, seven wounded,
and two captured. The encounter, really a skirmish, was referred to as the Battle of Cheat Mountain. Many wondered
why the Rebels had not attacked while they had the camp
surrounded, just before Coons arrived, and theorized that
heavy rains during the night had wet the Southerners' powder. When Coons' men approached, the Rebels believed that
they had themselves been surprised by the entire army. As
they fled, they littered the hillside with knapsacks, blankets,
and other possessions; but Houghton and others complained
that the Fourteenth got little of it. "The Ohio regiment stole all
our plunder," he said.[30]

E Company had advanced down the pike late in the skirmish; Sergeant August Junod of the Crescent City Guards had
been killed. After the Rebels' retreat, Brooks called for volunteers to secure Junod's body from behind the enemy lines.
Four men volunteered, among them Isaac Crim, the school-
boy from Loogootee. Daringly, they slipped through the lines
and brought back Junod's body for burial on Cheat
Mountain.[31] Another soldier, a private, had died with a ball
through his forehead and twenty wounds from balls and
bayonets in his body.

Now Reynolds decided to try to force Lee from the Green-
brier, or at least to give the army a real test of strength.
Reynolds' forces were superior; he had been reinforced by the
Twenty-fourth, Twenty-fifth, and Thirty-second Ohio regi-
ments and other units. He made ready to attack Lee on
September 26 and advanced two companies down the moun-

tain. Most spent the night without tents. As they waited to attack at dawn, an enormous ice storm pelted the area. Soldiers with tents took in as many comrades as they could, but not all could find shelter. Seven horses froze to death that night, and many men suffered from exposure.[32] The attack had to be temporarily postponed.

On October 2 all the troops received orders to prepare two days' rations. Landon estimated that after the hardships of the week before, only 600 were able to stand for duty.[33] Many were weak and unable to eat, the victims of "camp fever," which the surgeon described as an "exhaustion of the nervous system" with continued fever and bloating of the body. The causes of the sometimes fatal illness, according to an 1888 government medical history of the war, were "unquestionably protracted and exhausting labor, exposure to cold and incessant rains, insufficient clothing and sameness of food."[34] George Washington Lambert was covered with boils and could not stand or sit, let alone fight.[35] In Company C mess only Crim was fit; his messmates now told him, "You have been eating our food and now you must do our fighting."[36] Landon described the eve-of-battle preparations in camp, which in spite of the recent difficulties, were jovial.

> Up to 9 o'clock camp fires burned brightly; around them groups of soldiers gathered singing, laughing, "speculating" on the coming fight. There was a constant jing, jingle of iron ram-rods, snapping of caps, and sputtering of hot grease in sundry frying pans — notes of preparation for the morrow.[37]

The dissatisfactions of the past month were forgotten and the men were again a fighting unit.

About midnight, the men set out. Kimball rode among them, Lambert wrote, exhorting and cheering, stopping by F Company to tell them that

> unless they won the greatest honors of the day Pool should quit writing to the Express, and that he only wanted them to follow him, and if he should run toward camp he wanted they should

run as fast as they could, but if he should run toward the enemy he wanted them to see him safely through.[38]

With C Company in the lead, the regiment proceeded silently past several other regiments in dense fog, over the Cheat River bridge, eerily past their own ambulances and up to the slope of the mountain leading to the Southern camp. About 7 a.m. they encountered the Rebels' advance pickets, and as Crim described it:

> Col Kimball rode up and said, "Captain Brooks, deploy your Company and meet the confederate skirmishers." I will never forget how in perfect order our Company C deployed in the face of a heavy fire from the enemy, of both artillery and musketry, and at this time Amos Boyd, a young man, was killed and two others wounded.[39]

At about 10 a.m. the artillery was hauled into place and for about two hours the men exchanged fire until both sides ran low on ammunition. (A spy from the Fourteenth was in the midst of the Rebel artillery and was busy rushing defused shells to the cannonaders.) The order was given to the Northern troops to charge bayonets and the Rebels, with ammunition exhausted, ran up the white flag.

At that climactic moment in the battle, Rebel reinforcements arrived. The secessionists quickly hauled down their white flag and began peppering the boys with shell and shot. The Northern brigade withdrew, with fifteen killed or wounded. One of the spy's defused shells was taken from the shattered thigh of a Universalist preacher, who soon died as a result of the wound. The regiment's retreat was covered by the Thirty-second Ohio, which held off 3000 Rebel troops attempting to cut off the retreat at the Greenbrier Bridge. The men of the Fourteenth later complained that there should have been no retreat, that Kimball had wished to "storm the works [but] Gen. Reynolds would not grant that request, remarking that he had merely come out to reconnoitre the rebel position." Be that as it may, the men of the Fourteenth were undaunted by the lack of clear-cut success. "The loss on our side [was] trifling. . . .We captured 13 prisoners — our regiment 7, the Invincibles, 5. Bully!" Landon wrote.[40]

Beem and Jess Harrold captured seven Rebels, and Beem took for himself a "splendid rifle and beautiful pistol" worth forty dollars.[41]

On October 8 as the men again sat shivering around their campfires at the summit, the order came to strike tents; the regiment was going into winter quarters in the valley. The men shouted with ecstasy and yodeled the Hoosier yell at the top of their lungs. They were going off Cheat Mountain. Van Dyke was one of the ecstatic ones:

> From that time all was hurry and confusion, cooking grub, packing knapsacks, striking and packing tents. . . .I jumped upon one of the largest rocks and took a last survey of Cheat Mountain. . . ."Fall in Company G." Soon the line was formed and on calling the roll I found that all answered to their names for the first time since our advent upon the Summit. . . ."Forward march." With what a light step all started. Soon on the road turning at the brow of the hill, the Fourteenth took what I fondly hope is their last look at Cheat Mt.[42]

Houghton was realistic enough to know that Huttonsville, a "so-called town" in the valley, was not much better.

> We have hoped against hope that we who have stood the cold, wet and constant exposure of the mountains longer than any other troops, would be removed to some more congenial clime . . . .But we must not repine. Come what may, we must do our duty.[43]

The boys were leaving the mountain with the budding regimental spirit basically intact. They had learned in western Virginia that their particular kind of fighting unit was like a blade: it functioned best in use. In its scabbard, the Fourteenth rusted and tarnished into recklessness and even mutiny. The troops could be justly proud of their conduct in the skirmish at Cheat Mountain and the Battle of Greenbrier. They had deployed themselves as a smoothly functioning battle unit and had wanted to press on when Reynolds had ordered retreat. The spirit was beginning to solidify, and the mutiny and subsequent reorganization had cleared the air. From now on the regiment, resigned to the difficulties of war, would be at its best when it was in motion. Stonewall Jackson was soon to be on the move, and the men of the Fourteenth would have to push themselves to keep up with his erratic and brilliant ploys.

1. Lambert, Journal, August, 1861.
2. *History of Greene and Sullivan Counties,* p. 125.
3. Report of Nathan Kimball to the Secretary of War, March 20, 1864, in the Kimball Papers, Lilly Library, Indiana University, hereafter cited as Report of Kimball to the Secretary of War.
4. Letter of William Landon to the *Vincennes Western Sun,* July 17, 1861, hereafter cited as Letter of Landon to the *Western Sun.*
5. *Counties of Clay and Owen,* p. 628.
6. *Under Canvass,* p. 18.
7. Letter of Lewis Brooks to Thomas Jefferson Brooks, August 11, 1861, hereafter cited as Letter of Brooks to his father.
8. Letter of Beem to his wife-to-be, September 1, 1861.
9. Letter of Brooks to his father, August 11, 1861.
10. *Under Canvass,* p. 18.
11. Letter of McClure to his sister, September 18, 1861, in *Hoosier Farmboy.*
12. Ibid.
13. Letter of Van Dyke to "Folks at home," August 12, 1861.
14. *Under Canvass,* pp. 24, 25.
15. Letter of Beem to his wife-to-be, August 5, 1861.
16. *Under Canvass,* p. 35.
17. Ibid., p. 26.
18. Ibid., p. 28; Letter of Landon to the *Western Sun,* August 21, 1861; Lambert, Journal, August, 1861.
19. Diary of William Houghton in the Houghton Papers, July 10, 1861, hereafter cited as Houghton, Diary.
20. Letter of Beem to his wife-to-be, August 5, 1861.
21. Letter of Beem to his wife-to-be, September 12, 1861.
22. Letter of Van Dyke to "Folks at home," August 23, 1861.
23. Letter of John Coons, Captain of Company G, to Indiana Governor O. P. Morton, September 22, 1861, in Correspondence, Fourteenth Indiana Regiment, Archives Division, Indiana State Library, Indianapolis.
24. Bruce Catton, *Glory Road* (Garden City, New York: Doubleday and Company, 1952), pp 115-16. Catton does not identify the "Indiana troops in the West Virginia mountains," or the correspondents who complained to Morton, but the chief complainant was clearly Coons.
25. Letter of Van Dyke to "Folks at home," August 12, 1861.
26. Houghton, Diary, August 24, 1861.
27. The account of the battle is from Letter of Landon to the *Western Sun,* September 19, 1861; from *Under Canvass,* pp. 36-39; and from Report of Kimball to the Secretary of War, March 20, 1864.

8

8

28. Letter of Van Dyke, September 17, 1861.
29. Diary of John Kuppenheimer, September 12, 1861, photostated copy in the Indiana State Museum.
30. Houghton, Diary, September 13, 1861.
31. *Martin County Tribune,* January 29, 1897, in *History of Martin County,* vol. I.
32. Letter of Beem to his wife-to-be, September 19, 1861; Letter of Kimball to the Secretary of War, March 20, 1864.
33. Letter of Landon to the *Western Sun,* September 27, 1861.
34. *The Medical and Surgical History of the War of the Rebellion,* 13, pt. 3 (Government Printing Office, 1888), 273.
35. Lambert, Diary, October 2, 1861.
36. Crim, Memoirs.
37. Letter of Landon to the *Western Sun,* October 4, 1861.
38. Lambert, Journal, October 2, 1861.
39. Crim, Memoirs.
40. Most of the account of the Battle of Greenbrier is taken from Letters of Landon to the *Western Sun,* October 2 and 6.
41. Letter of Beem to his wife-to-be, October 6, 1861. There is an unexplained discrepancy in the total of regimental prisoners.
42. Letter of Van Dyke to "Folks at Home," October 18, 1861.
43. Houghton, Diary, November 6, 1861.

CHAPTER FOUR

VALLEY CAMPAIGN AND THE JAMES RIVER

The valley of the Shenandoah is a green patchwork of fields and woods nestling comfortably between the Shenandoah Mountains and the Blue Ridge range. Its strategic importance in the first year of the Civil War (not at all lost on the politicians in Washington) lay in the fact that it formed a natural high road to the nation's capital and certain Southern victory if the Confederacy were to use it.

The Confederates were well aware of the valley's military advantages. They did not, however, plan to use it to attack Washington in 1861. Instead, it would be the staging area from which to sabotage a major Union offensive against their own capital, Richmond. While Shiloh was being fought in the West, McClellan, with great caution and after long preparation, headed toward Richmond. His necessary reinforcements would have to go through the Shenandoah Valley, and Robert E. Lee planned to stop the arrival of those reinforcements.

Lee had been shifted from western Virginia to become the military advisor of Jefferson Davis. Now, in March, he helped devise a plan to save Richmond and put the South brilliantly on the offensive. The executor of the plan was to be Stonewall Jackson, the hero of Manassas Junction. With only a few thousand troops (the total was finally 17,000) he would come roaring into the Shenandoah Valley to confuse the two Northern armies trying to cross it to join McClellan, and put the fear of God into Lincoln in Washington.

The Fourteenth Indiana was squarely in the middle of the Valley Campaign. In March and April of 1862, they were a part of Banks' division, one of two divisions in the area, the other being that of General John C. Fremont. Jackson's strategy was that of many other commanders with small armies; he would face divided enemies, whipping each section of the opposing forces separately. After dealing handily with the West Virginia troops of Fremont, he then turned savagely and unpredictably on the army of Nathaniel Banks, 16,000 strong.

*   *   *

By this time the Fourteenth Indiana was eager to fight again. Now battle-ready veterans who had watched the Sixth Ohio, the Twenty-fourth Ohio, and the Fifteenth and Twelfth Indiana regiments all leave Virginia, the Fourteenth had waited through long months in winter quarters. Moving to Philippi and eventually to Romney, the regiment had commandeered houses and public buildings and were living in comfort which contrasted sharply with the rigorous conditions on Cheat Mountain. Still, life was dreary. Days passed in the routine of drilling and camp duty through November and December.

Van Dyke was comfortable in an oyster seller's log hut which he had confiscated. He used the long afternoons to rest and send many letters home. He berated the Denny family in Vincennes for not writing him, he arranged for his father and mother to move to Indiana, and he urged his family not to let his sixteen-year-old sister, Alice, marry so young. Most important, he mananged both to get engaged and break off this engagement to Eliza Shaw by letter. He had thought better of his eve-of-battle romance, as he explained to his father:

> I suppose you will wonder why so seemingly advantageous or eligible match was broken off. Well in the first place, she is older than I am. . .in the next place her Father, who was an Episcopa-

lian clergyman, very talented, but he proved to be a libertine and for some of his libertine actions in Texas he was *foully* treated from the effects of which he died. Two of the brothers are the worst reprobates in existence and the sister of whom I spoke is not cordially received in respectable society. . . . I wrote to her desiring that we should henceforth consider ourselves merely friends.[1]

Now that this engagement was off, he began to write longer, more thoughtful letters to Angie Kent, signing them "Your loving friend."

Houghton had been in bed with a swelling of the lymph glands and Dr. Clippinger, the regimental surgeon, had advised that a "good fire, a warm cot and plenty of blankets" would speed his recuperation. He was placed in a warm, friendly home and was cheered by it; but as soon as he returned to camp he became depressed about not being involved in the fighting.[2]

On the 28th of December he wrote his mother complaining of

the never failing routine of duties which have to be performed every day. Now that the holy days are here, I feel as if I *ought* to have one day to call my own.

Houghton was spending many days in his tent alone now, working. Brooks had returned to Indiana to recruit volunteers to fill the gaps that battle and resignation had caused; Houghton had had to assume many of his cousin's duties. One of his tasks was to sit in judgment in court-martial proceedings. A recent proceeding had included the sentencing of

two men for becoming intoxicated and disobeying orders; are to forfeit to the government ten dollars of their monthly pay and be confined to hard labor for the term of ten days, and imprisonment for one month.

The third forfeits five dollars of his pay only, on account of previous good conduct.

The fourth sentenced to a forfeiture of eight dollars of his

monthly pay for the period of one year, and to be imprisoned in
the military prison at Washington for the same period.

The first two are to have, in addition, a barrel placed over their
heads and be marched in front of the regt at Dress Parade on
two separate occasions, to the tune of the "Rogue's March."[3]

The period of inactivity they had experienced on Cheat
Mountain had not ended, but most of the men were finding
ways of occupying themselves. Beem complained, however,
that very few of them read books or found "improving"
activities.

Mostly they stay together and have considerable sport. When
night comes on, after they have had supper, and washed their
dishes (tin pans) they go into their tent and have fun and frolic
until the drum beats for bed-time; then lights must be blown out
and silence preserved, though they sometimes keep rather noisy
silence.

Mahala kept asking about the regiment's religious life and
Beem had to admit to her that it was slipping.

I tell you this is a hard place for men to live religious lives, not
only because there are a great many temptations, but because
there is little attention paid to it here, and the circumstances are
so unfavorable. You can form some idea about how we go to
church here when I describe to you our meeting today. Bro
Webb got a barrel which stood between two rows of tents and
read his text, sang and prayed and commenced preaching to
about half a dozen men. The small number present was owing
mostly to the fact that the mud where the audience had to stand
was just six inches deep. Now if Bro Dave had been here, I have
no doubt he would have lectured them for not turning out
better to hear the word of life, but I am inclined to think that
under the circumstances even he would have found any excuse
for staying away and would a little rather be in a comfortable
room enjoying the society of dear sister Lena than to stand in the
cold to hear the gospel preached.[4]

He assured his intended that he was not neglecting the means
of grace; he read his Bible still.

Beem had also devised a plan so that he and Hala could be married, but he was afraid that she might, as a pure woman, object to parts of it. He wanted her to come (with a chaperone, of course) to Wheeling; he would get a short leave. They would be man and wife before Christmas. He knew his wife-to-be well; Hala declined. Probably not only did it sound too much like "running off" to get married, but she also must have wanted to invite all her friends in to drink lemonade, eat ice cream and cake, and kill all the bad-luck "bats" at a southern Indiana wedding reception.

That Christmas for Beem and the rest of the regiment was cold and cheerless. Lambert and some friends sought to keep the old-time custom of shooting off holiday firecrackers by firing off an anvil, shooting muskets, and trying anything else they could think of to get the proper reverberations. Lambert, looking around "for something extra in the eating line," found some oysters for a holiday supper. He was glad that the band was at Philippi, where the holidays could produce even mild festivity.[5] At Romney, where many of the rest of the men were, all was generally spartan regulations and sheet-iron crackers.

Landon wished everybody at home a merry Christmas through the *Vincennes Sun.* "There will be no Christmas for us this year" — in the Hoosier sense of the holiday, with turkey and sage dressing and squash.[6] Actually, Indiana people would have been shocked to know how the boys did celebrate the Savior's birth — they became riotously drunk and disorderly. One soldier from the regiment drowned trying to swim the river with a bottle in his hand. One man was stabbed through the lungs, another in the arm, and others had their faces pounded up and their heads cut open. In reporting these events, Van Dyke added, "I am sorry to say Denny [son of his friend] is now under arrest."[7]

Lambert pondered the question of why soldiers drink.

Why is it our soldiers become more disipated in the army than at home? At first thought one might suppose it is the influences by which they are surrounded, and with some this may be, and unquestionably it is the case to some extent. But there are three great reasons why the soldier degenerates both morally and socially. First, the total isolation from the more gentle and restraining influences and surroundings of Mothers, sisters, wives and female society generally. Second—Disappointments occasioned by the nonreception of intelligence from friends from home. Third—examples of superiors in rank, and to stimulate the nerves for action.

He went on to add that the Creator had made men and women to be together and "when this great plan of the Creator is strictly adhered to, society moves on smoothly, and there need be no drunkenness or debauchery."[8]

Some of the officers in other regiments had solved the problem of obtaining female companionship in a time-honored way; they married another wife, temporarily forgetting the one back home. Cavins, in a New Year's letter to his wife, said:

> Quite a number of officers wives are out here. The most singular things about this is that in several instances the second wife has very unexpectedly appeared in the presence of the astounded husband.

Cavins appeared to be a man who needed female companionship, and his marriage was so sound and fine that he and his wife had long ago faced that fact that he *would* flirt. Ann Cavins tolerated his "conversations with several ladies" bemusedly, so long as they remained chaste (and there seems to have been no question about that). She was expecting a baby at any time.

The strength of the Cavins marriage, even in wartime, was shown in a January 1 letter in which he felt free to tell her, with some humor:

> You must not get jealous at what is now coming; you know I always tell the truth and the whole truth. The truth is that I stayed at Philippi so long that when I did leave, I had quite a big job of kissing to do up. It may be some consolation to you to know that I done it up right as I usually do.

It was to be a good while before Cavins and the other men experienced the genial restraining influences of the Victorian women they had left back in Indiana. Now, in late winter, while the drive to Richmond was underway, all that was to be seen in winter camp was guns, uniforms, and complaining moods. Houghton wrote:

> there had been nothing new transpired since my last — nothing doing — nothing intended — from the slow snail-like manner they had moved heretofore. I hope when General Reynolds gets here, that he will initiate a new program and give us something to do besides standing picket guard. We are looking for Col. Kimball back in a few days. His coming will be hailed with joy.[9]

Kimball was continuing to build trust by his dedication and by the small touches of humanity which seem to have marked him as a leader. Once Lambert was in his own quarters singing "Maggie by My Side" from a ballad sheet when, he reported,

> one of the boys spoke and asked me if I did not wish her by my side in reality. Yes, was my reply. Someone else spoke, "Pretty good. I wish you had her here too." The thought struck me that this last was not the voice of any of my tentmates, and on looking up, who should I see but Col. Kimball, who had entered directly I began, and advanced to the center of the tent, shaking his head at the other boys. My embarrassment may better be imagined than described.[10]

General Reynolds did not return from his trip to Washington, and General Frederick W. Lander was named brigadier. Lander was a firebrand of an officer, surely one of the most flamboyant and unpredictable in the Northern Army. In late February he took ill and died suddenly on March 2. The men of the regiment were to remember his three-hour funeral in the high tradition of military honor, for more than one reason.

Though he had been colorful as a man and officer, Lander had not really been popular with the men. Lambert described their reaction to his death and funeral.

About 4 o'clock in the evening their intelligence of his death occasioned considerable surprise, but not much sorrow. The boys, in fact, acted more like they had received more Ft. Donaldson news than that of the death of the commanding officer.

This morning the flags were all lowered to half mast and draped in mourning. We were ordered to fall in ranks at half past eleven with guns and accouterments which order we obeyed and stood there until we were almost frozen when "redtape" concluded it was not quite ready yet and sent us back to our qrs. Half an hour later, we were called out again and marched down to the Depot, where the whole Div. was drawn up in the lines, between which the corpse and escort were to pass. Behind these lines of infantry were the Cav. and Art. on the right and left respectively. Here we stood in this position full two hours and cold. O scipors! The boys repeatedly wished that no more Gens might die in this Division. Presently the booming of the cannons told that the procession had started from Hd Qrs. Nine minute guns were fired and the corpse approached carried on the shoulders of the Staff Officers—followed by field officers and preceeded by Chaplains. As the procession passed between the columns, it was saluted by the Div. with a "Present Arms" and when it reached the cars, the different Regts. separated and went to quarters keeping step to more cheerful music. The corpse was taken home for interment and thus ended the career of one of the most daring and strong headed men the world ever knew.[11]

Lander's death made Van Dyke philosophical:

It was hard to realize that the strong man we had seen dashing along the front of our line in every word, look and act a warrior was so helpless in death.... His greatest wish to die on the battlefield was not gratified. He seems to have had but one fear and that was of dying a lingering wasting disease, which had marked him for its own.... In our late skirmish at Bloomery Furnace he rode with headlong speed, along up the road and dashing up to a party of Rebels among whom was Col. Baldwin, threw himself from his horse and demanded their surrender and they, surprised at such audacity gave themselves up as prisoners. He was one of the most wicked men I ever saw. Profanity seemed to be to him a recreation and no time or place was sacred from his oaths. . . the remains went East on the Rail road to Washington City.[12]

Brigadier General James T. Shields came to command the division in Lander's place, and Kimball was given command of the brigade which would make a name for itself and stay together for the rest of the Fourteenth's time of service — the Fourteenth Indiana, Fourth and Eighth Ohio, and Seventh Virginia regiments.

The Bloomery Furnace incident, which Cavins and some others always wryly referred to afterwards as "Lander's Midnight Bloomery Dash," occurred on February 13 and 14, when the Fourteenth was helping to clear the Winchester Pike. Now, as March progressed, Shields began to take the division on the offensive again, having been informed that the Rebel force which had been holding Winchester was greatly reduced by the recent departure of the short-term enlistments. Jackson also was stirring, returning to the area he had recently left, readying himself to block any Northern advance.[13] McClellan was moving 58,000 men to Fort Monroe, preparing to move up the peninsula to Richmond. The shifting perspectives of the Valley Campaign were coming into focus.

On March 22 Jackson stationed his troops on the hills above Winchester to meet the advancing Shields' division. The Fourteenth, eager for action, moved onto the Strasburg Turnpike hot on Jackson's heels. They were as strong physically as they were ever to be; morale was high and the men were healthy, with a few exceptions.[14] About 4 p.m. the two forces met. The Battle of Winchester Heights (Kernstown) was on. As Kimball led the brigade into the action, he came upon General Shields being borne from the field wounded. Shields told Kimball to take command of the battle. Then night fell and the action stopped.

The next day Jackson's men fought gallantly, themselves backed against a stone wall in the heights of Winchester. Kimball was fighting a defensive battle, directing his troops in response to Jackson's actions, because he believed that "not only was the force of Ashby present, but the entire army of Stonewall Jackson, with that general in command, in person." When, from his hospital bed, General Shields sent a message suggesting an encircling movement which would cut off the small force *he* believed to be present, Kimball was not pleased:

> Convinced that the general did not comprehend the situation, the strength of the enemy nor the position held by the respective forces, and satisfied that from his bed in the city five miles to the rear he could not properly conduct the movements which might be required. . . I determined to remain on the defensive and in the position now held my line.[15]

The Northern forces, heavily reinforced, fought well. Houghton related the circumstances at the climax of the Battle of Kernstown:

> Tyler's brigade was moved to the right, where the rebels were trying to turn our flank and in a half hour we heard the battle open. It was one of the most terrific fires I ever heard. . . . Soon, however a messenger from Gen Kimball galloped up and told us we were wanted to support Tyler's Brigade. We immediately marched by flank to the right. . . . Our course at first lay through an open field. . . then into a strip of timber broken with hollows, after which we came again into an open field, where the rebel fire played upon us. Our Regt moved in solid columns up to the scene of the battle and I can safely say that no men ever found a more trying danger. The 87th Penn whom we were sent to relieve had stood a terrific fire for nearly ¾ of an hour and were almost cut to pieces. They were almost panic stricken and many were running towards us. Their Colonel (Murray) was borne through the ranks of Company C with his brains dropping out of his broken skull. The Fourteenth, true as the Spartan band and noble as the cause for which they fought, marched up to their places as deliberately as if on drill. The first fire the standard fell. The color bearer snatched it up and waved them both above him in two seconds. He too was down and two others snatched them up and still bore them on triumphantly.[16]

The Fourteenth had been firing from a distance of about eighty yards. Houghton acknowledged the courage of the enemy: "Most gallantly did they sustain their reputation that day." Finally, hard pressed by the Hoosiers, the Stonewall brigade broke ranks as dark fell. Cavins described their retreat:

The Confederates fell back in great disorder, and we advanced in disorder just as great, over stone walls and over fences, through blackberry bushes and undergrowth. Over logs, through woods, over hills and fields the brigades, regiments and companies advanced in one promiscuous, mixed and uncontrollable mass.[17]

That night the Fourteenth lay on the battlefield with the dead and dying all around. What the men did not know, because Jackson did not want Northern intelligence to know it, was that Shields' forces had been vastly superior in number to those of Jackson. Kimball, who won his brigadier generalship because of the Battle of Kernstown, had fought against only 4200 men.[18] But the men of the Fourteenth and the rest of Shields' division were exultant that they had stood against the famous Stonewall.

By mid-April, however, Jackson's will-o'-the-wisp tactics had stunned them and left them gasping for a few days of rest and relief. Early in the war Jackson had told his brigadier:

Always mystify, mislead and surprise the enemy if possible; and when you strike and overcome him, never let up in the pursuit so long as your men have strength to follow; for any army routed, if hotly pursued, become panic stricken and can then be destroyed by half their number.[19]

Jackson was in the business of "mystifying" the enemy so that he could delay the march of McClellan's reinforcements to Richmond and then pop up himself a few days later, to the complete astonishment of McClellan, on his right flank at Chickahominy. The checkerboard moves that followed were made so rapidly that the men of the Fourteenth had little time to eat, sleep, or find replacements for the boots and pants that were again wearing out, let alone discern the reasons for the cat-and-mouse strategy Shields' division was involved in.

(1) (May 15) Shields' division, which, much against the will of both Banks and Shields, was ordered to Fredericksburg to be nearer to Washington, proceeded in an exhausting forced march of six days.

(2) (May 23) Having disposed of Fremont's troops in the mountains, Jackson's men pounced on the remaining Banks troops (9000 men) at Front Royal and drove them from the valley.

(3) (May 25) Lincoln and Stanton, fearful of Jackson's escape, attempted to close the gap between Shields' division and Fremont's and Banks' troops, and Shields' division was ordered to retrace their steps and make another forced march to Front Royal.

(4) (May 28) Almost at point of exhaustion, the Fourteenth Indiana and the remainder of Shields' division arrived at Rectortown. Less than twenty-four hours later the following communiqué was received:

> Colonel Kimball, commanding First Brigade: You will march immediately; leave your teams and wagons, take only ambulances, ammunition, wagons, and provisions, as much as on hand in haversacks. SHIELDS, BRIGADIER GENERAL COMMANDING.[20]

(5) By a series of moves which were incomprehensible to Kimball, the division was sent in the opposite direction from the fleeing Jackson, to Luray.

(6) Jackson, in a brilliant final ploy, secured the bridge at Port Republic for his escape, and as Shields' division advanced to oppose him, cut Samuel Carroll's and Daniel Tyler's brigades to ribbons. The men of the Fourteenth rushed to reinforce the rest of Kimball's brigade but arrived just in time to meet the "worn and defeated comrades of Tyler's and Carroll's command."[21]

Jackson had slipped the noose.

Beem had missed most of this. He had left the regiment in April on a mission to Indiana and had achieved two of his long-sought-for goals: he had received his commission as captain, and he had finally married Hala. Then, after a brief home stay, in mid-May he tried to catch the regiment, a difficult job in light of the erratic movements at the time. When he returned after Port Republic, he calculated that the Fourteenth

had marched 339 miles between May 15 and June 23 and had
lost more men through "unnecessary hardships and expo-
sures" than it had lost in battle.[22]

Though his assessment was fairly accurate, there was little
complaining, except of mismanagement of the campaign by
the men at the top. But in fact the men had a good deal to
complain about on this score if they had wished. At Luray,
even when the wild marches had finally ended, the men could
not draw on quartermasters' stores, and as a result of a special
order from McDowell, they could not even forage. Shoes were
worn out. On the last march "it was customary to parade the
shoeless and put them under the command of a special officer
and let them pick their way," Beem said. He reported seeing
fifty or more men at this time marching barefoot, some with
bleeding feet. Many men fell along the road, weakened by
dysentery and exposure. Many others deserted. Cavins wrote
to Ann June 12:

> Every decent or honest man has been disgusted with the man-
> agement of this division of the army. The army has become a
> marauding party, plundering everyone — Union men, women
> & children as well as rebels. Not leaving anything for them to live
> on. Horse stealing and passing counterfeit & bogus money are
> every day occurrences. Officers are required to buy their provi-
> sions from the Brigade Commissary, instead of regimental, and
> they have to pay cash down and make their own change. And
> they are charged about 25 percent more than the law allows.
> Heretofore we have bought our provisions on credit, paying up
> each pay day. We will soon be out of money. I have only $10
> now. And then we will have no means of getting anything to eat,
> unless a change is made in affairs. The result will be that unless
> we are paid or credited for something to eat, that some of the
> officers will be at home in about a month from this time. I am not
> in a humor to write today, so you must excuse the lack of interest
> in this letter. Don't show this letter. I will write again in a few
> days if we stop marching long enough. My love to all.

Among all these difficulties one cheering interlude had
occurred while the group was at Fredericksburg. On May 23,
as the regiment "rested in the arms of Morpheus" according to

Lambert, a grand review featuring "Uncle Abraham" in person along with Secretary of War Stanton was announced for that day. Lambert wrote in his journal:

> Having never seen Old Abe of course I was not loath to make the necessary preparations. I jumped up, blacked my shoes, washed my hair and combed my face and was soon in the parade ground, where the whole Division assembled in a clover field . . . .The president, being mounted on a large white horse, and tall himself, was easily distinguished from the escort. He rode by with his hat off, but he is a better looking man than I expected to see.[23]

And, in "Beulahland" (Luray, Virginia) at the end of the long ordeal, Beem basked in appreciated relaxation and wrote his "dear wife":

> Luray is a small town 25 miles south of the Manassas Gap RR in the Blue Ridge range of Mountains. Our camp today is in a beautiful grassy field, in the midst of magnificent scenery. Within three miles of us, the tall peaks of the Blue Ridge rise away up above the clouds, for the clouds literally hid the summits of many of them. Close by runs a fine stream of pure mountain water, affording an excellent place for dirty soldiers to bathe. I confess that such scenery has peculiar attractions for me, and sometimes in viewing it I almost forget that these lofty hills hide a hostile foe in their bosom, only a few miles away.[24]

It was the mocking fate of Lincoln's army to be fighting a bloody war in the midst of some of the most picturesque scenery in North America.

Now, in their unmatchably cocky style, the correspondents in the regiment were spending their time helping the home folks catch up on the army's doings. Pool had gone home to Terre Haute and would not return, but Landon actively continued to record camp and field gossip. Items:

The "Tiger Tail Mess" of G Company had been enjoying flapjacks after a ration of flour came through.

Henderson Simpson had gone home on furlough.

Youthful Adjutant Blinn, who had departed in a huff because he was not appointed a field officer, had returned to the regiment.

Private John Racine of B was court-martialed for robbery and sentenced to six months at hard labor.[25]

And there was always "regiment watching." For the first time, the Fourteenth had an opportunity to see some of the Eastern regiments, many of them dandified and unfriendly, at least to the Western mind. Landon wrote:

> The band of a Maine regiment, having played a few tunes for a public celebration, at Martinsburg, had the "cheek" to pass around "de sasser." D—n these "Down East," money-loving, Yankee band-box Provost Guard regiments! Dressed out in full rig, with all the extra [brass] touches on, and polished boots, they take possession of the little towns along our line of march as fast as we run the rebels out, strut about like turkey goblers with guns that have never fired a shot at sesech (nor ever will) and woe to the unlucky soldier that is absent from his quarters without a permit— "Halt-ah! What Regiment-ah? Fourteenth Indiana, damn you!" "Got a pass-ah" "no!" "Fall in the rear-ah!"[26]

At another time a guard from a New England regiment commented on the dirtiness of Shields' division, who would not have water for washing from Luray until after the Seven Days' Battles. During this time, the men's rations were severely limited. John McClure commented that they had marched 400 miles and

> are fed on half rations and the very poorest at that. I have seen, while on some marches, I would not see a bit of meat for two and three days. Nothing but sheet iron crackers and coffy with no sugar in it and scarce at that. Well if you have money you can get a meals victuals for from twenty-five cts to fifty. . . .If you get a pair of boots out here, I have to pay $7.00 for them.[27]

The pay for a private was $13.00 a month.

Foraging was providing its usual supplements to the diet of the Fourteenth, in spite of strong orders to the contrary. It was sometimes dangerous. Beem described one incident, "one of those calamities which I have done my best to prevent" as follows:

> a wagon broke down in the mudhole, and I detailed six men to stay with the wagons to assist him along. When they got the wagon fixed and started on the road, two of the boys. . . . instead of coming along the road with the rest, left it and went some two miles off the main road. . . . these boys stopped at a cabin to get something to eat, high up on a mountainside. This was near night, and Randleman being tired, laid down on a bed while the woman of the house was cooking. Very soon the house was entered by a number of rebel scouts. Bonfanti was at a window when they came to the door and made his escape, though they fired at him. Randleman was lying down and had his shoes off, and of course, was seized. . .you can let his father and mother see this and tell them this is all I know. . . .[28]

And after Jackson's escape did away with the tremendous pressure for haste, better food and clothing finally began to come in. Then on June 23, the men prepared to leave the valley. They were to join McClellan. Boarding the cars at Bristow Station for Alexandria, a historic town not far from Washington, the men saw for the first time the lower Potomac River, its waters covered with sail and steam ships. Here also Shields' division, whose bonds had been forged through three months of difficult marches and combat, was split; Kimball's brigade was attached to the Army of the Potomac and ordered to join McClellan immediately on the peninsula in front of Richmond.[29]

The brigade was to go by water on the steamship Columbia and the men were ordered to stack arms and remain near the wharf for an estimated departure time of 4 p.m., June 30. But the veterans of Kernstown and the Shenandoah Campaign could not be restrained, and many headed for Washington. Some had to be dragged from taverns, as Lambert reported.

> Impossible to keep the boys in camp and in less than one hour I believe half the men in the Regt were either downtown drunk or

in camp drunk, and I am sorry to say Lieut. Col Owen, which is not the first time by many, but I have always hesitated to expose him.[30]

Other indulged their famished senses more mildly, buying cake and coffee and pork, which they cooked over a small forge on board the Columbia. Finally all were aboard, and the boat left. The men, looking back at Washington, could see across the gold waters of the river at sunset the skyline of the historic city and all of Fairfax County from the decks. Houghton, forever abstracting meanings, mused that this panoramic, over-the-shoulder view was

> as we sometimes look back over our life, and see it depicted in all its varied phases, checked scenes, chances and changes, good and evil.[31]

The boat steamed past Fort Washington and Mt. Vernon, for which the men of the regiment expressed real respect, and after an overnight trip on Chesapeake Bay, arrived at Fortress Monroe, where the flags of ships of many nations were waving in a slight wind. As soon as dawn came, many of the men went swimming near the fortress; later the steamer proceeded eight miles up the James to Harrison's Landing,[32] the site of McClellan's supply station and headquarters.

On July 2 they found the Army of the Potomac, which they had come to join, exhausted after the miserable last stages of the Seven Days' Battles. McClellan's attempt to push to Richmond had failed, and he had marched back to the James after the Battle of Malvern Hill. There his army stayed, almost as spent as the Rebel defenders of the city.

The Fourteenth, placed on picket duty beyond McClellan's headquarters, was almost immediately in the midst of sniper fire and shelling. About dawn, the left wing of the regiment underwent heavy shelling, and the entire brigade was ordered up to support them in an engagement called the Battle of Haxols. The troops advanced to the enemy pickets through a hellish barrage of grapeshot and cannister. Men dropped, mortally wounded, around Beem, and a cannonball fell near his foot. Houghton, who commanded C and D companies in the action, and who was one of the regiment's sternest critics, was unstinting in his praise of the Fourteenth's conduct as a fighting unit:

> I never saw the Fourteenth behave so nobly and the whole brigade was complimented by General Keys and his staff for the whole affair. . . . I cannot say too much in praise of our brave noble and enduring boys. That they were brave I always knew, but on every new field they show their powers more. They were void of fear.[33]

The Fourteenth was in excellent fighting fettle. The vicissitudes and physical hardships of the Valley Campaign had toughened them spiritually and physically. They had arrived at a degree of independence as a fighting unit and as individuals that many of Lincoln's best troops eventually possessed; they decided their own fate now, as at Alexandria, when they simply refused to "stack arms" and wait.

They had not much left but bone and sinew, but compared to the veterans of the Seven Days' Battles, the Fourteenth looked strong and vital, according to Houghton:

> The troops here have suffered greatly and the Regts are greatly reduced by different causes. Our brigade with all its hardships is the finest looking one I have yet seen.

He added, however, "War is a lottery and the lucky ones draw the prize." Soon the lottery would be drawn at a small Maryland town named Sharpsburg, where the odds would be heavier than they had been so far for the Fourteenth.

1. Letter of Van Dyke to his father, December 28, 1861.
2. Letter of Houghton to his mother, November 28, 1861.
3. Lambert, Journal, November 4, 1861.
4. Letter from Beem to his wife-to-be, November 17, 1861.
5. Lambert, Journal, December 24, 1861.
6. Letter of Landon to the *Western Sun*, "Christmas Eve, Dec. 24, 1861."
7. Letter of Van Dyke to "Folks at home," January 5, 1861.

8. Undated sheet attached to Lambert's Journal.

9. Letter of Houghton to his mother, December 29, 1861.

10. Lambert, Journal, January 13, 1862.

11. Ibid., March 3, 1862.

12. Letter of Van Dyke to his wife-to-be, March 4, 1862.

13. Material on military movements and strategies in this chapter comes from Kimball's description of the Kernstown Campaign in "Fighting Jackson at Kernstown," *Battles and Leaders of the Civil War*, 2 (New York: The Century Company, 1884), hereafter cited as *Battles and Leaders*, 2.

14. Letter of Beem to his wife-to-be, March 15, 1862. The exception was William C. Hord of H Company, who was chained to a bed with hydrophobia, seemingly contracted earlier from a dog bite. Hord died just before the Battle of Kernstown.

15. *Battles and Leaders*, 2, 305.

16. Letter of Houghton to his father, March 27, 1862.

17. *Battles and Leaders*, 2, 307; Letter to Kimball, July 9, 1887.

18. Bruce Catton, *The American Heritage Picture History of the Civil War* (New York: American Heritage Publishing Company), p. 150.

19. *Battles and Leaders*, 2, 297.

20. Ibid., p. 311.

21. Ibid., p. 313.

22. Beem, "History of the Fourteenth Indiana."

23. Lambert, Journal.

24. June 6, 1862.

25. Letter of Landon to the *Western Sun*, April 28, 1862.

26. Ibid., April 29, 1862.

27. Letter of McClure to his sister, June 26, 1862, in *Hoosier Farmboy*.

28. Letter of Beem to his wife, June 11, 1862.

29. *Counties of Clay and Owen*, p. 630.

30. Lambert, Journal, June 29, 1862. Philander Owen was lieutenant colonel of the Fourteenth.

31. Letter of Houghton to his father, June 30, 1862.

32. Letter of Landon to the *Western Sun*, July 8, 1862.

33. Letter of Houghton to his mother, July 1, 1862.

CHAPTER FIVE

ANTIETAM

As they waited on the shore of the James in July of 1862, the soldiers of the Fourteenth had new time for reflection. As provisions arrived (potatoes, onions, and dried apples) and the sanitary commission went around the camp sprinkling chloride of lime over the stinking ooze outside the tents,[1] the men considered where they'd been so far and where the long road ahead was leading.

One thing certain was that the regiment itself had changed; it had undergone a consolidation process. Chaff had been winnowed, and many men who had signed the rolls at the emotional recruiting meetings were no longer in the ranks. The ones left, however, had drawn together and were conscious for the first time of a spirit among them not based on rhetoric and romantic dreams but on their performance at Cheat Mountain, Kernstown, and the Shenandoah Valley against Jackson. They had fought well. They could look at themselves as a fighting unit worth bragging about.

It is risky, of course, to speak in terms of the "spirit" of any group. No group has one will (at least not for a very long time). There are always the sulkers, the evaders, the psychologically unfit, the summer soldiers. In fact, it is likely that only about one-third of the men built the regimental spirit, really were the regimental spirit in fact: the Beems, Houghtons, McClures, Harolds, who cursed the war (except for Beem who never cursed) but stayed on, exerting leadership and who if

87

wounded came back as soon as they could. The second third followed their leaders. Sometimes indifferent, they did their duty because it was easier to do it than to get out. In the Civil War regiments, these members of the rank and file were exceptionally tough, but in the Fourteenth they often did their job with some distinction. In a war which furnished native timber far above that of most armies in the history of war, the Fourteenth still had an advantage: they had skimmed the first cream of the Indiana countryside for both officers and men of strong character. The bottom third of any army is always those who do not make it for one reason or another — those who were Copperheads at heart, those who looked for discharge on slight grounds, those who were misfits or were physically unable to stand the rigors of camp. Included in this category, perhaps unfairly, are the ones about whom we will never know: the ones who early were wounded or succumbed to camp disease.

The process of war had effectively eliminated this bottom third by the time of the stay on the James after the Seven Days' Battles in August, 1862. It took a little more than a year, then, to reduce the regiment to about 700 men. Antietam and the trouble after Antietam took a toll of about 200 more in a short time. Company G is a good example. By August, 1862, twenty-four enlisted men who had been mustered in June of '61 were no longer with the company. Three had died in battle or of disease, five were "discharged disability," and of the remaining sixteen, ten were deserters or dishonorably discharged and the rest simply listed as "discharged" (those with connections in the military or in Washington pulled the strings necessary to get the term "deserted" taken from the record).

By the end of the year, after the devastating battlefield losses at Antietam and the resignations and transfers following in its wake but not really related to it, fourteen more were gone. *No* desertions occurred in G Company after September, 1862, and losses were the result in large part of woundings and deaths through battle. These losses, of course, were heavy in G as in all companies of the Fourteenth. When the regiment fought at Spotsylvania and Cold Harbor, its last battles, there were only thirteen men in G Company, twelve in A, and twenty-four in H.[2] Since the dead wood in the regiment had been cut away early in the war, its losses, though heavy, were largely all "honorable" after the Valley Campaign.

Officers had left, too, in about the same proportion as enlisted men. For them, however, it was easier to leave when they wanted to without the disgrace of desertion. Many left seeking that elusive pot of gold at the end of the advancement rainbow; for some the Fourteenth could not offer sufficient challenge for their talents.

Brooks was not returning, and the men in C Company felt his loss sorely. He had come back for just a month during the Valley Campaign but had resigned because of continuing ill health. When a call came in August for 300,000 men, Brooks agreed to help form another southern Indiana regiment, received a commission as lieutenant colonel (later colonel) of the Eightieth Indiana, and led the regiment during Perryville and the Knoxville campaigns until August, 1863, when ill health forced him to resign.[3]

Major William Harrow of Vincennes and Lieutenant Colonel Philander Owen of Clinton were continuing causes of controversy. Owen's drinking made him the object of scorn. Harrow's temper and arbitrary officiousness caused irritation.[4] He was foul-mouthed, his swearing sometimes being compared to Lander's. (Lander was supposed to have been asked by the Methodist chaplain of the Fourteenth during the evacuation of Romney, "What arrangements had been made to transport the sick of the Fourteenth Regiment?" Drunk as a beast, he had replied, "God damn you, the 14th Regt, the whole army, everybody and everything and if I have forgotten anything, God damn it too.[5]) Van Dyke had claimed that when Harrow was unable to curse any subject sufficiently he told his orderly to send for General Lander. Now that Lander was gone, one would assume that Harrow had to curse on his own. But the charges were more serious than just that Harrow was foul-mouthed and officious. Cavins contended that Harrow was so drunk at Kernstown that he didn't know anything.[6] In addition, he had hounded the apparently capable and well-respected Captain Jonathan B. Wood of B Company out of the service on charges that Cavins and most of the other officers believed were "frivolous." Cavins wrote his father on December 15, 1861 that Harrow was possessed "of a malign spirit" and that he (Cavins) had urged Wood to resign or Harrow would see him ruined. Finally, incensed by the resentment and antipathy of the independent Fourteenth Indiana, Harrow resigned. After his resignation letter was read to the men on July 2, Lambert of F Company wrote in his diary: "I guess the boys could not cry, at least I could not. I guess Col Owen will leave us soon too."

First Lieutenant William Denny, the son of Van Dyke's friend, who had been arrested for drunkenness, had been "promoted" to the Fifty-first Indiana and was thus out of scorn's (and temptation's) way as far as the Fourteenth was concerned.[7]

As far as the men at the top went, the army's leader, George McClellan, was in most of the men's eyes still "the idol of the West," even in the face of defeat and inactivity. Houghton, for instance, proclaimed:

> We all have faith in Gen McClellen. All our troops who were with him on his retreat seem to think that no other man in the world could have done as well. Also the press applauds him except Frank Leslie who gives him and Halleck one of the most scathing lectures I have ever read— But it does not do well for men in New York to tell how General McClellen ought to have moved 100,000 men.[8]

There was, however, a strong faction among the troops that distrusted McClellan, a faction which grew as the men became more fully aware of the disaster that the retreat from the James had really been. Augustus Van Dyke wrote:

> Nobody knows though everybody inquires where [the Army of the Potomac's] young chieftain who was to prove himself a Second Napoleon is or what is to become of him now that his

army seems to be upon the eve of dissolution. It seems to me that
it must be extremely humiliating for him. . . it is true that he
fought and won, perhaps, several brilliant battles, but without
any decided success, because they weakened his force without
accomplishing any good. Many think he will be deprived of
command. . . . I think he may be a splendid engineer and a good
man to plan a campaign but he is not a fighting man.[9]

Houghton and many others still clung to the temptation of
being irresistibly near Richmond, which they felt should still
be taken.

We will maintain ourselves till reinforcements come that will
enable us to move successfully and when we move Richmond
shall be ours. Though it takes thrice as many days to reach it as it
took the Rebels to drive our forces from there and though every
day be stained with fields as bloody as "Malvern Hills."[10]

Hatred of the Rebels as a group had reached an intensity in the
Northern Army which would persist as long as the war lasted.
Knowledge of personal losses of friends on the battlefield, the
sad waste of war in general, and the defeats they had witnessed
in the gloomy swamps made the men of the Fourteenth bitter
and vengeful. Vindictive and angry actions from then on
through the sacking of Fredericksburg to Reconstruction revealed the depth of their emotion. As Houghton put it:

We often ask if there has been blood enough poured out to
atone for the great sin, but it appears not. The South must be
made a wastefield — her cities become deserts and her business
towns will soon be among the things that were.[11]

One thinks of the stark, gray, end-of-the-war picture of the
ruins of the Galengo Flour Mills in Richmond and the newspaper correspondent's description of a city like "the stillness of
catacombs. . . a vista of desolation" and remembers the thousands of dead and dying that the Fourteenth saw on the
Malvern Hill battlefield. No one in the Army of the Potomac
wept for Richmond once the end finally came.

But their hatred was not only for the secessionists. Word was filtering in that Martin, Knox, and Greene counties were again plagued by Southern sympathizers. When vigilante justice took its own private toll of the Copperheads in Martin County, Houghton wrote:

> I don't know what our men who used to be in the service are doing, that they allow open mouthed traitors to pass unpunished. It wouldn't do for Comp C to be at home and hear men avow themselves for the South. There would be more dead men around than men to bury them—They've suffered too much—endured too much and risked too much on account of this infernal Rebellion to allow a man to enjoy life and liberty under the Stars and Stripes secretly wishing success of our enemies.[12]

Misunderstanding on the home front of the soldiers' dangerous and desperate life and of the trials and sacrifices necessary to win the war poured salt in the wounds of those in camp on the James. John McClure's sister did not seem to understand why he was not sending more money back home. He wrote her an exasperated letter:

> The way you write it seems as though you don't put very much confidence in me, you are afraid I will go gambling. I thought that you knowed that I had more sense than go gamble my money away. . . . You must reckon that you folks are seeing good times to what us fellows do out here.[13]

Certainly the fact that back on the home front folks continued to enjoy life as usual was one of the most ironic (although at the same time comforting) aspects of the war for the common soldier. Lambert's sister and brother sipped punch at parties, the Young Americans (ranks somewhat depleted and with many new rushed-up marriages) attended their church socials, and Beem's relatives intently discussed "shocking" small-town scandals and lawsuits, all as if a thousand miles away men weren't wasting away of Chicahominy dysentery and trying to recover from brutal amputations.

Mahala Beem wrote to her new bridegroom, whose company had recently been in mortal danger and who was worried about the command of men whose morale was being sapped rapidly by heat and sickness, that she did not believe she could stand the separation from him any longer. He wrote her his sternest letter:

It is not my intention to write you a lecture this beautiful morning, my dear wife, but I do intend to write you something about your way of thinking concerning certain things of which you speak in nearly every letter I get from you. I think I haven't got a letter from you without your saying in it that you couldn't stand it to be separated from me so long, that it is so hard for women to be separated from their husbands and so forth. Well, of course it is or ought to be, and I am glad you say you will stand it the best you can, but you must remember that this world makes us experience a great many things disagreeable to us and that the more cheerfully we endure hardships and disappointments the better it is for us. Besides, your situation is favorable compared to that of many other women, and if you think that your case is hard, many others have reason to despair. How is it . . . with at least a hundred other men in Owen County who have large families to take care of? If they can stand it, as they must, you can do the same. Were I a woman, I would be ashamed of a husband who would not fight for his country. . . . A good government is the best thing on earth. Property is nothing without it, because it is not protected, a family is nothing without it because they cannot be educated. Hence, every man ought to defend it and a man who refused to do so when he can is no man at all. . . . I would have a low opinion of myself if I were not in the army. I thank God for the impulse that caused me to take up arms at the Commencement of the war. Had I not done so then, I would certainly feel it my duty to do it now and if I were too big a coward to shoulder a musket under the last call, I would hide my head from the face of men and pray for rocks and mountains to fall on me to cover up my disgrace. . . . Now my dear wife, you may think that this is plain talk, but I say just what I mean, and I think you will say it is right. This war has a great many hard features about it. Friends have to be separated for a time at least, perhaps forever; a great many die of disease, thousands fall off the field of battle and a great many sweet little wives like yourself have to be left at home. . . all I can ask of you is to be patient and

cheerful like a good Christian ought. For my part, I have no
doubt I am a good deal happier than I would be at home and lie
down at night with a mind lighter and more grateful heart than
many a big lazy pup at home who is too cowardly to come out
and defend the old flag of Freedom.[14]

Church going, watching sailboats and steamers on the bay,
and reading the periodicals were about the only entertain-
ments during this time. Again inactivity began to weigh on the
men. They commented that they couldn't take much more of
this "stand-still" policy. The weather was close and oppressive
and men suffered from a wide variety of agues. Myriads of
flies forced them to retire under mosquito netting to write
letters.

Now assigned to Sumner's Second Army Corps, the men
broke the routine with a reconnaissance in the direction of
Malvern Hill, but returned to camp without encountering the
enemy. They were, however, encountering the Rebs infor-
mally if one record written years later is true. This writer
described hailing Jackson's men on the nearby Southern lines:

> We traded them Washington papers for Richmond papers and
> good government coffee for Virginia tobacco, and had a real
> nice time for a short time. We were always friendly with Jack-
> son's men when not engaged in actual argument with guns or
> chasing each other.[15]

John McClure of G Company seemed wary of this type of
friendship. "I never tried the experiment," he wrote his
sister.[16] McClure was, as usual, finding the lighter side of "all
quiet on the James." He and others finally convinced Mart
Johnson, a cohort from the old neighborhood, to join them as
one of the new recruits. McClure wrote to his sister July 13:

> Mart Johnson is getting along as well as could be expected. He
> don't like hard crackers and fat meat verry well.[16]

On August 15 the lumbering army finally got on the move
back north, leaving Harrison's Landing and proceeding down

the peninsula to Newport News. Kimball's brigade was among
the last to get on the road, following a trail of dust in heat
which had already taken a toll of horses and men ahead of
them. The Fourteenth watched the rest of the Northern Army
move onto the retreat trail for a full sixty-four hours, day and
night, before they at last took their turn.[17]

The first night, after many hours of hot, dusty marching,
the regiment halted near a 100-acre cornfield, which they
stripped "to the nubbins" for supper, comparing themselves
gleefully to the disciples in the Galilean wheatfields. The next
day they pressed on past Williamsburg and Fort McGruder's
strong defenses, and noted that when the Rebels had "skedad-
dled" they had left behind a considerable quantity of sound
shot and two heavy guns. Coming to Yorktown, they "pulled
about fifty acres of corn for another man," bathed in the salt
water of the York River, and caught clams, oysters, and crabs,
some of them gorging until they were ill. Beem looked for and
found "the spot where the British General gave up his sword to
the Father of his Country." On each of the final two days of the
journey, the troops were aroused at 3 a.m. to complete the
march to the James.[18]

The regiment boarded the "splendid steamer" *Illinois* for a
pleasant trip up Chesapeake Bay to the Potomac River. The
men "enjoyed the trip up hugely," Van Dyke said; in the
well-furnished cabin, reserved for the sixty officers of the
brigade, Houghton, Beem, Van Dyke, Kelly, Coons, and the
rest relaxed, hobnobbed with the general and his staff, and let
the steward wait on them. It was a far and welcome cry from
the tents in the Chickahominy. Everyone stayed up late playing cards, having mock court-martials, and joking.[19] The enlisted men did not fare so well. Lambert complained of
hunger; the trip seemed to take longer than had been planned
and food supplies ran low. Finally on August 23 the steamer
arrived at Alexandria. The men, in no mood to be "taken,"
headed to the sutlers for supplies. When one sutler grew
saucy, his cart was overturned and the men helped themselves.

The regiment went on the march for Rockville, Maryland.

The prospects of renewed battle made them edgy and soon they met on the road the remnants of the broken and retreating army of Pope, who had been trying to effect a junction with the rest of the Northern Army. His wagons and wounded men choked the roads, and movement forward was tortuous as the regiment wound its way past abandoned wagons stuck in the mire, two ammunition wagons which had collided and spilled their contents all over the road, and ambulances and cavalry units which kept crisscrossing the muddy track.[20]

Amid constant shelling, Kimball's brigade moved out to cover the retreat of Pope's forces and then recrossed the Potomac by way of a chain bridge. Harrow, now reassigned as colonel of the regiment, helped lead the retreat. He had evidently decided to swallow his pride and had accepted a recommissioning which recognized his instinctive ability as a soldier without dealing with his personality problems. Cavins had been advanced to major and Coons was now lieutenant colonel. William H. French was commander of the division.

The men arrived at Rockville apprehensive, but not fully aware of Lee's serious threat to the North — an intrusion into Maryland which could be the beginning of a grand sweep through the Union. Although the regiment longed only for rest and sufficient time for their invalids to regain strength after the grueling stay in peninsular Virginia, the men found instead that they were to march on immediately. The Rebels were at Frederick City with a reported 100,000 men. Lee had to be stopped at once.

Houghton, confronted by the order to march, was dismayed. Men unable to stand a hard march were to be left, and many were put into a makeshift hospital at Rockville (John McClure and Henderson Simpson among them). Some of Houghton's men and others in the regiment again had no shoes and also had to stay behind. Surveying Company C, Houghton found he had forty-three men, eleven of whom were new recruits and had never held a gun. Some of the forty-three were assigned to details, leaving him thirty-seven men able to fight.[21]

The brigade began a slow march through what seemed, again, almost mockingly picturesque countryside. Houghton praised its beauty:

> I think at that setting sun I witnessed the most beautiful scene of my remembrance. The valley of Frederick lay like a map before us with its beautiful groves and fields — its circle of mountains all around its pretty villages, sparkling streams and the spires of the city — five miles distant, flashing in the departing sunlight. . . so quiet, so lovely, so homelike that it seemed impossible that the thunder of artillery should ever wake the sleeping echoes of these lovely hills.[22]

The regiment camped in the darkness, and when dawn came it revealed the vast Northern Army sprawled over the hillsides, a dormant giant of 87,000 men, wounded but powerful still. The column formed and marched toward the sound of distant firing in the mountains ahead. As they neared the city of Frederick, Maryland, they halted and General McClellan and his staff rode past. Along mile after mile soldiers' hats were thrown into the air and the men of the Fourteenth said that the shout was deafening. To Houghton "he looked fine and there was a glance of triumph in his eyes at the knowledge he had outlived his maligners and still lived the Soldiers' Deity — they loved him."[23]

As the column passed through the town, regimental flags flying and Lambert and the rest of the boys in the band playing loudly, Frederick women leaned from windows to display Union flags, as Barbara Fritchie had done in defiance of Stonewall Jackson. The women of the town left no doubt, at least in the minds of the men of the Fourteenth, that theirs was a Union city.

Lee, involved in a daring strategy to capture Harper's Ferry, had left D. H. Hill to fight at the passes of the mountains beyond Frederick and on September 15 fought the Battle of South Mountain, in which the Second Corps (including the Fourteenth Indiana) was in a reserve position. After the battle, the brigade crossed the field, through a sea of dead men, and camped at the summit of the mountain. On the night of September 16 the regiment camped on the banks of "an unspeakable creek," as Houghton said, within two miles of the Rebel camp. Unavoidable confrontation loomed and the men slept very little that night.

At dawn on September 17 the soldiers awoke and, boiling water from Antietam Creek, they quickly made and drank their coffee. The Fourteenth marched from the field where they had bivouacked, apprehensive and aware that the sounds and feelings of a cataclysmic battle were all around.[24] Heavy artillery thundered to the right as the men of the regiment crossed the creek and piled their knapsacks on the other side. The fighting at Dunker Church had failed to break the Rebel left, and at 8:30 a.m. French's division of Sumner's corps was forming in line of battle in front of Roulette's farm. McClellan's plan was straightforward; he would hurl most of the army at Lee's left until Lee folded. Kimball's brigade (the First) of French's division was part of the hurling power. The Third, the First, and finally the Second brigades of French's division were ordered forward, toward a ditch and a sunken road which would afterwards be known as Bloody Lane. The battle had begun at dawn and was at a fever pitch; Rebel shelling was incessant and nerve shattering. As the tension built, the regiment in front of the Fourteenth, the Northern Sixth Maryland, broke and ran toward the woods in the rear. The men of the Fourteenth began to yell taunts at them, charging them with cowardice for letting the flag be captured. Some of the Maryland men reluctantly returned, but for those who could not be shamed, the Fourteenth gave three groans and followed them with three cheers for the Union. Then they gave the Hoosier yell raucously and advanced to the ditch within sixty-five yards of the enemy.[25]

From 9 a.m. until noon Kimball's troops held the Bloody Lane position, without relief, in an unremitting inferno of death and noise, with grape and cannister, shot and shell, screaming and whistling and turning the air dark. On that Antietam morning casualties were incredibly high. Beem saw his friend Jess Harrold, the blacksmith from Owen County, shot four times, first in the right thigh, next in the left elbow joint; then, while he held his wounded arm and leaned over, the third shot struck him in the back of the head splitting it from base to crown. When he threw his right hand to his head, the fourth shot entered the point of the left shoulder. Incredibly, Harrold would live to fight again.[26]

Then Beem watched as Lieutenant Porter Lunday, his tent-mate and "better half," was shot beside him. "He never spoke after he was struck," Beem said.[27] Van Dyke, too, saw the man next to him die with his brains shot out and turned away from the sight only to see another comrade cut in two by a screeching cannonball.[28] Houghton watched as his men were eliminated like garish caricatures of men, targets in a shooting gallery:

> I saw my brave boys fall like sheep led to the slaughter. Bryant was shot through the brain. McCord was shot near the heart, and while the life blood was gushing from the wound, he sat up and with an almost heavenly smile playing upon his features, he told us he was dying but to mind him not, he was happy and we must go and avenge his death. "Farewell boys, farewell Captain," he exclaimed as I reached him and he fell forward to the earth.[29]

Officers dropped as rapidly as enlisted men. Orderly Sergeant W. D. Mull took command of A Company when other officers were laid low although he himself had five separate wounds.[30] A Company was decimated; after the battle Mull reported that only seven men were able to answer roll call, only three of them unwounded. The ten rounds of ammunition per soldier were exhausted by 10 a.m., and the men of the Fourteenth began to rise like specters through the gloom as they searched the bodies of the dead for ammunition. At one point, as the line on the right gave way and the enemy screamed around the right flank, Harrow received orders to fall back. Jumping onto his horse, he commanded, "Attention, Fourteenth!" But the men ignored him. In a few minutes, he

again attempted to command the retreat, but when the Fourteenth once more refused to listen, he abandoned the idea of
falling back, roaring at the men, "Shoot, God damn you,
then!"[31] Then he hurried to the rear to find more ammunition.

As Lieutenant Colonel Coons was carried off the field, badly
wounded, E. H. C. Cavins took command, although he was
painfully wounded in the hand. He exhorted the men to
remember Indiana and fight on, beyond despair and isolation
from the rest of the troops, beyond the frustration they must
have felt as segment after segment of the wounded line gave
way and battle flags from fresh units could be seen in the Rebel
lines, beyond anger as men from other units ran in the face of
the enemy ten times their number. They stayed on and at
12:30, desperately assembling one final time and somehow
sensing the confusion in the Southern ranks as orders were
going astray, the officers of the Fourteenth (along with the
paltry remnants of other regiments at Bloody Lane) charged
up the hill with hats in hands and swords in the air and, as
Houghton recalled,

> the men yelled like demons and fought like infuriated mad men,
> the Rebels at last broke and ran like sheep from the squad that
> was left of our brigade. Relief came up gallantly after the danger
> was over.[32]

McClellan sent his congratulations (but did not do them the
honor of following up the opportunity they had won) and
General French gave them a sobriquet that they ever after-
ward carried: the Gibraltar Brigade.[33]

The battle at Bloody Lane was over and the Fourteenth fell
back, leaving its wounded on the scene along with the 12,000
other men of the Northern Army who were killed or wounded
at Antietam. It was a long and terrible night, with a cold fall
wind blowing and pitiful cries of the delirious and wounded
coming to the men lying sleepless on their arms on the very
battlefield where they had fought.

The desperately wounded Harrold had been carried back to
the field hospital, but no one could give him attention. He was

propped up against a fence corner. Half delirious from his
head wound, he rose to find a blanket from his knapsack but
lost his direction and stumbled onto the battlefield. He spent
the night wandering into the Rebel pickets until he suddenly
awoke near dawn and took himself back to the fence corner at
the field hospital.

Harrold's further experience was typical of that of the
wounded after Antietam. He lay for five nights with his only
medical attention being seven stitches taken to close the head
wound. He and the rest of the wounded nearly froze to death;
medical details were busy everywhere not only treating the
living but also burying the Rebel dead as well as their own.[34]

Houghton had been wounded early; but his admonition in a
letter, "Don't start, Mother, 'tis but a scratch" was an under-
statement. A surgeon squeezed a ball from the same hole near
his elbow that it had made in entering. Coons was removed to a
hospital nearly dead, but he too would recover, slowly, and
return to the regiment. All the letters home had the same
strongly poignant and ringing tone; through the pain and loss
shone the pride in a cooperative effort that had succeeded.
"We never gave an inch. Tell them that, Mother, when they say
we were all wounded." The lessons of the Bible and Shake-
speare and Napoleon (and their own Indian-fighting parents)
had come true for them on that dark, bloody morning. All had
taught something different but all had urged them to play the
man in a world where their actions had real significance and
tragic meaning. The Fourteenth Indiana lost 210 men, killed
and wounded, which all accounts agree was well over fifty per
cent of the men sent into battle. Of Houghton's thirty-seven
men in Company C, twenty-eight were killed or wounded.
Sumner added his congratulations to the only part of the
Northern line that did not give way at Bloody Lane.

The battles and events before Sharpsburg built the regiment; Antietam gave it, like many other Northern units, glory.
Glory is not a fashionable word these days; the men of the
regiment would have well understood it to mean that they had
distinguished themselves, that they had earned through com-

munal effort an honorable fame. They had been able to show
grace under fire and they had done it together for a cause they
still believed in as clearly as they had the day they had enlisted.
The Athenian men at Marathon, the Romans of the Republic,
and the Americans at Saratoga would have understood this
type of glory.

Beem wrote to Mrs. Lunday, the wife of his best comrade in
arms:

> I have now to perform the most painful duty of my life and one
> which fills me with grief and sadness. . . . Tell his children that
> their father died a glorious death. When they arrive at maturer
> years, they will know they lost an affectionate parent in the great
> struggle for a priceless government. . . . I am filled with regret at
> our inability to send his corpse to you at present. The great
> number killed and the want of facilities for embalming have
> rendered it absolutely impossible. Myself, Col Harrow and Gen-
> eral Kimball did all we could to have it done. . . it may be a
> satisfaction to you, however, to know that we buried him de-
> cently in a county cemetery under a beautiful tree.[35]

The sense of glory was, of course, mixed with an over-
whelming sense of tragedy and horrific loss. If Houghton
began his Antietam letter home with a line from *Hamlet*, "I
could a tale unfold" (I.v.15), it is because he, like the ghost, had
passed through the world of death, personal and immediate,
and had, unaccountably, returned to talk about it. The horror
of continual, unrelieved slaughter at Antietam was acute and
chastening to men's spirits. "May I never again see the horrors
as I saw that day," Van Dyke wrote to Angie, his wife-to-be.
[36] "Oh the rush and roar of the battle," Beem wrote. "I wonder
if the dreadful sounds will ever be out of my ears." Fifty years
later they were not; writing about Antietam after the turn of
the century, Beem still used words like "frightening," "desperate," and "awful":

> Who can describe the emotions that stir within when every
> sound that strikes the ear, and every sight that attracts the eye
> are those of close and deadly conflict? The conflict was dreadful
> and the carnage awful on all sides. . . .[37]

When Beem talked about his feelings at walking "many rods" over the corpses of the dead enemy, it is obvious that he, like so many others in both armies, had finally realized what the Civil War was all about. For weeks the horrors of Antietam floated in the minds of many of the soldiers of the Fourteenth, a hideous, distorted magic-lantern show of mechanized death and human misery.

Antietam profoundly affected the regimental spirit by instilling in the men a deep new sense of comradeship. In a few minutes scores of regimental or lifetime friends were gone — shot to pieces or left to die untended on the darkened field. The sense of anguish and helplessness on the part of their comrades was great. But for the living comrades a new feeling was born, a sense of debt and respect. These men from southern Indiana had held the line for the Union and for each other on the greatest day of slaughter in the Civil War. They had found ammunition for each other, helped the wounded off the field, and after four hours of holocaust followed their madly brave leaders, hurling the Hoosier yell directly into the teeth of the Rebels. They looked at each other and saw that they were touched with a certain greatness surpassing any medal or commission that French or McClellan or any other part of the military machine could award to them. On the banks of the "unspeakable creek" the Fourteenth Indiana and many other units of the Army of the Potomac learned about war's essential nature and what they themselves were. That was their real portion of glory — the conscious confidence of courage against unbelievable odds. Antietam would confer many other legacies, most of them bitter, but that confidence would always remain. And, like that of Lincoln himself, this sort of glory was for the ages, and those who shared it could never really be separated again.

1. Lambert, Journal, July 2, 1862.
2. *Report of the Adjutant General*, 4. Only three desertions occurred in the regiment after January 1, 1863.
3. *Brooks Memorial Booklet*.

4. There was a general code of "silence" in letters home about matters that might cast a poor light on the regimental mystique. This is clear from many instances in private letters of instructions not to "show this letter around." Many letters were printed in local papers. Drunkenness in the regiment was one of the subjects not to be spoken of to the home front; thus Van Dyke dutifully revised a letter about Owen in this way: "The only field officer we now have is Lieut. Col. Owen, who is *either* sick most of the time *or* [sic]." The italicized words were crossed out in this letter, sent to Van Dyke's father, August 3, 1862.

5. Letter of Van Dyke, February 8, 1862.

6. Letter of E. H. C. Cavins to his wife Ann (hereafter cited as Letter of Cavins to his wife), April 6, 1862, in the Cavins Papers, Indiana Historical Society Library.

7. Van Dyke said, in a letter dated March 4, 1862, to Angie, "If Will and John were not being clothed and fed by the U.S., I do not know what they would do for a livelihood. . . . We have heard nothing from Will since he left here, I suppose that he is at Vincennes yet. What an awful captain he will make. Just such a captain as any other ignoramus and most consummate coward would make." Will Denny's later career as captain and later colonel of the Fifty-first Volunteers seem to indicate that Van Dyke's comments were not very well founded.

8. Letter of Houghton to his father, July 14, 1862.

9. Letter of Van Dyke to his brother, Mandeville Van Dyke, August 23, 1862, hereafter cited as Letter of Van Dyke to his brother.

10. Letter of Houghton to his father, July 14, 1862.

11. Ibid.

12. Letter of Houghton to his brother, Walter Houghton, July 26, 1862.

13. Letter of McClure to his sister, June 26, 1862, in *Hoosier Farmboy.*

14. Letter of Beem to his wife, July 27, 1862.

15. James William Edwards, *A Brief Biography,* photostated copy in the Indiana Historical Society Library, hereafter cited as Edwards, *Brief Biography.*

16. Letter of McClure to his sister, July 13, 1862, in *Hoosier Farmboy.*

17. Beem, "History of the Fourteenth Indiana."

18. Lambert, Journal, August 17, 18, 19, and 20, 1862; Letter of Van Dyke to his brother, August 23, 1862; Letters of Beem to his wife, August 23 and 24, 1862.

19. Letter of Van Dyke to his brother, August 29, 1862.

20. Ibid., September 9, 1862.

21. Letter of Houghton to his mother, September 20, 1862.

22. Ibid.

23. Ibid.

24. Ibid.

25. Ibid.

26. "The Soldier Shot to Pieces."

27. Letter of Beem to Mrs. Porter Lunday, September 20, 1862.

28. Letter of Van Dyke to his wife-to-be, September 21, 1862.

29. Letter of Houghton to his mother, September 20, 1862.

30. *History of Vigo and Parke Counties,* pp. 26-27.

31. Lambert, Journal, September 17, 1862.

32. Letter of Houghton to his mother, September 20, 1862.

33. William H. French, Report, *The War of the Rebellion,* Official Records of the Union and Confederate Armies, 1st ser. 19 (Washington: 1880-1901), 324.

34. "The Soldier Shot to Pieces."

35. Letter of Beem to Mrs. Porter Lunday, September 20, 1862.

36. Letter of Van Dyke to his wife-to-be, September 21, 1862.

37. Beem, "History of the Fourteenth Indiana."

CHAPTER SIX

FREDERICKSBURG

It took several days to bury the dead at Antietam. Lambert of F had climbed a hill to see what the Rebels were doing. He was angered when he did not see burial details at work; he counted six clouds of dust in the area of the river and concluded, quite rightly, "The rebels were making off and leaving the dead for us to bury." Ironically, the Fourteenth drew the burying detail, and Lambert himself was soon at work.

> Our boys were all tolerably decently buried today, but it took days to enter the rebels merely by throwing them in rows and covering them with a little dirt. And they began to smell very bad before we got done with them,[1]

he wrote in his diary.

Cavins wrote to his wife on October 1 that he had urged the men to arm themselves with good rifles from the 30,000 or 40,000 dead on the battlefield. He told them to stack their old muskets on the field. "We have a rifle regiment now," he reported.

The men gladly broke camp on September 22 and marched to the river. They passed through devastated Sharpsburg, with its sheared-off trees and blasted houses and waded the Potomac at Harper's Ferry to make camp at Bolivar Heights. Here they pitched their tattered summer tents, prepared for a long recuperation stay, and hoped for clothing and money; the paymaster was long overdue. Many of the men were scattered in hospitals in the area and word came into camp about them daily; Coons of G was so badly wounded that Vincennes people came to take him home to live or die.[2]

In the encampment at Harper's Ferry began a serious period of dissension in the regiment which is not easily explainable except in terms of the men's long-endured frustrations and weariness, including battle fatigue. Certainly the trouble that arose cut into the solidarity welded at Antietam and lasted longer than it should have, until finally it almost broke the regiment. And just as certainly, it was precipitated by one unfortunate incident.

On October 1 Colonel Kimball ordered reconnaissance toward Leesburg. His orders were vague. Harrow claimed that Kimball did not state whether the action was to be a scout or a change of camp, and he therefore had no choice but to order the regiment to take all their gear — to travel heavily laden with knapsacks.[3] The men left at 7 a.m. and were ordered to move rapidly. Soon in the sultry heat, they began dropping out of the ranks, unable to continue with their loads. Still the march went on. When the men arrived a few miles outside of Leeburg at midnight, only seventeen men were able to stack arms in the Fourteenth and ninety-six in the brigade.[4]

The infuriated Kimball called the officers together on the spot, and either unable or unwilling to face the realities of the situation, threatened to arrest every one of them for allowing the straggling on the road. An angry session followed, with the officers daring him to "pitch in, we would like to have the affair investigated."[5] No enemy was at Leesburg; Kimball ordered the men to get a few hours' sleep and then to march at 8 a.m. the next morning. They arrived back at Bolivar Heights at 3 a.m.

The officers of the Fourteenth, who had willingly faced death only two weeks before at Bloody Lane to carry out their orders and indeed had initiated desperate orders of their own when the circumstances called for it, were outspoken in defiance of Kimball's rashness. Beem later wrote:

> General Kimball on this occasion accomplished the feat of marching his command until all but 25 in the 14th and less than 100 in the brigade had been run down and fell by the roadside . . . . Nothing whatever was accomplished and the march was conducted in such an outrageous manner as to win for Nathan Kimball the hearty hatred of every man and officer in his command. . . about 100 of our best soldiers, with feelings outraged by this inhuman treatment, which was excused by no palliation, took advantage of the order allowing volunteers to enlist in the regular army and thus escaped the future outrages of this shallow brained and heartless officer.[6]

The men were beginning to perceive that Kimball was a little superficial; his personal papers reinforce their opinion. Kimball seems to have been a very conscientious and courtly if not overly brilliant officer. The men of the regiment did not deny his obvious devotion to duty, but at this period they strongly believed that they were being sacrificed to it, and to what they thought were his increasingly evident political aspirations. Van Dyke was sure that Kimball would run for lieutenant governor once the war was over.

Not everyone took the straggling incident seriously. Some of the men, like Lambert, survived the march and indeed much of the worst of the war by not troubling themselves too much about "duty" at certain strategic moments, doing pretty much whatever their survival instincts told them. Hoosier pragmatism never served Lambert (and some others) better than on the ill-fated march to Leesburg. In fact, he seemed to have dawdled purposefully, reasoning, as he said, that if they met Rebels he would not be much use as a brigade band member. He detoured and allowed himself to be called aside at Waterford by a smiling young lady carrying a tray of pears and cakes.

> We could not eat all, but it was a very difficult matter to pass such unexpected kindness without stopping to bestow a few words of

gratitude at least upon the fascinating donors. Finally I was
conquered and inveigled into conversation with three beautiful
girls and am ashamed to acknowledge the fact, but it is the truth
nevertheless that I actually so far forgot myself and my duty as
to find to my great astonishment that I was "sitting on the stile,
Mary, as we sat side by side" with one of them.[7]

The lady asked him to stay the night with her folks, but he
finally bade her goodbye and double-timed it after the regiment, which was now fully five miles ahead of him. He had not
been missed.

When the regiment returned to Bolivar Heights, they heard
that Lincoln had reviewed the troops. Landon of G believed
that they had been sent off "on purpose," for the Gibraltar
Brigade was

> the hardest looking one in Sumner's corps, but the old regi-
> ments in it ("Shields' foot cavalry") 7th Virginia, 8th Ohio and
> 14th Indiana are *some* in a *skirmish* like Antietam; though they
> do present a rough appearance on parades.[8]

The Fourteenth was continuing to take a rough pride in the
fact that they were no "bandbox" unit like many of the new,
well-equipped ones they saw. Even without shoes, shirts, socks,
or caps, they could fight like jackals. But they would not march
uselessly.

Exacerbating the Leesburg incident was another controversy. Harrow had been placed under arrest, and for once the
regiment stood behind him. Immediately after the march he
had spoken for the men in urging that the brigade commissary
Collins be investigated for graft. Cavins had written to Ann on
October 20, "Collins is playing as strong a game at swindling as
Buntin used to play. The arrest of Col Harrow is an outrage
upon common honesty, and he will make some of the generals
feel it yet." The men were eating wormy crackers while the
commissary enriched himself, and they were enraged to think
that Kimball had seized the wrong man in the controversy.

Harrow was soon released, but the Leesburg event would
not die down. On October 20, as Beem reported, a recruiter

from the Fourth U.S. Artillery came to the camp, claiming that
he had authority from the War Department to recruit men
over the protest of their officers, for the federal artillery.
About seventy left that day, and thirty more followed within
the week when a recruiter from the Sixth U.S. Cavalry came to
town. Kimball was chagrined but could not prevent the transfers. He posted heavy guards around the camp, but it did little
good; the men of the Fourteenth, completely battle proven,
came and went as they pleased, for, as Lambert said:

> [the guard] does not amount to much, for the boys have become
> most too old soldiers to be kept in camp by guards. . . . One
> thing certain, we have been very much imposed upon and
> Kimball in all past cases has had recourse to a few soft words of
> blarney to get the boys all right again. . . this time the scale is
> turned.[9]

This is probably a good time to draw the difference between
"regular" and "volunteer" in the Union Army, because the
Leesburg incident is related to that difference. The United
States maintained a regular army before and during the War
Between the States. It consisted of cavalry, infantry, and other
typical military units. Most of the war, however, was fought by
volunteers. They had originally been recruited in Indiana by a
loosely organized volunteer statute which had been passed in
1852 and which had called for the organization of militia with
honorary commissions conferred upon local citizens who were
in the militia. After Sumter this loose legislation was replaced
by an authorizing act passed at a special session in the state
capital,[10] but it left a great deal of power in the hands of the
volunteer units; they remained products of the people
throughout the war, self-impelled, self-recruited, and self-
managed to a large extent. As the war progressed, great numbers of volunteers no longer came forward, and the nationali-
zation of both the troops and the country itself became a real
factor. All of the volunteer units, however, remained quite
independent throughout the war. "Regular," therefore, was
the opposite of "volunteer." To the soldier "regular" meant

different from them, less exuberant and unpredictable,
bound by more spit-and-polish regulation. To some extent,
then, the volunteers in the Fourteenth in their determined
transfers were making a statement: those particular men were
fed to the teeth with the volunteer war, with its corn-fed
leaders, its small-town politics, and its uncertainties. It was
their belief that a "regular" commander would never have
made them make the ridiculous march to Leesburg. They
were opting for professionalism as they saw it. For them and
the other men, the ones who stayed, Leesburg was symbolic of
the whole mismanaged, amateurish effort they were involved
in — in short, the whole rotten volunteer war.

To Kimball, Cavins, and others who understood the vitality
and uniqueness of the volunteer army, the new recruiters
represented something else. Their appearance signaled an
intrusion of the federal government into an area that had been
sacrosanct. The Indiana regiments were units of the state;
when they needed aid or direction or promotion they turned
to Morton. The interference of Washington did not please
Kimball, who rightly interpreted it as the beginning of a new
turn in the war and resisted, to no avail. The recruiters carried
papers signed by Lincoln and would not be put off. Kimball
then tried the appeal mentioned by Lambert; he promised the
men white bread and warned them gently that the wounded
from Antietam would return and find them missing. But the
men were unmoved. It would take many recruits to fill the
gaps and many weeks to ease the tension.

Morning reports for G Company during this period show
this tension quite clearly. They were made out first by Landon
as first sergeant, then, when he was promoted, by William H.
Jackson. The underscoring is Landon's.

> Oct 1 Absent Sick 17; Present & Absent aggregate 74. Expedi-
> tion (with knapsacks) to Leesburg distance 32 miles. Returned
> October 3rd 4 a.m.
> Oct 2 Pvt. John R. McClure detailed at Teamster to Division
> Train.
> Oct 4 Cpl. Robert Ewald returned to regiment.

Oct 6 Pvt. John P. Connelly, Wm. H. Javins, Fred Bryer, John
Shahan and Joseph Wilmer, *deserted.*
Oct 7 Private Nicholas Geise placed under arrest. Captain John
Coons promoted to Lieut Col, 14th Indiana Regt, Lt Wm. H.
Patterson promoted to Captain, 2nd Lt A M. Van Dyke pro-
moted to 1st Lieut, Orderly Sgt Wm. Landon to 2nd Lieut, Sgt
Wm. H. Jackson to 1st sg.
Oct 18 Private William H. Javins discharged by order of Gen
Wadsworth.
Oct 20 Private John Runnett detailed as ambulance driver.
Oct 21 Transferred to Regular Battery No 4 privates Adam Alt,
John Muth, Nicholas Geise and John Bussells.
Oct 22 Gideon Munch discharged by Order October 22 to go
into Regular Battery No 4.
Oct 24 Joseph Campbell, private, was discharged by order to
join Regular Battery, No. 4.
Oct 25 Pvt Jacob Bower Discharge by Gen Order War Dept No
154 and this day enlisted in 1st Cavalry.
Oct 30 Pvt James H. Simpson discharged on account of disabil-
ity from U.S. Gen Hospital Washington City, D.C.[11]

Life was not all bad in spite of the depletion of the ranks and
the growing chill in the drafty two-man tents. G Company had
acquired a "contraband" runaway slave who cooked their
meals. Van Dyke had picked him up after the old man had
made off from the area around Culpepper Court House, and
he served succulent stews made from good onions and meat
and the newly arrived (as per Kimball's promise) white "soft
tack."[12] In general the Fourteenth were applying themselves to
eating while they rested. As they marched about the countryside or while they were in camp, they bought whatever was
cheap and hearty. Captain Patterson of G and Landon bought
a "gallon" of potatoes, cooked them without salt, and ate them
on the spot. They cost twenty-five cents. For two dollars the
soldiers could buy "turkies" or four chickens, but since the
paymaster was late more often the men "flanked" the unfortunate birds in their home barnyards by night.[13]

On October 30 the regiment packed the tents and was on the
march through Maryland to Upperville, Rectortown, Salem,
and Warrentown. At Warrentown on the morning of

November 10 McClellan was finally relieved as general of the army. As he rode along the lines he had so long commanded he was cheered from every side, and when at last he handed over the command, he said to the men, "I only wish you to stand by Burnside as you have stood by me and all will be well. Goodbye."[14]

Houghton, who had always been one of McClellan's staunchest supporters, probably expressed the sentiments of many of the men in the regiment and the country (certainly of Abraham Lincoln) when he offered this reappraisal of the general:

> Concerning McClellan, as I always did, I could not but feel mortified on seeing him disgraced. But his losing campaigns, his fruitless victories, his *"masterly inaction"* after the battle of Antietam, the golden days which he allowed to pass by while lying at Harper's Ferry after having been ordered to *move* by Gen. Hallack, with the general imbecility shown in all his subsequent movements convinced me that something was wrong and a change of commander necessary.[15]

He believed Ambrose Burnside was well chosen and wished him luck. The other men in the regiment grumbled for a while about the removal of the general they had respected for so long, but finally they accepted the new man and hoped only that he would press for action soon.

Action was exactly what Burnside himself wanted. Hoping for a break through to Richmond, he urged a move through Fredericksburg, Maryland. Lincoln approved that strategy but insisted that speed was the key to success; Burnside was going to have to hurry.

Both the Army of the Potomac and its new leader had some trouble with this requirement. They made a good start; no one could deny that. When Sumner's Grand Right, of which the Fourteenth was now a part, arrived opposite Fredericksburg, only a fragment of the Rebel army was nearby. Burnside told the city to surrender or else be taken with artillery. But "it rained and turned cold," as Lambert said, "so that the demand was not enforced."[16] Many of the officers thought that the Northern Army should stand behind its demands. Van Dyke wrote:

> The time has always so far passed by without any noise from the hundred or more cannon pointing towards the city. The last time appointed is nine o'clock this morning. I think both sides are inclined to let the Sabbath pass away quietly.

He compared both the armies to schoolboys playing "touch me if you dare."[17] The men were well aware of the stakes of the game. The Rebels, Van Dyke felt, would not allow the crossing of the Rappahannock. They could not leave open the road to Richmond, "only sixty miles with a railroad all the way which can be repaired as we advance."

Yet, with everything seeming to call for decisive action on the part of the Northern Army, Burnside did nothing. They had to cross the river, of course, and the pontoon boats needed to ferry them did not appear. The men believed that the battle had been postponed and began to build stout winter quarters. For more than a week they felled trees to build log shelters, keeping out the cold with mud fireplaces and using the shelter tents and ragged oilcloths for roofing.[18] On December 10 the quarters were finished. At almost that very moment the order came for the Fourteenth to be ready to move at 6 a.m. the next day. Battle was on the horizon.

There was little sleep that night as the artillery carriages rumbled toward their positions. About 4 a.m. as firing began, the men formed and marched to the river and then lay under cover of the hills all day as cannons boomed about them.[19] Burnside was trying to dislodge the sharpshooters who were firing down from windows and roofs of the town on the harried engineers laying the pontoon boats for the crossing. The shelling accomplished little, however, until volunteers from the Seventh Michigan rowed across and drove the Rebels from the bank. Soon Howard's division also crossed, but the Fourteenth spent the night on the north bank.

Early the next morning all of Sumner's Grand Right crossed

the river and marched into Fredericksburg, stacking arms on
Caroline Street, which had been old in George Washington's
time. They raced into the basements of some of the graceful
eighteenth-century homes — for tobacco, which had been extremely scarce. The part of the village nearest the river had
already been rid of Rebels and the troops spent the rest of the
morning driving the Confederates from their strongholds in
the lower end of Fredericksburg. Gradually the Rebels retreated back to their works on a hill at the rear of the town and
strengthened their positions. They were supposed to be
75,000 strong.

As the Northern Army took full command of Fredericksburg, Van Dyke looked approvingly at the pockmarks in
the masonry caused by Yankee cannons. Then came the looting. Men ran up street after street, seizing whatever they
could, because, as Beem said,

> The inhabitants had all fled and left their houses, furniture and
> goods completely at our mercy. Our men were not slow in
> helping themselves to whatever they fancied.

Van Dyke wrote:

> Our soldiers took what they wanted and destroyed what they
> could not use. The streets of the city were filled with women's
> clothing and broken furniture and in some cases a piano was
> tumbled out of doors.[20]

Officers watched (and in some cases may have helped) as men
found a bank safe and took out several hundred dollars. A
soldier from the Fourth Ohio broke into a jewelry store and
stole thirty-seven watches and a variety of other jewelry. Beem
watched the scene and recorded it:

> The town clock is on the Baptist Church, an elegant fine old
> building. A ball passed through the steeple a few feet below the
> dial plate, but the good old clock not in the least frightened went
> on to tell the hours, calm and faithful as ever.
> But the destruction of houses was not all. The citizens had all left

AFTER THE BATTLE.   From the original Painting by Capt. James Hope, from a sketch taken by him on the spot.

"BLOODY LANE," ANTIETAM.

The Fourteenth prided itself on being the only part of the Northern Line that did not yield at Bloody Lane during the Battle of Antietam. 1889 engraving by James D. Hope based on his on-the-spot sketch and subsequent painting.

The competent General William French, whom Cavins called "old whiskey tub" and whose strike force at Antietam included Nathan Kimball's brigade.

Colonel S. S. Carroll, the leader of the brigade at the Battle of Gettysburg and later a general.

City from South M.

E.H.C. Cavins probably took this picture of Harper's Ferry.

The controversial citizen-soldier John Coons, who won the colonelship of the Fourteenth Indiana through his own determination and military record.

Colonel E. H. C. Cavins of Greene County, a prominent attorney and lady's man.

William Houghton as he led a Memorial Day parade in Martin County before the turn of the century.

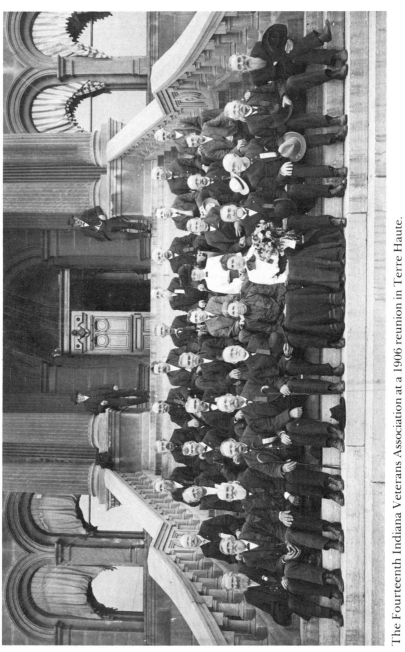

The Fourteenth Indiana Veterans Association at a 1906 reunion in Terre Haute.

Indiana Historical Society Library

Four white-whiskered veterans, Captain J.S. Harrold, Captain J.S. Sullivan, Major William Houghton, and Colonel E. H. C. Cavins, rehash old battles.

The Aaron Houghton home, a mill owner's mansion that is one of the two remaining structures from Mt. Pleasant, Indiana.

several days previously in a panic. Houses were abandoned with valuable goods in them; fine furniture in the yards and in exposed places; splendid bureaus and pianos, elegant setees and fine chairs, costly mirrors, all abandoned in wild confusion. When our troops entered, they helped themselves to all they wanted and destroyed much they ought to have left alone. Almost every house was ransacked; fine parlors were strewn with all kinds of dirt and filth and even ladies clothing thrown in confusion or torn to pieces.

In the streets, sights strange and shocking might be seen. So much destruction of elegant property I hope never to see again. Citizens had left their finest furniture in the yards . . . our troops quartered in the streets. On Saturday morning I took a stroll before the battle — I saw fine offices of lawyers and doctors literally ruined together with their books and papers. Some soldiers had split up a fine bureau of mahogany and were making coffee on the fire made of it in the street. For seats around their cooking fire, they used fine cushioned parlor chairs. Many other things I saw in keeping with this. . . . This was one of the most cruel necessities of the war; and whatever I may witness in the future, I pray I may never be called upon to behold another ruined city.[21]

The opinion of Beem (a civilized man in the midst of barbarity) was the only voice from the Fourteenth Indiana which has survived to condemn the looting of Fredericksburg. Everyone else recorded deep satisfaction. Van Dyke, for instance, considered the sacking well done and a "solacing fact" after the loss of the battle which followed "that the city was almost completely destroyed and pillaged."[22]

This attitude should not really be difficult to understand. First and most importantly, even though extreme, it was simply a continuation of the long-standing foraging practice of the regiment. Its premise should, again, be understood in terms of pioneer ethics: Fredericksburg was part of the enormous survival situation of the entire war. Traditionally, when one went from an Indiana stockade to a deserted Indian village, one made sure that the Indians knew he meant business by leaving signs of destruction. One might protest that the owners of the velvet settees were not Delaware Indians, but to the tough-skinned veterans of Antietam, it was all the same. Those may have been historical and beautiful homes, but their owners were traitors and proud to be so. Unlike its sister city of Frederick, Maryland, Fredericksburg had no patriotic matron like Barbara Fritchie to defend the republic's flag. Matrons and maids alike had welcomed the gray coats; let them pay by having every piece of Regency furniture in their parlors smashed.

In addition, the men were motivated by a bitterness that went beyond their desire to retaliate against the enemy. The Army of the Potomac was in a surly mood, "demoralized," as McClure called it. They had lost too much, too often; their energies had turned sour, passing from cider to vinegar in about three months' time. They were lawless and on the rampage — like a gang of tough boys who find the soda shop closed and go to smashing windows. It is not an unfair comparison considering that many of them *were* boys who had been through more than any men should have to experience. So the bonfires that night lit the faces of boy-men frustrated by an enemy they could not beat. Their bitterness was also increased by one final realization— the knowledge, gradually dawning, that the Northern position in the battle tomorrow was probably hopeless.

Lee's men had used Burnside's delay to assemble a strong army of veteran fighters on a hill at the edge of town. The army stood before a farmhouse of a man named Marye. Burnside's strategy, which had not changed even when the conditions calling it forth had changed, was as simple as it was impossible: they would take the Rebel position by storming straight up the hill.

There seems to have been a kind of desperate bravado on the part of the men of the Fourteenth before Fredericksburg. One man in Company F was reading a novel, sitting on a cracker box. A shot came over, struck the building in front of him, and rolled down the roof and into the end of his cracker box. When someone told him about the shell, he got up still holding his book, raked out the solid shell with the toe of his boot, and nonchalantly sat back down on the box.[23] Van Dyke and the other officers were surveying the "battle-ready" troops that they were to pit against Lee's best in the morning. Recruits had not filled all of the gaps in the ranks since the recent resignations, and many men were back at the hospital across the river or in Washington (including Harrow and McClure). They spoke together about the order to storm Lee's positions and, as Beem recorded it, "Everyone who viewed that strong position felt it would be rushing into a slaughter pen, but each men resolved to go as far as any other."

John Craig of H Company was one of those resolved. He left the medical care of the field hospital and rejoined the regiment at the last moment. Craig would be wounded on the field at Fredericksburg and die from the wound a few days later.[24] Also returning were some of the men who had joined the cavalry; B Company welcomed back John Hutchins just before orders were given to fall into line.[25]

The best account of the Fourteenth's part in the battle is the report by Kimball's courier to the wounded general immediately after the battle.[26] The attack against Marye's Heights was to begin about noon, with Sumner's Grand Right leading the charge. Kimball was to take the Gibraltar Brigade in first. The men marched down the main street in Fredericksburg into "an alley running straight to Marye's Heights," passed the depot buildings on the edge of town, and crossed the canal which wound its way through the countryside. In the open field immediately beyond the canal three large shells burst among the tightly packed ranks of the Fourteenth, killing, among others, Captain Kelly, the popular officer of Company A, and blowing off the leg of the unfortunate Hutchins only minutes after he rejoined his company. It was a horrible moment, but discipline told and the men did not break ranks. "Torn and bloody," they pressed on "through that struggling, writhing mass of flesh" to form in line of battle.[27]

The Fourteenth was on the left. Kimball ordered the men toward the heights. As they crossed plowed fields on the double quick, they tore down fences and tried to avoid the grape and cannister falling everywhere and raising clouds of amber smoke that could be seen for miles around. Houghton and Beem were soon wounded, and just as the men approached a slight depression in the field, only 100 yards from the stone fence where Rebel sharpshooters aimed deadly fire at them, Kimball was badly wounded in the thigh. As he was carried off the field, he gave a final order, "Charge bayonets forward and do not stop until you reach the top of the hill."

It was not to be. The men dropped into the depression, which was the advance position of the Northern line at this point. They could go no farther (although a few from the regiment tried; one man from I Company was found dead against the stone wall). There they stayed, using up the ammunition, waiting for reinforcements which came and then melted away, watching the Rebels dart up from their breastworks and then return to the safety of their superior positions. The courier told the general:

> No one could get beyond our line — the fire was so deadly with grape in front and shell the whole length of the line, battalions melted away like dry grass before the fire — while Frenches Div was coming up the enemy had thrown two lines of infantry at the foot of the hill in a ravine and behind a stone wall and every man who stepped onto the plateau in front of them fell. As Hancock's 2nd line passed the crest of the hill under which all the Brigades formed Col Mason ordered me to report to Gen French that we were out of ammunition and were holding what we could at the point of the bayonet. The enemy had charged twice our center but had been driven back — I immediately found Gen French who informed me that the brigade had been ordered off the field. . . the order [was] not given to them.

Three color-bearers fell in a few moments, causing one of those heroic moments the men loved later to relate. Beem reported that when the color-bearer of the regiment, Sergeant Wingert, was killed, Corporal Tom Gibson of Company H seized the colors. Gibson, too, soon received a wound in the neck but refused to leave the field when an officer ordered him off. "This is what we are fighting for," he said.

Finally Cavins, who after some confusion had assumed command, ordered Gibson off and the young man obeyed.[28]

For two hours, the men lay in their exposed and bitterly contested position, the dangerous depression so near the stone wall. They could not retreat when they received the order; going was as dangerous as coming had been. Some men did leave as the afternoon wore on, slipping away singly with the hope that the Rebels would not bother to fire at one man. Finally, under cover of darkness, the Fourteenth and all the rest of the troops retreated to the city, leaving 9000 dead and wounded on that terrible field at Fredericksburg. Tensely, they waited for orders to renew the attack in a different way, and then the truth slowly dawned. Burnie was "giving it up so, Mr. Brown," in the words of a popular song. Taking their heavily wounded along, the Fourteenth, with the rest, evacuated the town. The Indiana regiment left behind four killed in battle. Seventy had been wounded and eight were missing from their ranks.

On December 21, under a flag of truce, three men from each brigade in the corps reentered Fredericksburg to bury the dead. William Hall of G Company was one of the detail, and he returned to tell the rest of the regiment what he saw. In Fredericksburg the Rebels held full sway, with the Thirteenth Mississippi acting as provost guards. Gray-clad soldiers were showing the ruined houses to many of their owners who had returned after their flight from the city. On the battlefield Yankee corpses had been stripped naked and the Virginia cavalry was galloping over the field, paying no attention to where the horses' hoofs fell, whether on field or bodies. The corpses were in an advanced state of decomposition; only Clay Welch's could be identified by Hall, and this only because of a tattoo on his arm as he lay pinned against the stone wall. Here, while the Thirteenth Indiana, acting as a guard for burial detail, held off the disdainful Confederate cavalry with bayonets, the men buried the dead, placing them three layers deep in a long ditch which ran the entire length of the battlefield. Landon commented, "The sight Fredericksburg and

the battlefield presented would have made even the old hell-
hound Horace Greeley cry 'Peace.' "[29]

The men of the Fourteenth left more than their dead behind. They left a ruined city and the bitterest memories of the
war. In a string of losses, this was the worst. "It was a grand
failure," someone wrote, as through bitter cold and driving
rain the regiment moved into the camp they had made before.
"Bull Run, the First or Second, was nothing compared to this,"
they said.

1. Lambert, Journal, September 18, 1862.
2. Letter of Landon to the *Western Sun*, October 6, 1862.
3. Lambert, Journal, October 2, 1862.
4. Ibid.; Letter of Van Dyke to his father, October 6, 1862.
5. Letter of Van Dyke to his father, October 6, 1862.
6. Beem, "History of the Fourteenth Indiana."
7. Lambert, Journal, October 1, 1862.
8. Letter of Landon to the *Western Sun*, October 6, 1862.
9. Lambert, Journal, October 23, 1862.
10. *Indiana in the War of the Rebellion*, pp. 2, 7.
11. The G Company morning reports were kept by Orderly Sol Gundrum and are
in the John McClure Collection.
12. Letter of Van Dyke to his father, November 23, 1862.
13. Letter of Landon to the *Western Sun*, November 20, 1862.
14. Lambert, Journal, November 10, 1862.
15. Letter of Houghton to his father, December 3, 1862.
16. Lambert, Journal, November 21, 1862.
17. Letter of Van Dyke to his father, November 23, 1862.
18. Lambert, Journal, December 4 and 10, 1862.
19. Ibid., December 11, 1862.
20. Letter of Van Dyke to his father, December 23, 1862.
21. Letter of Beem to his wife, December 18, 1862.
22. Letter of Van Dyke to his brother, December 23, 1862.
23. Edwards, *Brief Biography*, pp. 23-24.
24. Beem, "History of the Fourteenth Indiana."
25. Letter of Landon to the *Western Sun*, December 19, 1862.
26. The writer of the report is unknown because the first page in the Kimball
Papers in the Lilly Library, Indiana University, Bloomington, is missing.
27. Ibid.
28. Beem, "History of the Fourteenth Indiana."
29. Letter of Landon to the *Western Sun*, December 21, 1862.

CHAPTER SEVEN

WINTER OF '63 AND CHANCELLORSVILLE

Who or what was the nebulous amalgam known as the regiment after Fredericksburg? What relationship did it bear to that original bunch of young Hoosiers who had signed up at the heated recruitment meetings at Loogootee and Rockville? The answer was — not much of one. The original desertions and discontents had sapped the regiment after Cheat Mountain and in the Valley Campaign; Antietam and Leesburg had reduced it further. After Fredericksburg, probably not even half of the original men were left in the ranks.

Cavins, Beem, George Washington Lambert, Coons, Patterson, Van Dyke, Landon, and Houghton stayed on. So did a surprising number of enlisted men and noncoms, among them McClure and Amory Allen, the young man who had sent a lock of his hair home. They watched recruits come and go, generals fade in and out of fashion, uniforms fall apart and be replaced by the surprisingly better equipment now supplied by the Army of the Potomac, new regimental colors come to replace the battle-shredded old familiar standards.

What then was the regiment? It was certainly not an unchanging group of 1000 men definite in time and place. Instead it was a fluctuating mass with a sound, immovable southern Indiana core of a couple of hundred good men who had decided to stay and survive the conflict no matter what and to do so with reasonable honor. The desertions which plagued many other regiments during the time after the Marye's Heights fiasco did not involve the Fourteenth.[1] They had bitten the bullet earlier, in the confusion of the Shenandoah Valley and on abominable Cheat Mountain, and had made their pact with war. Now they would keep it if they could.

To do so, the old soldiers of the Fourteenth looked to the past reputation of the regiment. By now its fame had grown considerably. Part of the mystique had evolved in Indiana, where the Fourteenth was viewed with respect on its old stamping ground. Pool had published his reports from Cheat Mountain in a tributary booklet dedicated to General Kimball (its dedicatory poem, "All Hail the Gallant Fourteenth Brave," appears as the first page of this book). Landon in the *Vincennes Western Sun* had portrayed it as a coolly capable, tough unit praised by generals for its bravery in combat and ability (which Landon shared) to surmount the trials of camp life with assurance and good humor. Beem often wrote to the *Indianapolis Sentinel* and Houghton to the *Martin County Tribune,* extolling the brave actions of members of their units or commenting on some political aspect of the war. Most hometown papers during the Civil War had news of individual engagements on the supper tables of area families before soldiers' letters could hope to arrive. The front-page dispatches rarely mentioned the officers' arguments, the drunken, murderous brawls, the shoddy, petty jockeying for positions of power. Not only the Fourteenth but most other units were well reported on and were building their own fan clubs. Many thought they were among the top fighting units in the army; certainly the Fourteenth did, even now at the midpoint of the war. How right were they? Certainly the Fourteenth was well above average (even outstanding) in an army of fine fighting units. But whether they were among the "top ten" is not important; what counted was that they thought they were. They thought they were tops. Assuredly that attitude could not help but be a sustaining one in the difficult months to come.

The men themselves cultivated the regimental image which

had coalesced at Bloody Lane and had been decisively reinforced in the charges at Marye's Heights. They found in it a
reliable code to which they could refer their own personal
standards in times of stress: the Fourteenth never ran; it was
generally sent in first and given the dirty work for good
reason; it stayed when others left.

The individual esprit de corps of Civil War units on both
sides was a triumph of idealism and image making, but it
played a conspicuous part in determining creative and consis-
tent action on the battlefield. It was a point of reference for the
Fourteenth: we have always acted this way; I am going to act
this way, too, even if I don't really wish to. All the soldiers
needed to do was to look at the regimental pattern and act the
way the reputation dictated, at least after Fredericksburg. The
ultimate in esprit de corps had been achieved; highly indi-
vidualistic men had been persuaded to submit themselves to a
code; the Fourteenth Indiana Regiment had become an ideal
instead of a physical battle unit.

*   *   *

Let us suppose for a moment that we can view a cross section
of the mind of the Fourteenth at this nadir of its experience in
the war — the disaster at Fredericksburg. If we could miraculously scan a soldier's ideas over the years through the pages of
letters and diaries, this is what we might see.

There was, first, cynical disillusionment that was bitter but
not always despairing. Sometimes the disillusionment was cold-
ly ironical. Van Dyke was able to calculate that the position of
the Army of the Potomac at Falmouth now was advantageous
for the Rebels: a few of them could hold off the entire army
while their leaders "can saw off men enough to drive Gen.
Foster out of North Carolina, to drive Rosecrans back into
Kentucky to the defeat of Louisville and Cincinnati."[2]

As it became increasingly obvious that nothing was going to
happen for the rest of the winter, the men's frustration with
the state of affairs in the Army of the Potomac intensified into

a real torrent of abuse and anger, and the thought scan of our typical soldier by the end of January, 1863 would have been fairly abusive. All the talk was of the fiasco at Fredericksburg following the fiasco after Antietam following the Seven Days' fiasco. Van Dyke's letter just before Christmas of '62 should be read in full, because it distilled the feelings that were beginning to spread among the men of the Fourteenth:

Dear Brother
    Affairs remain in the status quo in the Grand Army of the Potomac. It is not only grand as an army but is also one of the grandest humbugs that has been imposed upon the public since the palmiest days of that prince of humbug Barnum. Have you read the reports of the "investigation Committees" and the proceedings of the "Courts in Inquiry" in the cases of Porter and McDowell? I have read all of them and a great many other articles regarding the "conduct of the wars" by this Army of the Potomac and after mature deliberations and canvassing of the opinions of others I have come to the conclusion that the object of this war in this department has not been only the speedy suppression of this rebellion. That such is merely a secondary consideration of that of political agrandizement upon the part of some parties high in authority, military and civil. This army went to the Peninsula 100,000 strong splendidly armed and equipped, one of the grandest armies in point of discipline that was ever commanded by any General. At the end of five months campaign, they hastened to the defense of Washington, leaving the bones of nearly 60,000 soldiers in the swamps of the James and the Chicahominey and having expended $300,000,000 of our people's money. It then appears at the scene of our first disaster, Bull Run, only to take part in another worse if possible than the first, and retreats ingloriously before an inferior foe, falling back to the protection of the strongholds of Arlington Heights. In order to leave something for these political hucksters to work for the Rebels must be driven out of Maryland. In the inordinate lust for peace and power their "vaulting ambition had near oer leaped itself" and a dishonorable peace was near being forced upon the country. The army showed at South Mountain and at Antietam what it could do if led earnestly to the work of crushing the Rebellion. But the enemy in defeated *Washington* was safe, and it would not do to fall upon the disheartened rebels and destroy them utterly for that would end

the war before all the political triggers were set ready to be sprung.

The enemy must be allowed to escape with all his material into Virginia, there to collect his scattered forces, receive his reinforcements and prepare to meet us again with superior numbers. In consequence of this the pages of history are reddened with blood of ten thousand men, slaughtered in vain upon the plains of Fredericksburg. "There is tide in the affairs of men, which, if taken at the flood leads on to fortune." There is also a tide in the affairs of nations which if taken at the proper time will insure the success of and the permanence of its institutions. When I look back over the history of this war for the past year and notice particularly the relative position of the two armies, the one of the Peninsula the other this place in June last and see what *might* have been done, had the "tide been taken at its flood," by McDowell cooperating with McClellan, I curse from the bottom of my heart the imbecillity or the treachery of those who prevented our destroying the army of the South and occupying the strong hold of treason. If anyone at Washington prevented this success, or if any one in the army was the cause of this non-success, he or they merit the eternal damnation of perjured traitors and murderers.[3]

These strong words assuredly apply to Abraham Lincoln. For him, in these dark days, the collective mind of the regiment reflected nothing but hatred. The suspicion that he was somehow traitorously refusing to defeat the Rebels was only part of the fury directed at the President by the army. The Fourteenth certainly despised him even more for the Emancipation Proclamation. Lincoln had prepared a first draft the summer before, and word of that had had some impact on the troops; he had issued the proclamation after the victory at Antietam, but it was not until after Fredericksburg that its greatest impact was felt among the troops of the Army of the Potomac. Idle in camp with time for speculation, and embittered by their defeats, they transferred the blame and frustration for the faltering war effort to the man who had freed the slaves. John McClure wrote about the proclamation in a Christmas letter home:

What kind of Christmas and New Year did you have. I expect
you had a better time than I. I had fat pork and crackers for
dinner and crackers and fat pork for supper. . . . I think the
Union is about played out. I used to think that we were fighting
for the Union and Constitution but we are not. We are fighting
to free those colored gentlemen. If I had my way about things I
would shoot every niggar I come across.[4]

The most vitriolic tirade against Lincoln (with insulting jibes
at Negroes in general) was a dispatch from Landon printed in
the Vincennes newspaper:

> Old Abe's "free papers" to all, including Africans and the rest of
> mankind, also the apes, orangoutangs and monkeys in South
> America caused me an hour's hearty laugh, two hours tender
> cry, four hours big with mad, and I am swearing in all the
> languages known to Americans and Europeans. . . . I laughed
> because I am now certain of seeing the old piece of political
> party mixed with wool, in an insane asylum at no distant day. I'll
> be the *visitor*, "mind that." He the animal on exhibition. I cried
> because he did not kill himself when a youth splitting rails on
> bets. I choked with wrath to think that he has command of the
> old ship of State for twenty six long months to *come*— hence the
> "tall cussin."[5]

Not everyone in the Fourteenth Indiana opposed the proclamation: Houghton was only vaguely unsettled by it and Beem
supported it as necessary and wrote to Hala not to listen to its
detractors at home (and there were many).[6]

The Emancipation Proclamation was only one of several
problems of national interest that drew intense heat from the
Fourteenth Indiana. The composite mind of the regiment had
at all times a strong political cast. Curiosity on the subject of
politics was fed by the thousands of written words on national
and international events that reached the information-hungry
soldiers. Newspapers poured into the camp at Falmouth — the
New York Herald and *Times*, the *Philadelphia Enquirer* — and all
were avidly read and discussed. Every week during this period
an eccentric new political story from Washington or abroad
surfaced and made the grapevine hum.

Almost all of the stories were odd combinations of fact and fantasy, whatever was nearest to the reporter's hand or ear. They were hardly dispassionate. One week Sumner's division was to be sent to Washington to guard the city as a reward for their services so far. The next week Eli Thayer was to be made military governor of Florida and to command a unit composed of 300,000 newly arrived immigrants. Finally, there was the intriguing possibility that the South might really win. Three letters appeared addressed to foreign powers (Russia and France) by a turncoat lieutenant in the Rebel Army. This official believed that the great "North and West will again break loose from New England and the Middle States unite with the South." Van Dyke in his discouraged state at that moment said he for one would not object. He despised the "Puritans and Yankees of New England" almost as much as he did the Southerners. They had managed the war badly so far; let them burn in their own self-righteous hell when the South won.[7]

Landon had no faith at all in the papers or the intrigues they discussed; their correspondents were, after all, Easterners. He wrote:

> If I could only occupy the President's chair for one day, I would devote the entire twenty-four hours to the hanging of five hundred fools and all the correspondents of the daily New York and Philadelphia papers. To see how a battle looks to a "man up a tree" two miles off and half scared to death, to know exactly the day and hour on which Richmond *must* fall, to learn all about the secret movements of the army. . . one has only to read the effusions of these "daily specials." They know all about it *before and* after — in an hour.[8]

If most of the regiment was politically minded, there were some who resisted the temptation to speculate about congressmen and ambassadorial intrigues. Pleasure-loving Lambert, for instance, thought politics "a humbug," adding, "I have been trying to dispense with politics and do my duty as a soldier."[9]

The final characteristic of the regimental mind had never really changed. It was the strong frontier practicality they had grown up with, the wry acceptance of life that could transform anger into laughter, failure into food for future action. It also included the idealism which never really dimmed, taught by scores of Hoosier schoolmasters in one-room schools in Indiana and the rest of the Midwest, the lofty patriotism and almost religious sense of duty of McGuffey and the Bible and Mother. That idealism was never so sorely tried than after Fredericksburg, when the accents of Brutus rang across the nightmare scenes of horror and naked death at the foot of Lee's hill: "There is a tide in the affairs of men. . ." (*Julius Caesar*, IV.iii.215). It was a long way from the serene recitations in a Mt. Pleasant schoolroom, while the bees hummed in the clover outside, to the angry snarling of the brutal guns at Falmouth.

The men of the Fourteenth looked at the regimental creed, scraped the bottom of their souls for the courage to live it, to carry on, and somehow found what they needed in what they had brought with them from the counties of southern Indiana. They fed on the strength and meaning of home, and nostalgia softened their days. Landon remembered the old schoolhouse (his happened to be in Kentucky, but it was all the same) where he was "long ago taught the usefulness of the rod and the Rule of Three by one Snow & Sons. Fond recollections have I of the days when the boy 'marvelled,' studied 'Loss and Gain,' 'Tare and Tret' and [played postoffice]. Nearly twenty years have flown, but in connection with those happy fleeting hours there is a green spot on memory's table time can never affect."[10]

But for the men of the Fourteenth, wily Midwesterners that they were, Oliver Wendell Holmes of the Massachusetts volunteers was only partly right when he wrote:

> In the midst of doubt, in the collapse of creeds, there is one thing I do not doubt, and that is that faith is true and adorable which leads a soldier to throw away his life in obedience to a blind

accepted duty, in a cause which he little understands, in a plan of campaigns of which he has no notion, under tactics of which he does not see the use.

The Fourteenth understood the basic strategy; they simply rejected it as flawed. And by this time it was not even the cause that kept them and the other Midwestern boys going. They had looked the worst in the face; even if the Army of the Potomac was a floundering failure and worse, even if the cause died and the South won, they would keep on going. But Holmes was right about duty. Duty and obedience, pure and simple and learned in a simple society: when things were bad you stayed because there was nothing else to do. And the men were bound by pride, in homes that counted on them and kept on the parlor tables pictures of their boys with strong shoulders and bright eyes glaring defiance to the enemy and confidence in their own manhood. The frontier had taught them to count on themselves and to curse at weakness in others, and it was this lesson above all that got them through the hardest days after Fredericksburg. They would keep on going, they would pick the worms out of the crackers, because they had to and because that was the way it was done "way back in Indianner."

*   *   *

Meanwhile the business of war went on as usual in camp. Landon describes a typical day in camp at Falmouth:

Sunrise—guard mountings, drills, reviews, inspections, the "gas bag" at headquarters swinging in mid air with basket suspended beneath, a human head or two visible above its rim, to catch a glimpse of ye rebel pickets and see that they continue to wear grey uniforms and carry guns. Sunset—watch fires innumerable blaze on every hill, their red glare reflecting on the dark pine forest and exposing the erect forms of the sentinels as silent and watchful they pace their beats, the ever changing but always welcome face of fair Luna. . . her cold rays resting alike on the mound of earth beneath which sleeps one who has fallen

in the bloody strife and fills a hero's grave, on the bivouac of the
sleeping picket guards and on the numerous rude huts composing the camps of the "Right Grand Division". . . . the loud, shrill
blasts of bugles, the incessant roll of drums and screams of fifes,
the swelling music of full bands mingled with the piteous cries of
thousands of half-starved half frozen mules and the harsh "caw,
caw" of the carion crow. . . .[11]

The "numerous rude huts composing the camp" at Falmouth which were home to the Second Division presented an
interesting, well-organized scene in which a man could be
comfortable, at least (especially if he was an officer). Cavins
wrote February 4 to Ann describing life at Falmouth:

> Get up in the morning—eat a very good breakfast—spend
> time on official business—read my bible an hour (unless I have
> some other book)—talk to friends until dinner—eat a very
> good dinner composed of potatoes, onions, fresh beef or ham,
> light bread, cornbread, tea or coffee—sometimes soup or hash
> —and sometimes stewed apples and fresh peaches, cherries or
> blackberries. After dinner I spend the day as in the forenoon,
> except that 4 ock. we have dress parade, after which we have
> supper. My evenings are spent in reading newspapers, and
> writing letters—and when I receive them, reading letters.
>
> My bedstead is quite substantial and after the primative style.
> The bed posts are posts driven in the ground, leaving about two
> feet above the surface. Cross pieces are fastened across the head
> posts and foot posts, on which are laid rough hewed truncheons
> —and thereon I sleep, and calmly and sweetly repose. To one
> unaccustomed to such a bed it might seem rather hard, but to
> me it is about as comfortable as any. Thus day after day passes
> away, with no prospect of an early change. I have tried to get to
> go home but can't. If all the field officers were here I could get a
> leave for 15 days, but I being the only one able for duty, it is
> impossible for me to go. If I could go for 15 days, it would be
> very short, as it would take fully 5 days to go and 5 to return,
> leaving me only five at home. Still if it was possible, I would go
> anyway, because it would be a relief to be away from camp.

Breaking the routine at camp were the many furloughs to
Washington as men were sent to get the mail or carry mes-
sages. The men were willing to be impressed with the capital

and went with hopes high of attaining even a few days of exposure to its cultural and historical elegance. Lambert attended a "tragedy Media" and "Pocohontas and John Smith."[12] Van Dyke went to the theatre and during an intermission had the good fortune to recognize Ohio Representative John A. Gurley. Gurley, from Cincinnati, whom Van Dyke had written to before, invited Van Dyke to drink ale with him after the performance and then asked him to call next day at Willard's restaurant. Van Dyke wrote that he proposed to take the representative up on his invitation: "I shall try to see if I cannot get him interested in my behalf to procure me a leave of absence which must be done through the War Department."[13]

Van Dyke's official mission in Washington was to pick up shipping boxes, including an overcoat and other clothing of his own. When he finally found his box at the express station, he saw that rats had attacked a rock-hard cake that his mother had lovingly enclosed. They had also destroyed the seat of a pair of trousers and one whole shirt. Fortunately, the coat was untouched.

Although there was much to see in the capital, none of it pleased the seasoned frontier soldiers very well. The city itself "don't amount to anything," Landon wrote.

> Country town like, there is but one street deserving the name, and the surroundings are anything but what one would be led to suppose those encompassing the capital of this country should be. Stagnant pools of filth, hospitals, and the barracks of thousands of soldiers and contrabands — the former are perhaps needed to cover the city, and their presence *indispensible* but I could not see it — the latter are nuisances anywhere, even in South America, where they are hairy all over and have claws.[14]

The city was a sea of army blue and gold, much of it on officers. Van Dyke marveled wryly: "At the hotel table, at the theatre, on the public walk, at the bar rooms, nine tenths of our men are officers, whichever way you turn you see nothing but shoulder straps."[15]

Van Dyke also surmised that three-quarters of all the officers that one saw were under the command of the "Mackeral Brigade General." He scornfully described these Sunday officers grouped on porticos of hotels, wearing polished boots, brass buttons and gold lace and discussing

> with the silly twaddle of a four year old, the President's Proclamation and last night's play at the theatre. They are farther from home than they were before and were their heads pressed the milk of their mother's breasts would still pour from their noses.[16]

Landon could not believe how many enlisted men he also saw visiting bake shops, parks, and restaurants in this time of crucial war.

> Why are not the 50,000 soldiers I saw between Washington and Cincinnati Ohio sent to the front? Surely we have need for their help. . . to relieve us of incessant fatigue and picket duty.[17]

The men of the Fourteenth had their ways of dealing with Washington's red tape. They laughed at the provost guards' pretensions. Van Dyke told the first guard he met, "Just arrived — going to get my pass," and brushed past him. Of the next guard he demanded to know, "By what authority you question me?" and when no papers could be produced, Van Dyke roughly moved past. More often Van Dyke and the others played hide-and-seek with the provost, slipping out of sight to avoid being confronted. Often the passes were in perfect order; the Fourteenth was in its usual mood of irascible challenge of Eastern authority.

Van Dyke's pass did expire, and he found means to stay in Washington the one extra day he desired. It happened on the spur of the moment:

> I was at the theatre, and my pass had expired. I saw the Lieutenant of the Guard approaching. I thought I was gone sure; suddenly I thought of a certificate that Col Coons had given me certifying that "Lieut Col John Coons, 14th Indiana is under

treatment for a gun shot wound." I showed him that and he left me with the remark "that's all right colonel." I thought so too. . . . I have as good right to look like a Colonel as a great many of that mark who I have seen.[18]

The feud between Van Dyke and Coons had never really died. That spring Beem also made a visit to Washington city, as a result of a chain of circumstances he could not have foreseen. Hala's brother Jack Joslin, who had been a young recruit with the Fourteenth, had unfortunately contracted typhoid and, in spite of all the doctors could do, had died. Hala's mother was dangerously ill herself, and Beem's wife was even more depressed than usual. When she pleaded with him to come home now that she needed him, he anguished over her problems more than at any other time during the war. He had made arrangements for sending the embalmed corpse of Jack home, but soon a letter arrived from his mother-in-law telling him that the body had arrived in a "sorry state," adding to the home folks' grief. After walking seven miles to the embalmers to deliver a piece of his mind for the poor care of the remains, he determined to go home for a short time to comfort his wife and mother-in-law.[19] That visit came in March, and it was on his way back to camp that he stopped off at the nation's capital. His letter home is included.

My dear Wife:
I arrived in camp safe and sound yesterday Tuesday evening, about night and found everything pretty much like it was when I left two weeks ago. I got here the day my leave expires, though they did not look for me until the next day. But as you know, I was very anxious to be here *on time*.
I wrote to you from Washington on Monday evening last. Do you recollect what I said in that letter about going to the theatre? Well, my dear, I will tell you the whole of the truth. I did go to the Theatre, and witnessed a very nice literary performance, and everything was conducted in a decent style. In fact, the best society in Washington attended it, and I never could see why it was in any way wrong to go to an exhibition conducted like this. But I would not go to some of them. There were three of the Fourteenth's boys with me in Washington, and they wanted me

to go to a performance called the "Vanities," but I very respectfully declined, as I knew the performance consisted mostly of
dancing by ladies who, although they may be good looking, yet
exhibit too many *charms* to suit my eyes, and you know how *very
modest* I am.

When I got here, I found that President Lincoln was visiting
the army, and today we had a Grand Review of the whole Army.
This display was truly a magnificent one, and I wish you could
have seen it. The different corps were drawn up on one large
open space of country, and altogether the sight was a finer one
than I have ever witnessed before. General Hooker with the
President reviewed us, and we had a very nice time. The Army is
in excellent condition and the men all in good spirits. Mrs.
Lincoln was also present, and we marched past her carriage. She
no doubt was very much pleased with what she saw, and no
doubt it was all entirely new to her. Don't you think it very nice
for a lady to be a President's wife? I have no doubt it is much
nicer to be the President's "better half" than to be the president,
for I assure you that Abraham Lincoln looks like a man almost
weighed down by cares and responsibilities. . . .

I found Lieut Col Cavins and Major Houghton all well and
glad to see me. Col Coons was also very glad to see me, but he is
not so particularly my friend as the Lt Col and Major both of
whom I like very much. The boys in the company were all
getting along better than I expected to find them. Health better
than when I went away. The boys all seemed glad to see me, and
Shep Coleman among the rest, notwithstanding all he has said.

It seems very much like home to me here, and so natural to be
in camp. Last night I laid down on my soldier's bed and had a
splendid night's sleep notwithstanding the hard bed. But oh!
how much more pleasant it would be to be with my dear wife. I
would be happy indeed if this cruel war were over, so that I
could be with you all the time. Still, it seems this is the place that
duty assigns me. I do not know why it is, my love, but I can't help
thinking more about you than before I went home, and feel if
possible more anxiety about you. I suppose it is because you are
now more alone in the world than you were and it seems to me
that I ought to do more for you. Dearest, you are ever first in my
thoughts and I cannot express to you how much I desire to see
you happy. . . . I shall often think how very kind and loving you
were when I was with you, and I feel that if possible my love for
you has increased. I am glad that I can love you sweetest, it is a

real pleasure and one which I would not exchange for any other. I hope, I know that you feel the same way and that you are not sorry I went home. Darling, it will indeed be a happy time for us when we can meet to stay with each other. . . .

My love, I believe I have nothing more to write. Let me hear from you often. But why do I say this again, when I know that you always have been so very kind and punctual in writing letters to me? Also I want that picture *sure*. I think I must have it. If I can't be with you, I must have what looks most like you.

It is getting late, and is bed time for me. The bugles have already blown their last and with a kiss my love, I bid you goodnight. God bless and take care of you is the prayer of your loving husband.[20]

David

The return to Falmouth had been for Beem, as well as for the others, almost a relief. There had been changes, of course, as the spring weather brightened and warmed the camp. General Joseph Hooker had replaced Burnside. Kimball would not be returning; his Fredericksburg wound still troubled him and he resigned his commission, only to be later recommissioned and reassigned in the Southwest, where he became a major general. His successor was not immediately named. Coons was colonel of the Fourteenth. Cavins was lieutenant colonel, and Houghton had been named major and was now the youngest field officer in the Army of the Potomac. Van Dyke, who was, of course, an officer in another company and not close to Houghton, wrote of the latter's promotion:

The ranking captain who would have been major by virtue of his date of commission was jumped and another captain promoted to major. No one is sorry, for Willard is a "copperhead". . . the fortunate one is Captain Houghton, a young man of 24. He is one of the bravest men I ever knew and a gentleman.[21]

There is no question but that morale was up. Hooker was purposely building it with inspections without end, grand reviews of the type Beem had mentioned, and a tightened organization of the Army of the Potomac in camp. Basically, life was a boring routine, however, and John McClure complained, "There is no use talking to me about me writing an interesting letter, for there is nothing to be seen only big headed officers and big guns."[22]

Falmouth really began to stir on the first of April. Colonel Samuel S. Carroll took command of the brigade and Van Dyke was named to his staff. Harrow was gone from the Fourteenth; he had resigned again as colonel and was seeking another command. Soon he would have it, and the regiment would see him at Gettysburg.

Governor Morton, ever playing the paternalistic leader to "his boys," paid a visit to the troops and announced that their ranks would soon be filled with recruits. "I think that will be about right," McClure mused. "I won't ask them to go through any more than we will."[23]

Meanwhile, the contending armies observed each other closely across the river. Landon attended prayer services in the beautiful old Lacy house on the river banks across from Fredericksburg, now operated as a headquarters for the river picket guard. While in this area, he also observed a brigade drill of the Rebels and commented:

> They maneuver and handle their arms well, but the variety of colors exhibited in the habiliments (cannot call them uniforms) presented a most grotesque and ludicrous appearance, no two being dressed alike in a whole regiment. Quite a crowd of the motley crew were engaged in a game of ball, and occasionally a bevy of damsels of an uncertain age would take a long look at the Federal vedettes pacing their beats on the "sacred soil."[24]

No doubt adding to the high morale was the fact that the men were eating better than ever before, supplementing the standard rations with the newest offerings from the sutler. Prices were high as always but there were many willing takers: oysters, fifty cents a quart; fresh sausage (dog meat and ham), forty cents per pound; butter, sixty cents per pound; eggs, sixty cents per dozen. Very weak whiskey was two dollars per pint.[25]

Lee's army across the way was short on more than just habiliments. The power and money of the Northern industrial machine during the last few months had been poured into building the Army of the Potomac. Lee had precious few funds or manpower with which to build up his diminished army, which by now had shrunk to 60,000 men. What his army lacked in supplies, however, it made up for in ingenious military engineering feats — the remarkable trenches were like underground villages and were continually being improved. They set a pattern for World War I trench warfare. Lee's army also had a reputation for being invincible. In fact, G Company long since quit calling itself the "Invincibles" and had applied that name to Lee's forces at Fredericksburg. The Army of the Potomac believed that Lee's army might be impossible to beat. And it was certain that they never would be beaten in their strong, well-fortified rabbit warrens by the side of the river.

Hooker knew he must draw the Rebels away from the defenses at Fredericksburg and into a field of his own choosing, where he could with finality dispatch Lee's entire army. This would mean heading above Fredericksburg, crossing not only the Rapidan and Rappahannock, but the wild forest area called the Wilderness. The plan seemed a good one in spite of its chancy elements: the need to move without alerting Lee, and the boggy, impossible terrain of the Wilderness.

Hooker put the corps of Generals Oliver Howard, Henry Slocum, and George Meade on the road on April 26; the Second Corps, now commanded by Darius N. Couch, advanced behind them on April 28 with the Gibraltar Brigade leading the division. Houghton described the action of the next few days.

Dear Father
    I received your letter per Joe Williams and haste to send you a scrawl in receipt. You perceive we *have moved* and are now several miles in the rear of the Rebel works in the Rappahannock. Where the rebels are I know not — You will know by the papers long before this reaches you. On May 28 we struck camp and at six o'clock a.m. started by the River our division leading

the corps, and *our Brigade* leading the Division. We marched to United States ford about 8 miles from Falmouth in right of the Rebel redoubts and awaited the pontoon trains — on the night of the 29th they came but a steadily falling rain prevented them getting to the river's edge that night as was intended — it was expected we would have a desperate fight in crossing and of course *our brigade* was selected to *lead the advance.* There were not many unanxious hearts in our veterans ranks that night, when we knew we were ordered to take the first line in the morrow and it was with a feeling more akin to anguish which the thought of the next day's slaughter would probably witness in our already shattered ranks — But the Rebels had flown — the guns were removed from the redoubts and at 4 o'clock yesterday evening, the 8th Ohio, followed immediately by the 14th Indiana and the rest of the Gibraltar Brigade took peaceable possession of the Rebel forts. The rest of the corps followed and we took the advance, pushed forward to join Mead at Chancellorsville, where we are now. Mead crossed without opposition at Kellog's Ford and having better opportunities. . . got the advance of us — As to the relative position of the two armies, I cannot give any reliable information — you will probably get the news of the dispatches — I know that nearly all of our army has crossed without firing a cannon. Some resistance was offered to Segwicks crossing below Fredericksburg but there was little or no loss. I know the Rebels have withdrawn from their strongholds above Fredericksburg along the River and I know that we are now in better position to defeat them than we ever were before.

Hooker sent a circular around yesterday that "the operations of the last three days have been glorious *achievements.* We have the enemy now in such a position that he will be compelled to come out and fight us on our own ground or save himself by an inglorious flight."

There is some bumpkin there of course but the main features I think are true. It would be folly for me to attempt to prophecy now.

Everybody is in glowing spirits and Nature smiles on us — the first time in 4 days, as if rejoicing at our success. The successful crossing of our army has been [wonderful] to us thirty thousand men and. . . people everywhere. We are lying still today — everybody seems to be taking the benefit of the glorious Mayday sun. The men are airing their blankets, rubbing and cleaning their guns and drying their ammunition. Some are reading,

some writing, some sleeping. Bands are making all the echoes of
the old hills ring with splendid music. Birds are seen in every
tree and we are again in a land of flowers. . . . I am expecting a
great battle soon and the sooner it comes the better it will be for
us. We are carrying eight days' rations and we could march to
Richmond without further supply. . . Your letter was very interesting and Col Lewis [Brooks'] picture a valued present. . . .
We are now in a fair country abounding in streams and well
adapted to soldiering. I am in splendid health and the best
spirits I've been in since the battle of Antietam. The Regt looks
fine has no sick reports today — I hope we will not be brought
forward — all the time this campaign we have had glory enough
— But Carroll is impetuous and unfortunately we have a great
name which will always ensure us the most desperate chances. I
have no fears for myself — they call me "death proof" in the
Regt but I don't want to see the remnant slaughtered. . . . All my
love to Grandma Poor and Eliza. . . and all the family
            Write soon and remember me as
            Your affectionate son Will[26]

At the time Houghton wrote, both sides were hunkering
down for an inevitable, and what had to be terrible, confrontation. On May 2 the Second Corps was shifted several times in
the clearings and groves near where it had camped on May
Day. Hooker seemed indecisive and the troops knew it; "the
general did not know where to place us," Landon wrote.
Finally they were positioned near Hooker's headquarters, and
they spent the late afternoon chopping timber and digging
rifles pits.[27] Behind them as they dug and chopped, the Battle
of Chancellorsville was beginning; Stonewall Jackson was completing his daring flanking movement on a little-used road out
of sight of the troops.

About five p.m., without warning, the Fourteenth heard the
sound of artillery and reverberations of gunfire crashing
through the woods, coming from the right flank of the army.
The battle had begun, that was obvious, but the shape it was
taking they could not guess. Flocks of confused birds flew
about, and animals disturbed from their dens rushed into the
clearing where Couch's division of the Second Corps was
bivouacked. Soon, to the chagrin of the Gibraltar Brigade,

men burst out of the woods; the disorganized and retreating Eleventh Corps, bringing with them incoherent stories of Jackson's surprise attack. The scene was chaos, men running without hats, teamsters in disorder, disabled artillery — Jackson had succeeded brilliantly. The Twelfth Corps was called out to relieve the Eleventh and the Rebel advance finally stopped.

The men of the Fourteenth Indiana spent the night in the clearing behind the woods, sleepless, listening to the sharp outbursts of rifle fire, reverberations of artillery, and the Rebel huzzas as the armies contended in the smoky darkness for Hazel Grove. It was a night of dread that would never be forgotten by those who lived through the next day. Not far from where the Fourteenth lay on its arms, Stonewall Jackson was being shot by mistake in the confusion of that eerie, moonlit night.

At dawn the regiment heard the battle commence with terrible fury on the right.[28] Hooker had ordered General Dan Sickles to withdraw, and General J. E. B. Stuart was pouring devastating fire into the tightly packed Northern ranks. The division was called up to aid the retreat and went into withering fire on the edge of Hazel Grove; as the Northerners fell back the clearing was a devilish scene of chaos and death.

French was with Hooker near headquarters, and the Fourteenth was nearby. According to Houghton, at the crucial moment of the battle the brigade had another fine moment in its career.

> The retreat was begun among the trains and the moment was truly awful. Hooker asked French if he had a brigade who could *check* the Rebel line. French said he had and looked at *Carroll*. (We had only our 4 old regts and the 8th Ohio was taken to guard a battery). Carroll rode to his place in line and in his soul stirring voice called "Attention! Battalion. The battalion of direction — column forward." The bugle sounded *March!* and the column moved. It was the finest sight I've witnessed. Hooker, Mead, Howard, and French were all looking on and the interest was intense. We moved in splendid line and came on the

Rebels as soon as we entered the woods. We gave the first volley and the first cheer. The rebels ran like a plague had fallen among them and we drove them unsupported all the way through the woods — ran two brigades out of their entrenchments and had struck such a panic into the whole force that had we been supported we could not have failed in routing the whole line. . . . But we were sent in to gain time — we were expected to check and we drove them nearly a mile — we had no support on either side and were flanked, came near to being taken but formed back on the support which at last came and came off in splendid order from the field. We let loose two regts that had been taken the day previous.[29]

The battle was over, although the army heard the news, when it came, almost in disbelief. Their anger at Hooker was strong. French later told the brigade, "The general was whipped, the army was not,"[30] and commended them for their bravery. The cost to the dwindled regiment was moderately heavy — seven killed and fifty-seven wounded.[31] Many of the officers were wounded again, including Beem, Landon, and Harrold. The Owen County blacksmith Harrold was believed to be fatally wounded when bullets entered his bowels. The men of H Company carried him through the burning wilderness to the field hospital, from which he was sent home miraculously to recover. Charlie Gibson, the Mt. Pleasant boyhood friend of many of the men in C Company and Houghton's close companion for many years, had also fallen early in the battle. Gibson's wound in the groin did not appear serious at first to Houghton. It soon became apparent, however, that the bullet had entered an intestine; Gibson died and was buried near the river. The loss of Charlie was the greatest Houghton had to bear in the war.

Gibson's father had extracted a promise from Houghton before the company left Martin County that if his son ever fell, Houghton would return the body to Indiana. With the aid of George Reilly, who had also been Gibson's neighbor and friend, Houghton kept his word:

George Reilly and myself took an ambulance yesterday and went after him 8 miles over an awful road, exhumed him and brought him here. He had been buried 3 days and had decomposed so much that he could not have been recognized. We hesitated at first about bringing him but Mr. Gibson told me he desired him to be sent home in case he died so we did the best we could. He looked some better after being embalmed but was still a horrid spectacle to those unused to seeing corpses who have died of wounds and decomposed. We prepared him as well as we could under the circumstances but it was rough enough and those who are not acquainted with our situation might think we did not do our duty. He will be sent home tomorrow. . . . I am sure there never was a nobler, better or braver boy than Charlie was. He and I have lived together since the war began and I could not love him more if he were my brother.[32]

Another battle was over; another failure for the Army of the Potomac had been recorded. Ordinarily, the Fourteenth would have reacted with despair at the latest failure in leadership and tactics. The men of the regiment, however, took the failure with stoic calm; they focused at length and with real precision on the failure of the "nine days' campaign" and fixed on Hooker's problems as "too much whiskey, too little red blood."[33] Without emotion they calculated that Lee's army was dying of attrition, that their chance must come again, that the North's strength and industrial power was growing. They placed a good deal of faith in the constant upgrading of weaponry and supplies all around them; technology had moved ahead and they knew the difference it would make to them as they faced the hungry, ill-equipped forces across the breastworks in Fredericksburg.

Politics, they conceded, was controlling much of the war and eventually it would turn in their direction. All eyes were on Vicksburg, and Houghton appraised its importance as clearly as if he had written a centennial Civil War history article entitled "The Turning Point of the War."

Ever since the investment of Vicksburg by Grant, there seems to be a wavering on each side and I am anxious to see who will break first. Should Grant force Pemberton to surrender before

Johnson can reinforce sufficiently to make a successful attack, there can be no fears of the result in the South west. I shall feel very anxious till the result is ascertained. . . . I think our troops must have suffered greatly the day of the repulse from the city. But I was not surprised at the result, having heard so many descriptions of the strength of the works in the rear of the city. I have seen strongholds stormed, and I know that if brave men defend a redoubt it is physically impossible for flesh and blood to oppose solid earthworks and solid shot.[34]

In short, the attitude of the Fourteenth toward the war had grown completely realistic, even sophisticated. Political considerations, modern technology, the movements of large armies backed by powerful societies — these were the things that shaped this war as they now saw it. At Chancellorsville, at least for the Fourteenth Indiana, Victorian sentimentalism died. They were able to foresee for the first time the inevitable victory by the powerful nation they represented and the new age — whatever that would be — that they and the rest of the nation would be living in when the war ended. Now, in June, 1863, and about two years ahead of the rest of the United States of America, the Fourteenth was entering the modern world.

1. One of the major reasons was that the Fourteenth did not go on the notorious "Mud March" which disheartened the Army of the Potomac in the early part of 1863.
2. Letter of Van Dyke to his brother, December 28, 1862.
3. Ibid.
4. Letter of McClure to his sister, January 2, 1863, in *Hoosier Farmboy*.
5. Letter of Landon to the *Western Sun*, January 8, 1863.
6. Letter of Beem to his wife, January 11, 1863.
7. Letter of Van Dyke to his brother, December 23, 1862.
8. Letter of Landon to the *Western Sun*, December 21, 1862.
9. Lambert, Journal, January 27, 1862.
10. Letter of Landon to the *Western Sun*, January 8, 1863.
11. Ibid.
12. Lambert, Journal, March 19, 1863.
13. Letter of Van Dyke to his father, February 2, 1863.
14. Letter of Landon to the *Western Sun*, March 8, 1863.
15. Letter of Van Dyke to his father, February 9, 1863.
16. Ibid.
17. Letter of Landon to the *Western Sun*, March 8, 1863.
18. Letter of Van Dyke to his father, February 9, 1863.

19. Letter of Beem to his wife, March 3, 1863.
20. Ibid., April 8, 1863.
21. Letter of Van Dyke to his brother, February 22, 1863.
22. Letter of McClure to his sister, January 2, 1863, in *Hoosier Farmboy.*
23. Ibid., April 1, 1863.
24. Letter of Landon to the *Western Sun,* April 8, 1863.
25. Ibid.
26. Letter of Houghton to his father, May 1, 1863.
27. Letter of Landon to the *Western Sun,* May 6, 1863.
28. Letter of Houghton to his father, May 8, 1863.
29. Ibid.
30. Ibid.
31. *History of Greene and Sullivan Counties,* p. 128.
32. Letter of Houghton to his father, May 8, 1863.
33. Letter of Van Dyke to his wife-to-be, May 24, 1863.
34. Letter of Houghton to his mother, June 6, 1863.

CHAPTER EIGHT

GETTYSBURG AND THE DRAFT RIOTS

On June 5 Robert E. Lee was slowly moving his troops out of the lines at Fredericksburg and drifting northward into the Blue Ridge Mountains toward his inevitable fate in Pennsylvania. Lee could no longer wait to advance into the rich farm land of the North. His "Invincibles" were lean and hungry, and he realized that he could not allow the Army of the Potomac more months to grow stronger. Then, too, the vise around Vicksburg was tightening; perhaps it could be loosened if Lee could draw troops away toward a showdown in the Washington area.

He masked his withdrawal from the trenches in several ways. One of them was to shell the lines near the camp at Falmouth. The men of the Fourteenth listened to artillery booming and wondered what it meant. What their experience told them was that Hooker's slumbering, lumbering army would soon be moving again toward Richmond, which meant in this war discomfort, mistakes, and the repetition of defeat.

Could this be what was happening or was it something else? Was Lee attacking the flank? Or had Fredericksburg been occupied quietly by the Northern Army and was this demonstration a part of its capture? Van Dyke climbed up with the brigade surgeon to the heights on the Union side of the river to see what could be seen with field glasses; he espied "no stars and stripes afloat. . . in the city of Fredericksburg." So it was a false alarm. What he saw instead was, predictably, "diverse Butternuts" occupying their rifle pits.[1]

The heat was oppressive and dust thick in the air as the men waited in the Falmouth camp for something to happen. Rutted roads used to bring supplies into Falmouth had dried into powder and the top layers of fine dirt swirled up in the Atlantic winds which blew over the city of tents in early June. Not much rain had fallen since Chancellorsville.

Meanwhile, the men had watched the spy balloon go up and contented themselves with other small events to pass the time. Cavins was elected to present a sword to French; he wrote:

> I felt somewhat embarrassed to see such an array of officers there, but did not allow myself to show embarrassment. I made a short presentation speech about as follows: General, the officers and soldiers of the 14th Regiment Indiana Volunteers, desire through me their appointed agent to present to you this sword. The engraving on the scabbard exhibits a sufficient reason for the present. It reads, "Presented to Major General W.A. French by the officers and soldiers of the 14th Regiment Indiana Volunteers, as a testimonial of their appreciation of his gallantry and merit." The firm and unwavering position that the troops under your command, took and held during the long and bloody battle at Antitam, won for you and them the honor of being *chosen* to lead the charge at Fredericksburg; for the reason, as given by your commanding general, that your troops had never turned their backs to the enemy in battle.
>
> It must be a source of great pride to you that your division has never been driven before the enemy, nor lost a stand of colors, during the fluctuating results of battle for the last two years.
>
> Please accept this testimonial from the officers and soldiers of our regiment. . . . The general then made a short and very appropriate speech. Among other things he said, "I am proud to receive such a present, and especially from a regiment that has always been *foremost* among the *first* in battle — one whose colors are always planted in the very front. . . .
>
> After he finished his speech three cheers were given for him and for the Union. When the parade was dismissed, the officers

remained and partook of a treat of wine, champagne, etc. —and
afterwards a treat was sent over to the regiment. It passed off
remarkably pleasant. . . . I cut a considerable figure on account
of being in command of the regiment. General Hancock said he
wished he had a 14th Indiana Regiment in his division.[2]

Cavins had evidently forgotten that only a few months ago,
when he had been infuriated at French for participating in the
arrest of Harrow, he had called him privately an "old Whiskey
tub."

During this period, the men's thoughts were at Vicksburg.
Their Indiana relatives and friends were there. Beem wrote
that he would know that the war's end was coming if Vicksburg
fell. And Houghton said:

> It will be a glorious wreath that will crown the Vicksburg victors
> should they succeed. I wish I could wear it with them. My scars
> may be very honorable but the battles where they were received
> were but barren victories and will occupy places of secondary
> interest in the history of the war.[3]

It was impossible, of course, for Houghton to know that in a
curious twist of the public mind, attention would fix itself on
the dramatic struggles in the East; the glorious defeats at
Fredericksburg and Chancellorsville would afterwards over-
shadow the glorious victory at less glamorous Vicksburg.

Hooker confirmed Lee's northward march by intelligence
and was ordered to parallel that march, and to protect
Washington while he was doing so. He ordered the infantry to
prepare for a series of rapid forced marches forward, not
knowing that in the midst of the forced marches, he himself
would be relieved by Meade.

On June 14, the rest of the army having gone, the Second
Corps began to move through the stifling, sultry Virginia
night. The First Brigade marched all night, arriving at Staf-
ford Court House for a breakfast break. From there they
passed on, urgently, to Fairfax Station on the Orange and
Alexandria Railroad and then, with little rest, on to the
Potomac.

Heat prostration took its toll; some of the brigade's men fell by the wayside and some died. The brigade came through rain to Gainsville, not far from Second Bull Run, and kicked aside the skulls of the victims of the earlier battles. The men of the Fourteenth swore they saw signs of mutilations and atrocities on the bodies of Northern soldiers.[4]

At Centerville Lambert and the brigade band played for a dress parade in new uniforms and lorded it over two other brass bands. The First Brigade band, they said, had preferential treatment because it was dear to Carroll's heart.

One June 23 a carload of newspapers from Alexandria arrived as the men were resting by the roadside, and a crowding and pushing match ensued, the men of the Fourteenth coming up short and returning to their quarters "cursing" somebody or something, they hardly knew what."[5]

French was called away to command the Third Army Corps briefly and Carroll was put in charge of the division. This left Coons as brigade commander, and he ordered the troops back onto the road for the long, sultry march to the Potomac. The roads were slippery from rain ("marched by day and night, under burning sun and through torrents of rain" was the way Cavins described this march).[6] The men had nothing to eat but crackers and water; weary and disheartened, they arrived at Frederick City. Lambert bathed in the creek, but many of the other men went into the town and "notwithstanding the groceries were all shut up" bought enough liquor to get drunk.[7]

The worst of this forced march to Gettysburg was yet to come. After Brigadier General Hays relieved Carroll and Carroll returned to the brigade, the army moved on through the unrelenting midsummer heat. Men began to give out and fall by the wayside in large numbers. The band was particularly hard hit; and Lambert alone was left marching, carrying his drum with one man to help. By nightfall the drum was falling apart, so Lambert took it to a barn and the two men put it back together and got a good night's sleep on the hay. Next morning they hurried to catch up with the brigade. "But we would

not have known whether it was the brigade or a squad of
stragglers had not the flag been waving in the breeze."[8]

They were rushing, dog-tired, cursing, winded, and sweat-
ing to what? — they could only surmise, and their guessing
was dark and full of foreboding. It was July 1. The regiment
marched through a village called Harney. The townspeople
looked down the long column winding through their quiet
street, and one said, "Ah me! I can't begin to see the end of
'em." Another answered, "La me! I guess we will get to see
something now!" These Northern villagers, stranded in the
bywaters of the war, were gaping at an ambulance. The men of
the Fourteenth gaped at it also; it contained the body of
General John Reynolds.[9] The Battle of Gettysburg had begun.

Reynolds' men had been driven through the town of Gettysburg fourteen miles away. As Beem later described it, the
troops were told they must now rush to relieve the fallen
general's corps which had been crushed, "cut to pieces fright-
fully and greatly reduced in numbers." The men arrived in the
town late in the evening as both sides were preparing for
conflict:

> A part of the 11th corps under General Howard arrived during
> the evening and a new line of defense was formed, the right
> extending over a high ridge to the East, the left occupying an
> elevated slope of open country to the Southwest.[10]

The Fourteenth became a part of the efficient battle
machine of George Meade. Meade's army was filling out the
lines that Beem had described, excellent lines which Hancock,
who had set them up, believed could be used for defensive or
offensive battle.

With the dawn, the Fourteenth marveled at the speed and
efficiency with which Meade deployed the troops to the right
and left of the hill called Cemetery Ridge. None of the uncertainty of Hooker at Chancellorsville touched any of Meade's
movements.[11] The Second Corps — Hancock's — was in the
center and the Third Division, led by Alexander Hays now,
was on the right of the corps. Carroll was in command of the

First Brigade of Hay's division, which contained the Fourteenth Indiana. The regiment's controversial leader Colonel Harrow was nearby — in charge of the First Brigade of John Gibbon's Second Division in the same corps as the Fourteenth.

Positioning the troops took up the better part of the morning. Lambert went up to a hill where he could see the valley which separated both armies. Carroll was on the hill, also, on horseback, and Lambert was surprised to see the brigade's commander in real danger — a sharpshooter's bullet whistled past Carroll's head. The colonel turned and remarked to some of his staff with a laugh, "Did you see that damned rascal shoot at me?"[12]

The Fourteenth was ordered to its position to prepare for the afternoon charge, which started on the left and involved other parts of the troops in the Peach Orchard and the Round Tops. Eventually, after bitter fighting, the action ceased as the Rebel general Longstreet pulled back. The Fourteenth had not as yet been involved.

Then Johnson attacked Culp's Hill and the Second Corps braced for an attack on their section — Cemetery Hill. Two Rebel brigades stormed up the hill — North Carolinians and Louisianans who hurled themselves against rifle pits, lunettes, and stone walls, determined to capture the batteries on the hilltop. Supporting those batteries were the "Dutchmen" of Howard's Eleventh Corps. As the Rebels pressed hot and fast, the Eleventh again broke and ran in repetition of their cowardice at Chancellorsville. And again, as at Chancellorsville, the Fourteenth was one of the units to meet them as they fled. Beem was commanding H Company. Encountering fleeing officers as well as men, Beem drew his sword and collared an officer. He threatened to kill him on the spot if he did not return to the line.[13]

Ordered to support the exposed batteries, the brigade advanced through the dark on the double-quick with Carroll's resonant voice booming out orders above the sound of musket and artillery. In years to come, regiments that were nearby would remember that voice, radiating strength and security through the dusky confusion of that evening. The men pushed on into the chaos that surrounded the positions of the batteries, where the Rebels stood by the very guns.

The three regiments of Carroll's brigade detached from the rest were lustily cheered as they advanced, firing forcefully. Some of Jubal Early's men had intrepidly seized the guns; they had turned the horses' heads down the hill and were directing the seizure, but the brigade's rapid firing and unimpeded advance caused the Rebels to turn and retreat — some of them into the arms of the Fourteenth and eventually to Northern prisons. Several officers and men and numbers of small arms were captured. With this, the day's action was over.[14]

In this charge the Fourteenth lost six men killed on the field and about thirty-five wounded. Beem noted that as Isaac Norris was bearing the flag of Company H into the battle, his flagstaff was cut into pieces and a ball passed through his head. The men buried him and the others on the spots they fell that second night at Gettysburg.[15]

The next day the Northern troops waited apprehensively for what Lee would throw against the tremendous Northern force. He threw all he had, but Pickett's charge, so dramatic that it shook the very ground at Gettysburg, was not enough.

The Fourteenth Indiana was not with the rest of the Second Corps when they met Pickett's charge; they remained with Howard's corps, detached during that stupendous frontal movement. But they were near enough to witness the slaughter, to share the emotion and elation at its repulse. When it was all over, 23,000 men of the Army of the Potomac and 27,000 Confederates had been killed, wounded, or captured during those three days. The men were solemn, realizing the significance of what they had witnessed. Lambert, Houghton, and Van Dyke all recorded their emotions:

Lambert: You will have heard of the complete thrashing we gave the rebels. The army of the Potomac has redeemed itself. We have proved that we can whip Lee on our own ground. . . . The

Regt has 6 killed, 23 wounded and 2 missing. Captured a good
many prisoners and one stand of colors. The 8th Ohio detached
from the Brigade for the occasion and captured 1800 prisoners
and three stands of colors.[16]

Houghton: Capt. Blinn, our former adjutant was severely, sup-
posedly mortally wounded. You will see that we were honorably
mentioned in all the reports. We met old Gen. French yesterday
and gave three cheers for the old veteran.[17]

Van Dyke: The result of the three days battle at this point has
given an additional stimulus to celebrate this anniversary of our
Independence. The Army of the Potomac has nobly redeemed
itself and taught the insolent rebels what it is to fight on one's
soil. I know of nothing except what our own Division has done.
It has not only killed and wounded more rebels than it
numbered, but took 18 battle flags and captured near two
thousand prisoners. The Battle of Gettysburg is without doubt
the severest battle of the war.

It has been the most terrible battle it has been my fortune to be
engaged in during the war.[18]

But it was all in the viewpoint. McClure had been left with
the wagons. "We have had some very hard fighting out here at
least people say so. For my part I was not there."[19] He was
sitting in the rain, couched under a wagon. It was the same rain
that back on the battlefield was washing the blood off the
corpses of the soldiers of both North and South, the faded
flowers of the American frontier dream that would never
bloom again.

*   *   *

"Something unaccountable has turned up," Houghton ex-
citedly wrote his father in mid-August after the Battle of
Gettysburg. The Fourteenth had been in camp at Elk Run
when word came of the immediate departure of selected regiments for Alexandria to take ship — they were to be one of the
regiments.

All the western regiments have been taken from the Army of the

Potomac and are now here awaiting transportation to New York
City. . . the reason I can't fathom entirely. I suppose they want
us to quell the rioters but I think there is a secondary motive.[20]

That secondary motive, in Houghton's opinion (which was not
more implausible than the stated purpose), was that finally the
high command had appreciated the Western regiments as the
only real fighters in the army and were pulling them out for a
special expedition to the South to end the war somehow.

Certainly the action had been unexpected and surrounded
by confusion. Carroll, who had been away on leave, came
down for the day, assumed command, and then left. It was not
at all clear who was going, and because only Western regiments were to be involved, the Gibraltar Brigade would have
to split. The Seventh Virginia could not go. To Lambert's
dismay, the status of the band was left hanging. The order had
not called for bands and Colonel Snider, in command of the
brigade, was not going to send them. The brigade's officers
interceded, and at the last moment band members packed up
the horns and Lambert's drum and hurried after the troops on
the road to Alexandria.[21]

The threat to the breakup of the proud brigade seemed to
continue as the war machine tried to decide how to organize
units effectively for the draft riots. Would the Fourteenth
Indiana be allowed to remain with the Eighth Ohio and Fourth
Ohio? Carroll, determined to keep the group he had taken
through Chancellorsville and Gettysburg together, went to
Washington and as usual his charm prevailed.[22] When he
returned, he brought the news that two new regiments were to
be added to the brigade: the Seventh Michigan and the First
Minnesota. They were fine additions; the Seventh had bravely
forced the crossing at Fredericksburg and the First Minnesota
had been made famous at Gettysburg, when with 262 men it
had charged into a Confederate advance of thousands and
brought back an Alabama flag.

The men could hardly believe that they were going to New
York. Something must have gone wrong if they were to be

assigned this attractive duty with its promise of leave time, good food, and ladies. Lambert mused in his diary:

> It seems strange that we should be the ones selected for such pleasant duty when there are so many New Yorkers and Pennsylvanians. But they are sending all western troops. Good idea too. They won't fire blank cartridges.[23]

On August 21 the Fourteenth left Alexandria and steamed up the Atlantic to New York Harbor. Most of the men were seasick with the long, rolling swells which rocked the ocean. Lambert could not get out of bed for the whole trip. Only by lying perfectly flat on his back could he manage not to vomit.[24] When the band tried to play the next morning as New York Harbor came in sight, they had to give it up as a bad idea; they were too weak from being "over the side."[25]

Once in the harbor, however, they recovered miraculously and began to serenade the pleasure boats loaded with ladies and gentlemen who came nearby. After they had anchored opposite Governors Island and Carroll had received the orders to disembark, the men lay around on the island's beautiful grass until evening, wondering at fortune, which had brought them from the mud of the Rappahannock to the center of civilization in a few short days. Houghton thought Governors Island "one of the prettiest little islands in the world, whose only fault was that the sea breeze was rather too fresh to be always interesting."[26]

The first draft riots were over. While they had lasted, they had stunned New York City and concerned the rest of the nation. Conscription in the Ninth Congressional District in New York had begun easily enough; citizens were not happy about being drafted but accepted the routine in a law-abiding and orderly manner. Officials, then, were not prepared when on July 13 a mob in the city streets resisted the draft with a murderous riot, creating a "day of infamy and disgrace" for the city, according to the *New York Times*. The mob had sacked and burned the draft office and then had proceeded on a rampage which included the burning of a Negro orphanage.

During the several days the mob raged out of control, communications were disrupted, and there was a considerable loss of life. The Seventh New York Militia and police restored order only with difficulty.[27]

By July 18, order had finally returned, railway and telegraph service was restored, and "the police were everywhere alert," the *Times* reported. New York and Vermont volunteers were brought in on an emergency basis, but the situation was at all times a potential conflagration, ready to be ignited at a moment's notice. On August 3 the mayor of New York wrote to Lincoln protesting that arrangements for the draft had been badly handled in New York City. The fact that unknown people had drawn the names, people who could be accused of "special interest," had triggered revolt, causing "the most destructive riot in the history of our country."[28] He asked to have the draft suspended. Lincoln refused; the draft must and would recommence, and the President backed up his determination by sending troops to the city to enforce the enlistments. During the last two weeks of August the troops poured into the town to be present when the next conscription got underway.

Until it did, the Fourteenth Indiana regiment was free to rest and indulge in that great occupation of the soldier in the city — observing the big-city life. McClure wrote to his sister:

> This morning I thought I would write you a few lines. I am well at present and us boys are enjoying ourselves hugely. We landed on this island two days ago. I suppose we came here for the purpose of enforcing the draft in New York. We came here from Alexandria on the Steamer Atlantic. Had a long ride. Some of the boys got very sick but I did not. We was on board of the ship for four days. Glad enough when we got on the island.
>
> I think if we lay around New York verry long we will get fat. I can sit here on the grass in the shade and see New York & Brooklin and Jersy City all just across the river from us. There is a lot of foreigners come in here by the ship loads evrry week. One of our boys got hurt on board the ship. He was helping to unload the baggage and fell through the hatch hole of the ship from the hurricane deck to the bottom. I guess he will get well;

his name is Fred Yocum. . . . Tell Henderson I will write to him tell him he had better come and see us. . . . Old Abe is not giving any furloughs now.[29]

Houghton went to see the sights. Barnum's Museum he thought a humbug. But there was one interesting "natural" sight — a hornet's nest the size of a beer barrel. He saw Forrest in *Richelieu.* Forrest seemed to him old and worn looking — Booth must have been better, and he would have liked to see him too if he had the time. Houghton did not have much time to sightsee at any rate; the command of the regiment was on his shoulders. Coons was overseeing on a general court-martial and Cavins spent his time going to picnics. So the dutiful Houghton was shouldering the routine work, the petty cases of discipline, the supervision of the camp, and dress parade at night.[30]

The picnics and parties were an almost incredible respite to the veterans. For Cavins, it was an opportunity to indulge his mild vice of flirtation, as he wrote to Ann September 3:

Picnics here are entirely different from those in Indiana. They play so many different plays that I never heard before. One play called "Copenhagan" is particularly popular among all classes, and is played more than any other. Men, women, boys & girls all play it. It is played thus: About twenty or more or less form a circle facing the center, and hold a rope in their hands. Two or three (according to the number in the circle) get in the center. The gentlemen in the center (if he touches a ladies hand while she is holding the rope) he has a right to kiss her if he can do it before she gets inside of the circle. He goes to the outside of the circle after kissing her, or after trying and failing, and she takes his place.

The lady touches some gentleman's hand (which is not hard to do when I am playing) and then the gentleman has a right to kiss her if he can do it before she gets out of the circle, and he takes her place. It is a lively play, and the ladies kept me running considerably. It is hardly necessary for me to say to you that I kissed quite a number of pretty ladies — it would be out of the question to resist.

I attended these picnics with a linen coat so as not to draw too much attention, but it would soon be found out that a live Hoosier Col. who had been in all the war, was there and then, of course, I would soon have an abundance of friends.

It is so much like home to be at a picnic, and especially a Sabbath school picnic. I like it much better than the theatres, or the pomp of the city. We know that the ladies we meet at a Sabbath school picnic are virtuous and pure, while in too many instances at other places, they are not.

An officer can scarcely walk any considerable distance on Broadway of an afternoon, or visit Barnums in the afternoon, without having some pretty miss to smile sweetly at him and slip her card in his hand.

It will hardly be necessary for me to say to you that I never visit that class of females. But unfortunately for the morality of the army, many officers prefer such high society. I have accepted several invitations to dine and take tea in Brooklyn, and I think the people are very kind and hospitable.

The band was kept busy with the generous reception the citizens gave to the units in their midst; Lambert sensed that they did not come to listen to the martial airs the band "discoursed," but to see the seasoned veterans of Gettysburg playing in a band, like Mars, the war god, tamed. The band played as the regiments marched through the town from Governors Island to their camps — the Fourteenth being detached to Brooklyn and other regiments to Washington Park, where headquarters were established. Lambert complained, "I never saw so many children in my life. They followed the band so that we could do nothing."[31] The band played every evening, in the park, at picnics, and for Sunday-school suppers:

[We had] an invitation to a Tea Party at a church on Friday evening. I escorted [a] lady home this evening and passed outside the guard lines, but did not stay long. Though the guards are instructed to let no one out without a pass, they scarcely ever stop us, especially when accompanied by a lady.[32]

Lambert was in general surprised at the freedom which New York ladies exhibited and which Cavins also commented on. They crowded around the cooking fires and curiously eyed the contrabands, and if they had modesty, it was difficult to notice it. "The most wealthy and aristocratic ladies come into our camp and walk and talk with the private soldiers. It seems as though the people have never seen any soldiers. Any number of them are young women," Lambert wrote.[33] Besides the "ladies" whom he escorted home, Lambert had a "woman" he visited in a tenement several evenings when he was in New York.

Lambert was also impressed by the denseness of the New York population. One day, after attending Henry Ward Beecher's church and a dress parade, Lambert wrote in his diary, "What crowds of people, what crowds of people."[34] At the dress parade on Sunday, August 30, the crowds seemed to pose a threat, and the regiment had a taste of what the mob had wrought earlier. As Lambert described the incident:

> We got the regiments formed and could not get room to troop. The officers mounted their horses and tried to drive back the crowd. That also failed. The order was given to the Regt to charge bayonet and that made room, but they thronged round in the rear of the Rgt. . . . We established a line of guards to hold the ground in front and "about faced." Thus [we] got a little room.[35]

Houghton revealed the fear and antipathy that lay beneath all the surface politeness when he said:

> There seems to be no indications of another riot although the authorities are afraid. . . . I don't but wonder that the riot increased to such an awful dimension. . . . I would rather that such another riot would not occur. Should it be there will be more blood in the streets and more dead men in the sidewalks than the poor deluded fools ever imagined or dreamed of.[36]

Lincoln had picked the right group of men to enforce the draft.

Generally, however, duty in New York was easy and pleasant, but the idyll was over almost as soon as it had begun. The occasion of the new draft proved peaceful and on Sunday, September 6, the Western troops began to leave to return to the front. Lambert and the brigade band escorted the troops of the First Minnesota to the foot of Canal Street, where they embarked for the trip back to Virginia. Some were drunk; they had been "treated by the officers so many times that some of them got 'tolerably well, how come you so?' " and one man in the band in a drunken rage banged his instrument along the street until it broke, whereupon he was arrested. Drunkenness had not generally been a problem in the Fourteenth, at least since the first night in New York, when many of the men had forgotten the war in the pump rooms of the city.

Lambert stayed behind to get the drunken man's instrument fixed. It gave him time to "take tea with my woman again this evening."[37] The regiment steamed to Fortress Monroe, then marched through Virginia to Culpepper, where they found their old division and rejoined it in their former assignment (after Carroll again insisted) as the First Brigade. Soon they were all involved in a lively affair with the enemy at Bristow Station.

New recruits were being added to all the units, and some of them deserted as soon as they came. For these deserters, the Army of the Potomac took a hard line, and in September there were several executions. The Fourteenth witnessed two of these executions. On September 18 the entire division was ordered out,

> forming three sides of a square. An ambulance made its appearance in the center of the square, containing the prisoners (two deserters from the 14th Conn) and Chaplains guarded front and rear by soldiers and preceded by a detachment of the 10th New York Zouaves (Provosts of the Division) and the band of the 14th Conn playing a funeral dirge. The procession halted near the graves where the parties dismounted and were led to the coffins placed by the graves. The prisoners seated themselves upon their coffins and after the preliminary ceremonies were resignedly shot to death according to sentence. . . it was altogether a sad and melancholy scene — a most horrible butchery. But such may be necessary for the good of the service.[38]

It was chilly on the Rapidan that fall. As the boys lay in the open fields on the night they returned from the riots, a mid-September thunderstorm pelted them. Pulling his rubber blanket around him, one soldier remarked, "I wish the Brooklyn ladies could see us now. Ah, they might pity us." But the Brooklyn ladies might as well have been 1000 miles away. Such were the fortunes of war after Gettysburg.

1. Letter of Van Dyke to his father, June 7, 1863.
2. Letter of Cavins to his wife, June 5, 1863.
3. Letter of Houghton to his mother, June 6, 1863.
4. Beem, "History of the Fourteenth Indiana"; Lambert, Journal, June 8 and 23, 1863.
5. Lambert, Journal, June 23, 1863.
6. *History of Greene and Sullivan Counties,* p. 128.
7. Lambert, Journal, June 28, 1863.
8. Ibid., June 29, 1863.
9. Ibid., July 1, 1863.
10. Beem, "History of the Fourteenth Indiana."
11. Ibid.
12. Lambert, Journal, July 2, 1863.
13. Beem, "History of the Fourteenth Indiana."
14. *Counties of Clay and Owen,* p. 636.
15. Beem, "History of the Fourteenth Indiana."
16. Lambert, Journal, July 2, 1863.
17. Letter of Houghton to unknown correspondent, July 11, 1863.
18. Letter of Van Dyke to his father, July 4, 1863.
19. Letter of McClure to his sister, undated, in *Hoosier Farmboy.*
20. Letter of Houghton to his father, August 18, 1863.
21. Lambert, Journal, August 14, 1863.
22. Ibid., August 17, 1863.
23. Ibid.
24. Ibid., August 22, 1863.
25. Ibid., August 23, 1863.
26. Letter of Houghton to his father, August 24, 1863.
27. *New York Times,* July 14 and July 16, 1863.
28. Information on the draft riots is from issues of the *New York Times* for the rest of July and August, 1863.
29. Letter of McClure to his sister, August 25, 1863, in *Hoosier Farmboy.*
30. Letter of Houghton to his father, September 4, 1863.
31. Lambert, Journal, August 28, 1863.
32. Ibid., August 24, 1863.
33. Ibid.
34. Ibid., August 30, 1863.
35. Ibid.
36. Letter of Houghton to his father, August 24, 1863.
37. Lambert, Journal, September 6, 1863.
38. Ibid., September 18, 1863.

CHAPTER NINE

IN AND OUT OF THE WILDERNESS

Lieutenant Will Landon, the irrepressible "Prock," had been in the hospital in Washington ever since Chancellorsville. Now in the late fall of '63, he came into camp on the Rapidan with many tales of life in the "American Sodom."

He didn't like Washington city any better than he had the previous spring, although he admitted that the sights were more stupendous than Barnum's elephant. He had seen the "Rail Splitter" at the National B.B. Club directly behind the White House. The president, engaged in target practice, had used a smooth-bore loaded at the breech with the "largest cock I ever saw on any piece." Abe was a good shot, Landon said. Landon found the capital prison a great freak show:

> a motley crew of all ages, sizes and colors from every state in the Union and. . . a "right smart sprinkling" of Sambo. Europe was represented by some hard-looking chaps, among others I particularly noticed a Spaniard, that from his demoniac look no doubt entered upon his career by cutting the throat of his mother. In the female department were two persimmon eaters from North Carolina, dressed in the style of '76, waist two inches below the arm pits, no hoops, hair a la Indian squaw, snuff colored teeth, deep set, grey eyes, fingernails keen as a falcon's long fingernails; I thought of tendering the use of my knife to pare the claws but was actually afraid to.[1]

The bigger one asked Landon for a "chew bacc."

161

Everything was "dear" in Washington, at least twice the price of supplies in Baltimore; and Landon reported that all the restaurants ordered wholesale meat and produce from Baltimore.

The men of the Fourteenth had spent so much time in the hospitals around Washington that they seemed like second homes. Landon had nothing but praise for the sanitary officers and church nurses who patiently tended the wounds of the soldiers. But for the other visitors — the Sunday tourists who viewed hospital visiting as a spectator sport — he had unmitigated scorn.

There are three classes of visitors to the hospitals. First, and least important, are the *wordy* sympathizers of both sexes — the male portion of these "drones" are generally composed of broken-down, short-winded, long-faced seedy preachers of all denominations. They walk solemnly up and down the wards, between the couches of the patient sufferers; first casting their cadaverous looks and ghostly shadow upon all, and then, after a *whispered* consultation with the surgeon of the ward, offer to pray, do so, and retire, without having smiled on a single soldier or dropped a word of comfort or cheer. The females belonging to this [the first class] go gawking through the wards peeping into every curtained couch. . . [with] outbursts of "Oh, my Savior!" "Phoebe, do look here!" "Only see what a horrid wound!" "Goodness, gracious, how terrible war is!" "My, my, my!" "Oh let's go — I can't stand it any longer!" And as they near the door, perhaps these dear creatures will wind up with an audible "Heavens! What a smell! Worse than fried onions!"

Class No. two is composed chiefly of flashy youths, got up in the latest style and "perfectly regardless of expense" every "har" in its proper place, kids, canes and patent leathers, seal rings and an odor of musk. Accompanying these are wasp-waisted, almond-eyed, cherry-lipped, finely-powdered damsels carrying tiny baskets, containing an exquisitely embroidered handkerchief. . . and a vial or two of restoratives. . . this batch of "sight seers" do-nothing idlers, time killers, fops, and butterflies skip through the hospital and like summer shadows leave no trace behind.

Class three, he alleged, was the sincere encouragers who brought gifts and kind words and who were always welcome.[2]

Landon had returned to a regiment which was settling in for another long winter on the rivers of Virginia. After much investigating, the Gibraltar Brigade, like beavers looking for a choice spot for a lodge, had chosen to locate in "a huge hollow, with a dense pine and cedar thicket in front to keep the west wind off and a forest of heavy timber in the rear." Experts by now at building snug shanties, the men fell to with the enthusiasm only possible to those who must keep the arctic chills from their backs by their own building skill. Their tools were dull hatchets and bayonets to quarry rocks for the "chimbleys."[3] Here they rested from a series of November skirmishes. What was the Army of the Potomac really doing all that fall and winter? There were lots of guesses.

The politicians and generals may have had their own ideas about that, but John McClure, ever the rock-bottom pragmatist, summed it up his own way.

> Dear Sister:
> I cannot tell you where we are. I know this much we are camped in the woods across the river. This army has had great times this fall running around. Sometimes Mead will retreat and then old Lee will retreat. Each one trying to get the upperhand of the other. . . . It will only be six months and a few days until our time is out and if I live I think I will come to stay all summer any how. If ever Bob [his brother] wants to enlist I want you to keep him from it because it is not the thing it is cracked up to be. There is not so much fun carrying eight days rations. I don't know that he has any notion, but sometimes boys take fool notions. Although I can stand it — they can't hurt me — it don't make no difference now how hard they march me because I never had better health in my life. It is a good thing too because Mead marches men harder on less rations and more wormy crackers than any general we ever had.[4]

Some of the fights of November, 1863, were described in Cavins' account of the Fourteenth in the Greene County history written in 1884.

Had an unusual lively skirmish on the 27th of November at
Locust Grove and on the 28th at Mine Run. Drove the enemy
two miles. On that day, Lieut George W. Rotramel of Sullivan
County, one of the most gallant officers in the Fourteenth Regiment, was killed. He had gone out of his county to enlist in the
Fourteenth Regiment as a private soldier. On the 29th drove the
rebel skirmish line at a point about five miles from the former
engagement.[5]

Beem had been named acting brigade commissary. It meant
more comfortable accommodations and more interesting
work, although the hours were demanding. Colonel Carroll
was likely to command midnight conferences about supplying
the brigade, and for Beem those meetings meant five miles
over rough roads. The job, as it turned out, however, was
temporary and Beem returned to active duty with the regiment in time for the late fall skirmishes.[6]

Christmas came and went; the New Year arrived and grew
older. French ordered breechloaders for his favorite regiment, Landon reported, and they arrived. In January came
the "veteran volunteer excitement." Some sixty members of
the regiment, whose time would be expiring in late spring,
re-enlisted (among them Amory Allen, who had evidently
decided not to return to his "dear little children" for quite a
while longer) for service to begin in June. The inducements
were "great indeed," as Landon said. He signed the roster,
with the promises of $400 and thirty days at home with free
transportation to and from.[7] Many of the regiment would not
sign, however, and wondered what great push Meade would
inspire when the spring thaws came. Push they might toward
Richmond, and this time when they went, they knew they
would not be denied.

The first engagement of the New Year for the Fourteenth
occurred on February 6, 1864, at Morton's Ford near the new
winter quarters at Stevensburg, Virginia. Beem described it in
this way:

On the 6th day of February, 1864, the Second Corps left camp
for the purpose of making a strong reconaissance of the enemy's

position on the south side of the Rapidan. Wading the stream
where it was waist deep, and while the ice was running, they
found the rebels in full force a short distance south of the river
and a brisk engagement ensued in which the 14th was actively
engaged. . . . Capt. David E. Beem received a slight flesh wound
in the side and Henry B. Stoneman was seriously injured by a
shell which struck his knapsack and violently tore it from his
shoulders.[8]

Cavins said of Morton's Ford:

All the commanding officers of regiments in the brigade who
rode had their horses shot and all who walked were wounded
. . . . Jasper Sloat was killed there.[9]

One could be killed just as dead in a minor skirmish in the
middle of a stream as he could on the field of Gettysburg.

As they waited for the final push they knew would come,
small incidents made up the hours and days of the "skeleton
regiment" that was left (probably a few less than 300 men).
"Injun rubber" chickens cooked by the black cooks of the
officers. Van Dyke, now on the staff of General Webb, sending
whiskey to his old friends. McDonald of Company K killed in a
brawl with another man, his heart severed almost in two by
knife stabs. Houghton fretting about the reduced size of the
regiment. Several returning to southern Indiana on furlough
to see in person the "steamboat mania" they had all been
hearing about. "Darky" foot races featuring heavy, wild bet-
ting, witnessed by men on leave in Baltimore.[10]

And then, in May, just three short weeks before the time
expired for the first three-year regiments to go back home to
Indiana, one of the most horrible battles of all loomed like a
final, mocking test. Grant advanced, of course, on Richmond
and passed through the dark and impenetrable thicket known
as the Wilderness, which was an eternal nemesis for the
Fourteenth.

At 8 a.m. on May 4, 1864, the regiment crossed the Rapidan
for the fifth time. As the sun rose higher, the veterans began to
lighten their loads, leaving blankets, shelter tents, overcoats —

they would carry nothing but arms, ammunition, and haversack.

On the night of May 4 they bivouacked on the field of Chancellorsville. It was a mournful remnant of a regiment, like so many of the units in the Army of the Potomac at this time. The Fourteenth had recently suffered a real loss when Cavins left to command a prison camp. Houghton, who missed him grievously, called him "the most perfect man I have ever known." Van Dyke was with Colonel Harrow at Chattanooga.

Still, in spite of changes, the sense of identity remained. The Gibraltar Brigade looked over the field and identified the sights of the horrible night fight just a year ago. The woods were strewn with skeletons. The boys of Company I found the remains of Sergeant Tom Kidd lying where he had fallen, with his stripes still visible on his sleeve. "All that was left was decently interred," Landon said. All around were other memories: broken caissons, pieces of cannon, rotting haversacks, canteens, and shreds of uniform. The men stood where a year and a day before they had waited in line of battle. They saw General Couch's headquarters, shattered by shells, still and gloomy.[11] A tree where the red hospital flag still hung, splintered pine trees standing straight and tall — in this setting the Wilderness seemed a timeless, hellish stage of war on which was repeated Chancellorsville's play over and over again.

Grant's basic strategy was again simple; they would pound Lee, wherever he appeared, down turnpikes where troops were arriving, in thickets and ravines, wherever and whenever he counterattacked. At sunrise on May 5 the Gibraltar Brigade, now consisting of ten excellent "skeleton" regiments of veterans and including the Fourteenth Indiana, a part of Hancock's corps, pushed south passing Cobb's tavern. At precisely noon a brisk skirmish began and by 4 p.m. the Fourteenth was heavily involved in a battle which saw them blazing away along Brock's Road until dark. When the firing finally ceased, they slept on their arms in the position along the road.[12]

The next day the melee was spread across a five-mile front in the woods, the firing intense and continuous. Sixty-four men of the Fourteenth were wounded; seven were killed.[13] In the gloom and smoke McClure shot from behind a tree Indian-style, like Herkimer's troops at the Revolutionary Battle of Oriskany. He saw a gray hat, shot at it, and saw its wearer drop from behind a tree. Incredulously, for he had never in all his battles been conscious of shooting an individual man, he crept forward and knelt beside the unconscious soldier. The "Secesh" was young, a member of the Louisiana Tigers, and, as McClure watched, he gave one groan and died. McClure wanted to get out his wallet and papers to "let his people know," but the groan so frightened him that he ran back into the woods, where he himself was wounded within the hour.[14]

Then the woods caught fire, and some of the wounded were burned alive. The men of the Fourteenth fell back to the road and threw up a line of entrenchments. Stacking arms, they began to cook their first meal in over twenty-four hours when heavy volleys began to roll from the front lines. Longstreet's whole corps was making a grand charge on Hancock's center. The Confederate advance line had driven part of the division out of the hastily constructed breastworks. Then the Gibraltar Brigade's four veteran regiments heard the rallying cry. The Eighth and Fourth Ohio regiments, the Seventh Virginia, and the Fourteenth Indiana

> sprang to their arms, and with a cheer that made the woods ring, drove the bold soldiers of Longstreet over the structure again and broke their line. Many dead rebels were left lying across the breastworks — amongst them a major and two captains.[15]

Fire flared up along the breastworks and the men stopped fighting, and for the Gibraltar Brigade the battle smouldered into ashes.

But it would not end. Grant had determined not to rest until Lee's army was destroyed and Richmond reached — so the army of Meade would have to dog the Rebels and worry them and decimate them until the war was over. The men, sensing this resolve, fought like automatons — grubby, bearded, ruthless fighting machines. They ate whenever they could, cooking meals beside the dead bodies of comrades; they slept standing up. There were some strange interludes. On May 9, just after generals Meade and Grant passed through the lines, the Fourteenth came into the farmyard of one Giles C. Graves. While Rebel sharpshooters' bullets flew about, they calmly butchered pigs, chickens, and turkeys and cooked them. "Men. . . after a few days' constant fighting, care but little for life, and really don't mind the fire of sharpshooters or skirmishers but little more than people at home do house flies," explained Landon.

That night they bivouacked at Graves' farm. The next morning shells burst in the barnyard and the chimneys and board fences flew to pieces. The ten skeleton regiments of the brigade formed in a line on one side of the Po River while the Rebels poured solid shot, shrapnel, and railroad iron into the area around them. One of the "chunks of pig" cut down a tall pine tree two feet in diameter.

Advancing toward the enemy, the Fourteenth entered a thicket only fifty yards from the enemy line. Landon took a bullet in the foot and passed through the lines, out of commission. When Colonel Coons saw him, he said "Take my horse, Will, and ride him out — I cannot get along with him in this underbrush." Along the plank road, past charred and blackened remains of those who were burned and smothered in blazing leaves, past soldiers of all ranks lying together in muddy sloughs, past hills of Rebels piled up in careless death, Landon rode, through a literal hail of bullets, out of the Wilderness and out of the war.

Spotsylvania provided the next horror for those who stayed. Beem described this Virginia battle:

> At Spottsylvania, on the 12th day of May, the Fourteenth, then in Carroll's brigade, of Gibbon's division, Hancock's [Second] Corps, participated in the famous charge against the rebel breastworks. The intrenchments were very strong, and in front of Carroll's brigade were in the form of a sharp angle or salient.

The charge was made at 4:35 a.m. The column rushed forward and when about half way across the fallen timber in front of the rebel intrenchments, they burst into a cheer and swept onward in the face of a terrific fire, scaled the rebel intrenchments at the angle, where they had a desperate hand-to-hand conflict before the foe surrendered. The charge was a glorious success. The Second Corps captured 4,000 prisoners of Ewell's corps, and twenty pieces of artillery. The rebels made a desperate effort to regain their intrenchments, and the fighting during the remainder of the day at this point was kept up with great loss of life on both sides. Gen. A. A. Humphreys, one of the historians of the Army of the Potomac, says in speaking of the conflict at the angle: "The fighting was literally murderous." The commander of a Vermont brigade in the Sixth Corps says: "I was at the angle the next day. It was there that the somewhat celebrated tree was cut off by bullets; there that the brush and logs were cut to pieces and whipped into basket stuff; there that the rebel ditches and cross-sections were filled with dead men several deep. The sight was even more sickening than at the bloody lane of Antietam. There a great many dead men were lying in the road and across the torn-down fences; but they were not piled several deep, and their flesh was not so mangled and torn."[16]

Coons, the tough colonel who made it to the top of the regiment through his own guts and dependability and Morton's overcoats, died at Spotsylvania leading one of the last charges of the Fourteenth. D Company refused to leave and stayed on fourteen days after its time had expired. It was perhaps the final tribute to Cavins and the spirit of '61-'65; his boys kept the faith even when they could easily have left.[17]

Day after day the ambulance trains wound back toward Fredericksburg. One of them carried McClure, severely wounded in the shoulder, and Landon with a bullet in his foot that he would carry the rest of his days. As the train jolted through the pouring rain, it stopped several times to bury soldiers by the wayside. Then it passed on to Mt. Pleasant Hospital in Washington, where the fleas and flies and bedbugs in the wards and the nauseating smell of the death house next door reminded the boys (if they needed a reminder after the past three years) of the common mortality of man, especially in wartime. While they were in Washington, word came that the Fourteenth's time had expired. It was being mustered out in Indianapolis, from which it had departed three years earlier, before the Battle of Rich Mountain had even been fought and the war was still a thrilling dream.[18]

*   *   *

Henderson Simpson, McClure's cousin and a veteran of the Fourteenth's campaigns through Fredericksburg, had re-enlisted in the army. He joined the 120th Indiana Volunteers late in the war and wrote amusing letters home to his cousins John McClure and his sisters Mary and Annie, who were all living together now with McClure as head of the family. Simpson wrote May 19, 1865 of the time that they would all be reunited in Knox County:

> It will seem so much like old times, when I get home to visit you up there. It seems but yesterday since I used to walk up there — bare legged pants rolled up — Don't I remember! How glad I'd be when I got to the shady woods beyond Mr. Purcell's, and then when I got to the turn on the hill I'd raise a squawk and start on the double quick. Maybe some of you would come out to the fence to meet me. (You saw me so seldom!) I can see some of you yet, standing on the third or fourth plank while your toes stuck through the cracks like a row of turtle heads — But those dear old days can never come again. The past is dead. Let the dead bury the dead. . . .[19]

But Houghton, ever contemplative, had come to the end of a road and could only question the meaning of it all. Before the Battle of the Wilderness, when impossible responsibilities were being heaped on him, he had written:

> Our regiment will dissolve into nothingness and its name be forgotten, save in the hearts of those who remember the dead who sleep. In history it may claim a humble place. And I would rather that maligners would touch it gently — none others have been more true or have contributed more in blood and suffer-

ing to the common cause of our common country. Our banners can scarcely hold the inscriptions of our battles and our rolls show a sad percentage of those who are no more. I cannot tell what the coming events will be.[20]

Whatever they would be, the Fourteenth Indiana Volunteers as a fighting unit had passed into history. It sent its re-enlisted veterans to the 120th Indiana, its remaining men back to southern Indiana, and its battle flags, finally, to the Soldiers and Sailors Monument in the middle of the Monument Circle. Many years later, the last surviving comrades from Lincoln's army would drive round and round those flags in an unknowing tribute at the last encampment of the G.A.R.

1. Letter of Landon to the *Western Sun,* October 24, 1863.
2. Ibid., July 1, 1864.
3. Ibid., December 12, 1863.
4. Letter of McClure to his sister, November 12, 1863, in *Hoosier Farmboy.*
5. *History of Greene and Sullivan Counties,* p. 129.
6. Letter of Beem to his wife, September 10, 1863.
7. Letters of Landon to the *Western Sun,* December 12, 1863 and January 6, 1864.
8. *Counties of Clay and Owen,* p. 637.
9. *History of Greene and Sullivan Counties,* p. 129.
10. Letter of Landon to the *Western Sun,* January 6, 1864; Letter of Houghton to his father, February 1, 1864.
11. Letter of Landon to the *Western Sun,* May 18, 1864.
12. Ibid.
13. Ibid.
14. *Hoosier Farmboy,* p. 61.
15. Letter of Landon to the *Western Sun,* May 18, 1864.
16. *Counties of Clay and Owen,* p. 638.
17. *History of Greene and Sullivan Counties,* p. 130.
18. Letter of Houghton to his father, May 31, 1864.
19. Letter of Henderson Simpson to John R. and Mary Jane McClure, May 19, 1865.
20. Letter of Houghton to his father, February 1, 1864.

CHAPTER TEN

THE VETERANS' RETURN

When the Civil War soldiers returned to the Old Northwest, they found real change — especially in the cities. Chicago was a town transformed, a booming railroad mecca; Grand Rapids was swelling with increasing numbers of immigrants; Toledo and Cleveland were beginning to be great manufacturing centers. The war's demands had decisively begun to alter an agricultural society into a modern industrial society. In 1850 there had been 4300 manufacturing institutions in Indiana; five years after the war 12,000 factories were pouring out everything from woolen cloth and boilers to iron castings, Singer sewing machines to malt liquor.[1]

Soldiers returning, as Lambert did to Terre Haute and Myerhof did to Evansville, found that the towns had become thriving cities. Evansville had begun to grow rapidly just before the war due to its important position on the river, the influx of German immigrants, and its location on the railroad to Terre Haute. By 1870 it was the second-largest city in the state, according to the United States census.[2] When Myerhof returned to become a businessman in the town, it was flourishing; steamboat arrivals had almost doubled since 1861, streetcars made their first appearance in 1867, and a waterworks and a gasworks were being constructed to add to the comforts of home in the city.[3]

Terre Haute, where Lambert decided to settle and marry Mattie Shepherd and to take a commercial course and eventually enter the postal service, had nearly doubled its population. By 1970 it was the fourth-largest city in the state. Because of Terre Haute's railroads and manufacturing, it continued to grow after the war; as the pork-packing industry declined, iron manufacturing developed.[4]

If cities had grown, the quiet villages remained virtually unchanged in southern Indiana, at least in physical appearance. Dogs still lay in the streets in Wheatland and Carlisle as, indeed, they do today; and a child's shout could echo across half the town on a still Sunday morning. Southern Indiana, settled early in the history of the Old West, was slowing its growth at the close of the war while the younger states like Michigan and Wisconsin were booming. Michigan's rate of growth during the decade 1860-1870 was 58%, Wisconsin's 35.9%, Illinois' 48.3%, and Indiana's 24.4% (Ohio's growth rate was the smallest during this decade, 13.9%).[5] Even central and northern Indiana were growing more rapidly than the area to which the boys from the Fourteenth were returning. Most of the changes the boys found were personal, the necessary alterations of families separated for three years. Children had grown up, property had changed hands, and friends had married or moved away. Houghton's sister Net (Hattie) had disappointingly (to him) returned from college instead of completing her education. His younger brother Hilary, whom he had carried on his shoulders as a small child when he went to the Loogootee train station to go to war in 1861, was a rapidly growing ten year old. Houghton married (he never had children), went into the timber business for a while, and then, like many returning veterans, tried a variety of occupations: United States Internal Revenue assessor, miller, salesman, and manager for a wheel company. Finally he settled into banking, becoming the president of the newly organized White River State Bank.

Brooks, home since August, 1863, had bought a virgin stand of timber along the White River and cut and milled it. He named the plot Wildwoods, and he moved his family to it and became a prosperous farmer.[7] Cavins returned to his wife and children in Bloomfield, particularly concentrating on the education of his son Samuel, and took up the practice of law with his brother Aden. Beem also returned to his law practice in Spencer.

The fate of Will Landon, the ebullient and positive chronicler of the Fourteenth's saga, was far different and sadly ironic. Transferring to the regular army after the war, he was commissioned second lieutenant in the Eighteenth Regulars. During the summer of 1866, while he was at Fort Leavenworth, this seasoned veteran, who had survived the bloody battles of Antietam, Fredericksburg, Chancellorsville, and the Wilderness, drowned while swimming in the Missouri River. His body was never found.[8]

Van Dyke, too, continued with the military long after the Fourteenth was mustered out. He remained on General Harrow's staff and was at Kennesaw Mountain and at Atlanta in July of '64. He was then reassigned as captain and assistant adjutant general to Sherman, serving until September 19, 1865. Harrow wished him to join him in Memphis practicing law and Denny wished him to return to Vincennes, but of Vincennes he said, "I dislike the place."[9] Ultimately, he married Angie (Kent), moved to Ohio, and became recorder for the state.

Simpson and McClure took up farming in Palmyra Township of Knox County on the Revolutionary War acres of their families. Like that of so many returning veterans, McClure's life after the three years in Virginia became almost an anticlimax. He married Frances Purcell, his neighbor, had six children, and owned a prosperous farm. He himself, however, never actively supervised it, leaving that to his wife and the hired hands. In fact, according to his wife, he never did a lick of work on the farm except once each year. When it came time to slaughter hogs, he would take out his rifle, aim carefully at the head of the pig as if it were a Louisiana Tiger in the Battle of the Wilderness, and dispatch the animal with deadly aim.

This did not mean that he was not working elsewhere from time to time. He went into Republican politics; he served as a Palmyra Township trustee and a Knox County commissioner. But what McClure really did was to become a professional veteran. His type was well known in America up to the turn of the century and beyond. Around stoves in general stores in winter and on benches in front of courthouses in summer they gathered — men who had experienced the great drama and excitement of the battlefield and camp and for whom life could never be the same again. In McClure's case, the war had given his life a meaning it could never have had otherwise; he spent the rest of his days trying to recapture the sense of importance that had been his with the Army of the Potomac. There were plenty of informal occasions when veterans could talk about the "dad-burned war," as Mrs. McClure called it. When Simpson and his wife Lizzie Kelso (also a relative of McClure's) came down for dinner, the men refought the campaign on Cheat Mountain over the strawberry shortcake. Houghton and Brooks came by when they were in the area, and veterans of G Company stopped McClure in Vincennes to exchange news and ask about other comrades.

Then there were the G. A. R. functions, in which some of the men were more active than others. Founded in 1866, the Grand Army of the Republic sought to express the veterans' needs and wishes to the government as well as serve as a camaraderie club. At its height, its membership rolls contained over 408,000 names.[10] Indiana was one of its strongholds, Governor Morton having been instrumental in building its organization.

Beginning with the 1866 political campaign, the theme the Grand Army set and was to reiterate all the veterans' years was something like this: "Vote Republican. The Democratic Party was the party of war. It could even be viewed as treasonable. The only way to declare your loyalty to your country as we soldiers did in 1861-65 on the battlefield is to vote straight Republican." The G. A. R. welded the veterans of the North, including those of Indiana, into a solid, vote-delivery block.

McClure used the backing of the veterans to get himself elected to public office, calling himself a "Black Abraham Lincoln Republican." Houghton became a member of the Thomas J. Brooks G. A. R. Post 322,[11] formed in 1889 and named after the brother of Lewis Brooks (Houghton's cousin). Myerhof was commander of Evansville's Farragut Post 27,[12] and Beem eventually became the state commander of the G. A. R.

It was one thing to mix at the Grand Army functions with the veterans from many units in Lincoln's army and another to meet with the veterans of the Glorious Fourteenth (as they were now calling it). There was something very satisfying about being with the very men who had shared the rubber blankets in the rain at Falmouth, who had cursed the long march to Leesburg. A reunion of the entire regiment was held in 1872, and it must have been well attended.[13]

In 1887, a new era for the regiment began at Spencer when the Fourteenth Indiana Association was formed. The veterans of the Fourteenth now devoted themselves to preserving the memory of what had happened and to enshrining for themselves and for the future the Fourteenth's sacrifice. The psychological value of rehashing the war events was enormous; seeing the old familiar faces which had been illuminated by countless cooking fires was delightful in ways even they did not understand. Somehow seeing the other survivors reinforced the reality and put into perspective the enormity of what they had been through. They had lived a series of events so remarkable that at times they must have had the elements of a dream as they walked through the pastures of their home farms or sat tilting their chairs in their small-town law offices. They needed to touch again from time to time that emotional and personal epitome that had been the Civil War. The regiment, as it had been in the battlefield days, became a translating agency for their ideals and experiences in the war, its esprit de corps an almost spiritual force on which they could feed.

And so they met, elected officers, corresponded, and organized reunions. One of the first presidents was W. D. Mull of

Rockville, a vital young man who had left the regiment after Antietam severely wounded and gone on to become lieutenant colonel of the 149th Indiana.

The brigade also met, usually in Ohio, sending stirring invitations to their fellows in the Hoosier State:

> Comrades
> Yourself and family are cordially invited to attend a reunion of the Gibraltar Brigade Gen SS Carrolls consisting of the 4th and 8th Ohios, 7th W. VA, 14 Indian Vol. Inf. (and later eastern regiments) to be held 1st, 2nd, 3rd of September 1908 Summit St., Toledo, Ohio.[14]

Trying to decide exactly who the brigade was did present some difficulties, as did trying to fraternize with recruits in the regiment who had arrived after other veterans had been disabled and gone home. Sometimes the "old brigade" met separately so that its memories could be exchanged without the "outsiders."

The regimental and brigade reunions had several goals and activities. One of these was to keep alive the memory of sacrifice, particularly of the dead comrades, the Charlie Gibsons and Lieutenant Lundays, who otherwise had only their families to remember them. It was a sacred trust, one which could be tangibly demonstrated by a continued commitment to monument building both in Indiana and on the Eastern battlefields. Sometimes by themselves, sometimes in conjunction with the G. A. R., the unit designed, got subscriptions for, and supervised the erection of monuments. On May 25-27, 1900, for example, the men of the Fourteenth met with other local regiments in Terre Haute to dedicate the Soldiers and Sailors Monument in that city — a tall obelisk on whose point stood a soldier with a banner.[15] In Vincennes on October 8, 1914, John McClure rode a white horse at the head of a parade to dedicate the Soldiers' Monument by the Citizens of Knox County.[16]

At these solemn monument dedications high-school bands played "Battle Hymn of the Republic" and "Nearer, My God,

to Thee," and local dignitaries vied with each other to declare
their reverence for the veterans. Often there was more than
one service in the day. Sometimes the veterans traveled to
battlefields — to Antietam or Gettysburg — to look for familiar landmarks, trees, or shell-pitted houses and to supervise
the erection of state monuments. These were festive as well as
memorializing events, with church suppers and family visiting
the order of the day.

But it was not enough simply to join together to revive the
esprit de corps, to eat the ham and potato salad and sing
"Marching Through Georgia" (which, of course, they had
never done). They had to keep the flame of their reputation
alive. Thus they wrote battle chronicles. They wore silk ribbons, different colors for each reunion, listing their engagements. The list varied. Sometimes it was short and dramatic.

    Winchester
    Antietam
    Fredericksburg
    Chancellorsville
    Gettysburg
    Wilderness
    Spotsylvania
    Cold Harbor

The names were allowed to tell the story. But other times the
list grew much longer, as in 1908 when it proudly proclaimed

    In 72 ENGAGEMENTS
    Killed or Wounded in Battle
    392 or 52%

and then listed every battle and skirmish, too: Cheat Mountain, Greenbrier, Mine Run, Morton's Ford.

There was a subtle competition going on, a sort of top-
regiment-in-the-state contest, and the Fourteenth was running hot and heavy, at brigade reunions and over Thanksgiv-
ing dinner tables where relatives (many of them veterans)
would assemble from far-flung spots. And if one could

identify the top regiments in the state, what would be the top regiments in the Northern Army? The contest went on not only in southern Indiana, but in Gallipolis, Ohio, and Adrian, Michigan, and Albany, New York also. Points were awarded not only for prominence of battles (big names) but also for the percentage of killed and wounded. These were the means of judging "the bravest and the best," as Mrs. Stallard had called the boys from Vincennes and Martin County that first morning when the flag was presented. One's campaign theatre was important too: "I was in Virginia the whole war" was so much more impressive than "I was at Vicksburg." So? Everybody in Indiana had been at Vicksburg.

The position of the Army of the Potomac by 1900 had altered from that time in the depths of the war when Houghton had believed that its history would be merely a footnote in the military history of the conflict. Somehow, even if one intellectually grasped the strategic importance of isolating the Southwest and capturing Vicksburg, the last Mississippi stronghold of the war, one's heart inescapably fixed itself on Virginia, the field, dangerously near the Rebel capital, of brilliant, futile efforts of great bravery. The dramatic quality of their leadership troubles, the political difficulties they experienced, and their struggle as underdogs gave the veterans of the Army of the Potomac (relatively rare in Indiana) an aura of glory.

The attitude toward the Army of the Potomac was not the only one that changed in the veterans' regiment as the years went by. Many other red-hot issues blurred with time, and sometimes both sides did a complete about-face. The South remained hated as an historic idea that had animated men to undertake the unspeakable quest, but the brave adversaries of Gettysburg were readily forgiven. They never had been very mad at the Rebels, anyway, and regarded them by 1900 as "misguided" but "daring and brave." Former Confederate soldiers were by now meeting in their own regimental societies, recalling their own battles and brawls, and the bonds of fellowship transcended the Mason-Dixon. After all, they all had been soldiers, all fellow actors in the greatest drama in the nation's history.

The issue of slavery which had inspired few soldiers at the beginning of the war became more important as they looked back. Many of the men of the Fourteenth and other units identified themselves with that cause now that it was won. They became coat-tail abolitionists, so to speak. A 1903 poem found with some of Myerhof's papers evidenced the strange metamorphosis that had had to go on to turn black-haters into supporters of Emancipation:

> "The Button of the Legion"
>
> Then a health to its gray-haired wearers!
> And a health given silently
> To their comrades asleep in the North and the South
> Awaiting God's reveille
> Who fought — not for glory or conquest
> Not the wealth of the isles of the sea —
> But to win that birthright God gives to all,
> For their brother in slavery.[17]

Although it was true that some of the veterans of the regiment thought that way after the war, just as many probably remained unrepentant disparagers of blacks. But free blacks were increasingly a fact in their small towns after the war. Facing the reality and allowing their common sense and basic democratic instincts to prevail, they accepted them into the bosom of village life, practicing a grudging democracy that would percolate slowly into the social ideals of the next generation.

Thus, although the actual causes and political ideologies of the war softened into the background of the men's experience, like the outlines of people in an old sepia photo, the reputation of the regiment was highlighted by a variety of very specific means. By 1890 the regiment's story was a mystique, a *Beowulf*-type epic which was sung by veteran warriors in Hoosier halls. One line might have read: "To Houghton was granted great glory in battle" (being the youngest field officer in the Army of the Potomac in 1863 when he became a major). The epic had several elements which were always emphasized: the regiment was the first from Indiana to volunteer for three years' service; it fought (with bleeding feet) against Stonewall Jackson in the Shenandoah Valley and beat him. It lost half of those who went into the Battle of Antietam. It was christened the Gibraltar Brigade. Its dead were found closer to the stone wall at Marye's Heights than the dead of any other regiment. Part of the Battle of Gettysburg hinged on the Fourteenth's great performance. Its leader Kimball was a Christian commander.

Some things were never mentioned: the mutiny, the drunken deaths, the court martials, the deserters, the rage after Leesville, the ignoble search for advancement. The hell-bent, cursing, average Joe of Mailer's and Jones' World War II novels did not, could not exist for the Victorian men who manipulated the Fourteenth's image.

The Fourteenth was not the only regiment, of course, trying to memorialize its story. Regimental histories began to be written all over the country during the 1870's and 80's and even as late as the 1920's; the urge seems to have been widespread to put into permanent form the exploits of the military units in the Civil War. Corps histories, division histories, brigade histories poured from the presses. Most were published at the author's or unit's expense and circulated to members of veterans' associations and public and college libraries. Many times the circulation was much more widespread — the good ones were snapped up by veterans of other units and by a general population fixated by the conflict that was still fresh in their imagination.[18] Typical is a book written by Lieutenant Matthew J. Graham, *The Ninth New York Volunteers,* published in 1900.[18] It throws light on a literary genre that reflected the veterans' altered perspectives twenty or thirty years after the war.

In his book Graham told battlefield and camp anecdotes about his regiment, the Hawkins Zouaves, to supplement the dry details of troop movement. For instance, he recorded the jokes that the men cracked while standing in the food line. The last chapters were devoted to lengthy summaries of regimental reunions, with one of real interest being a reunion with the Third Georgia Survivors' Association. The Ninth New York had met the Third Georgia more than once on the battle-field — including at South Mountain — and they met again in 1889 and 1890 in reunion. The atmosphere of a sentimental and nostalgic testimonial dinner seems to have been typical of these affairs (as well as the books themselves), with jokes about how the Third Georgia wished it never had met the Ninth New York until that night, toasts, and recollections about specific campaigns.

Another book, *The Twelfth New Hampshire*, written by A. W. Bartlett, was one of the most colossal efforts made in regimen-tal history. In almost 800 pages the author detailed the regi-ment's career, including every movement of troops and change of command and histories of specific companies along with pictures and biographies of each soldier in the company who could be located. It is an impressive tribute on the oversize book shelf to the power of esprit de corps.[19]

For the Fourteenth Indiana David Beem was the chief chronicler. His regimental history was an ongoing venture for forty years. A summary, it never appeared in book form but was instead submitted to various papers on ceremonial occa-sions or made as speeches reported in the papers. He finally compiled an unfinished, twenty-four-page typewritten his-tory, but a better recounting of the regiment's actions is in the chapter Beem wrote for the *History of Owen County*. It is dignified, accurate, and honest (although one somehow wishes for the vital, off-the-cuff humanity of Landon's reports).

The epic of the Fourteenth as it evolved during the veterans' lifetimes had one major weakness: a gap in the story. The men had been present and suitably valiant at almost every major battle of the Army of the Potomac — Bloody Lane at Antie-tam, Sunken Road at Fredericksburg, the Wilderness, the Bloody Angle — but they had missed Pickett's charge at Get-tysburg. Beem, for his part, was always careful to point out that the Fourteenth was *not* on the hill when Pickett charged, as he said in the *History of Owen County:*

> The fact of the Fourteenth being detached to repulse the rebel
> charge on the evening of July 2 placed them on the right of the
> cemetery, where they remained until the end of the engagement
> and removed them where they did not hear the shock of the
> great charge of the rebels on the Second Corps the next day.

Others, however, could not bear to say that they were idle
and out of range when the great event occurred. The official
history of the regiment in the *Report of the Adjutant General*
states that the Fourteenth played a "conspicuous part in the
action of the third day." Reports after this are even more
hedgy until at last one very old man in the regiment, writing
when he must have been ninety years old, actually thought that
he had experienced Pickett's charge. What a vivid picture he
recreated from other soldiers' memories:

> Our corps commander, Gen. Hancock of the Second Corps
> had the right center of the line in front of the Gettysburg
> cemetery and immediately facing Pickett's charge. So we were
> (so to speak) strictly in it. We received them with open arms.
>
> I will in my feeble way attempt to give my personal remem-
> brance of the battle, or the part we took in it, or one instance of
> that awful slaughter of men and horses.

(so maybe he is allowing himself some leeway)

> After much maneuvering and placing of troops and artillery,
> and heavy cannonading on both sides, we took position behind
> hastily constructed breastworks of rails, stones, and dirt. Our
> artillery above and behind us, fired over our heads. Then came
> the awful silence or lull in firing of which all veterans know the
> meaning. The suspense was hard to bear. . . . At last Gen. Lee's
> signal gun was fired for the charge to commence. Pickett's rebel
> lines emerged from the woods about one and one-quarter miles
> from us, in splendid formation, as if on dress parade. Heavy
> cannonading commenced on both sides. . . it was quite a Fourth
> of July celebration. . . . They were coming on the double-quick
> at charge bayonets . . . when about forty yards from us we got

the command to fire, load at will, and keep it up. After our first volley it seemed as if their front line had melted away and lay before us in great heaps of dead and wounded human beings. . . .[20]

Finally a compromise was settled on in the Gettysburg issue which satisfied the Fourteenth's need to be glorious at all times and still served the interests of historical fact. Some of the officers, principally Myerhof, decided that the decisive moment at the Battle of Gettysburg had not happened at Pickett's charge: it was really the night before, when the Fourteenth had been instrumental in saving Rickett's batteries. So *Rickett's* instead of *Pickett's* became the official password. Myerhof, another unofficial historian of the Fourteenth, used for his argument in part a statement made by Colonel Harris of the Seventy-fifth Ohio, who had been commanding Ames' brigade.

The rebel army had hammered away at us until my brigade was so weakened it seemed that we would be compelled to fall back. We held out hoping for reinforcements. . . . About nightfall of July 2, 1863, the confederates prepared to charge the hill, at their head were the famous Louisiana Tigers. . . . At this crucial point the 4th Ohio, 7th West Virginia and 14th Indiana of Carroll's Brigade came to the rescue, charged the enemy. I would say in conclusion when that charge of the confederates was repulsed on the night of July 2 the battle of Gettysburg had been fought and won. And that the reckless and desperate charge of Pickett on the next day was foredoomed to defeat.

An important part of the epic-making process in addition to official regimental histories was the formal printed tribute. This was an assembling of praise, popular at the turn of the century, for someone or something, and the Fourteenth had its tribute (in this case for the brigade). It was not difficult to amass praise for the workhorse brigade's performance; many people had been complimentary about it.

Myerhof produced this typical tribute for the brigade, which he called *What Others Say of the Nathan Kimball and Later of the General S. S. Carroll Brigade.*[21] It is thirty-two pages of

effusive prose and poetry about the brigade from Generals
Howard and Walker and other commanders and com-
mentators on various battlefield actions. Several excerpts from
this little printed book, among them the passage quoted directly above, are included here because they capture the very
essence of the myth-making process just before and after the
turn of the century for the aging men of the Civil War
generation.

> On July 2nd, 1862, Gen. Nathan Kimball joined the Army of the
> Potomac with three regiments, all destined to win high distinc-
> tion in their 2nd Corps — 8th Ohio, 14th Indiana, and 7th
> W.Va. (and were treated as an independent brigade, at An-
> tietam were assigned as 2nd brigade, third division, 2nd corps),
> the buoyant, dashing and indomitable brigade of Western
> troops, under the command of Gen. Nathan Kimball.

> Antietam — Kimball's gallant troops, the 14th Ind., 8th Ohio,
> 7th W. Va. and 132nd Pa. dashed forward with enthusiasm and
> became engaged along their whole front in a contest of the
> utmost fierceness. Again and again the enemy assumed the
> aggressive and the greatest vivacity in counter attacks alike on
> Kimball and Webber. At last Kimball, following up a repulse of
> the enemy from his center, dashed forward, capturing 300
> prisoners and several colors and establishing his line a consider-
> able distance in advance.

> Chancellorsville, Va., Gen. Walker — Hays' brigade was half
> surrounded in the dense thickets, and the brave commander
> was wounded and captured with some of his men. But in this
> critical moment, upon the right of Hays' small and shattered
> command appears the brigade of Carroll, which its spirited
> commander handles with a dexterity and audacity all his own.
> Three of his regiments are flung freely and boldly against the
> left flank of the Confederates, which curls and breaks under the
> shock. Carroll not only takes three hundred prisoners, with two
> colors, but recaptures a regiment of our people.

> New York, Gen. Walker, 1863 — In consequence of the riotous
> resistance to the conscription act in New York City, S. S. Carroll,
> commanding the First Brigade, Third Division, 2nd Corps. was

in July ordered to the East, with the Fourth and Eighth Ohio
and Fourteenth Indiana. From the Second Division the First
Minnesota and the Seventh Michigan were also dispatched on
this duty. Unfortunately the ruffians who had burned orphan
asylums, pillaged defenseless houses, murdered stray militia
men, and filled the days and nights with terror, could not pluck
up enough courage to try conclusions with these veteran regiments from the front. Certain it is the "boys in blue" would have
liked nothing better than an opportunity to strike at the
scoundrels who had sought to stab the nation in the back, and
had they struck, it would have been for the admonition of
traitors to the end of time.

Myerhof, Beem, and others also involved themselves in a
constant debate over battle strategies that went on through the
country's periodicals. Typical was the exchange in the *National
Tribune* just after the turn of the century: a Lieutenant Peck of
the Seventeenth Connecticut had evidently written a letter to
the *Tribune* glorifying his (Ames') brigade (Seventeenth Connecticut, Twenty-fifth Ohio, Seventy-fifth Ohio, 107th Ohio),
which he said had stood like a stone wall that Gettysburg
evening on the hill with the batteries. The editor of the *Tribune*
had answered the lieutenant, but Myerhof felt he also had to
comment:

To the Editor, *National Tribune:*
You say in your issue of Aug. 12 Hancock who was keeping his
finger on every pulse of the battle, hurried Carroll's well tried
brigade to the rescue of the batteries. These rushed in with a
cheer, which sent the Confederates back in a rout.
   Will you kindly add what others said that were not directly
interested in Carroll's brigade? Gen. Hunt, Chief of Artillery,
said Carroll's Brigade, sent to East Cemetery Hill was a happy
inspiration. . . .
   W. H. Thurston, First Lieutenant Rickets Battery [present at
Gettysburg], says in his article [in the *National Tribune*], "But
relief was at hand and came in the shape of Carroll's Brigade,
which like a rushing current, swept through the battery, and the
famous Louisiana Tigers, who played so much havoc on that
fateful night, went out in darkness to molest no more that
night. . . . I ask Lieut. Peck of the 17th Conn. how the enemy got
into the battery if Ames' Brigade stood like a stone wall?

Myerhof finished his letter with a flourish:

> Truth is Truth and the gallant charge made by Carroll's Brigade
> on the evening of July 2, 1863, emblazons history's brightest
> pages and nothing can efface it.[22]

These arguments over the fine points of battle strategy were
stimulated by the many histories of the war published from
1870 to 1890. Written by commanding officers in the engagements themselves, these histories were based on official reports and personal journals. Unlike the regimental histories,
they tended to be painstakingly accurate and relatively free of
personal anecdote. The first and definitely the foremost of
these books was a series of volumes from the 1880's called
Battles and Leaders of the Civil War, a collection of *Century
Magazine* articles. Longstreet, McClellan, Franklin, Pope, and
Buell all wrote for the series, and it is truly remarkable both for
the quality of reportage and for the officers' unconscious
revelations of their personalities and characters as they looked
back over the engagements for which they had borne
responsibility.

Kimball was asked to contribute to the account of the
Shenandoah Valley campaign with an article which was titled
"Fighting Jackson at Kernstown," the battle which had won
him his brigadier generalship. Kimball, now surveyor general
of Utah, carefully edited his own notes and reports. He wrote
to Cavins, asking for help in reconstructing the battle and
campaign. Cavins' answer is enlightening:

July 12, 1887

Dear General
     Your letter has been received asking me to give you some time
to aid in writing an article concerning movements of Shields'
Division. After studying the matter for you two days, I am
unable to suggest anything that you would not be likely to know.
However, I send you a few items in pencil, but I can't say that
they will be any aid to you.
     A short time ago Captain Blinn and Lieut. Cox and some
others asked me to use my article about Winchester to write an

answer to Gen. Imbodens article published in July or Aug. 1885 in *Century,* where in he gives what purports to be a full history of "Stonewall" Jackson in the Shenandoah.

He entirely ignores the campaign by Shields Division in the Shenandoah Valley and does not even allude to it. I told these men that my article went so much into details that I thought it would not suit the Century Co. They insisted on my writing it anyway. When I received your letter I hadn't prepared, with the exception of adding names of the successor of Col. Murray.

If they should publish [this article] it would give your article a boon, because the article shows that you are entitled to the whole credit for directing the movements of the battle and gaining the victory.

There is another thing I wish to ask you about. I see in McClellan's book that he says that at Antietam two regiments of Richards' Division with help from the 7th Va. and 132 Penna charged to meet an attack on our right flank. This is an impossibility as there were not troops on the right of the 14th Indiana in the same line, then minutes after we passed the Rawley house. After we defeated the rebels in our front, and the remnant left in Bloody Lane surrendered, the 14th Indiana and 8th Ohio changed fronts to meet a fresh column of rebel troops that marched by flank movement and formed so as to sweep our line from our right flank. This was near the close of the engagement on our part. . . . Harrow was then in the rear looking for ammunition and Coons was off the field wounded and I had command. . . what I want to know is, what troops were those lying north of the cornfield? On what part of your line was the 7th Va. and 132 Pa? right or left? If these regiments were on the right of your Brigade, it was probably them, if they were on the left, it was some other troops.[23]

The letter illustrates the fascination with the minutiae of the battle's progress, the determination that the story be told accurately down to the last point, and the hope that the Fourteenth Indiana's part be portrayed in full (especially when it tended to glorify the regiment).

Kimball's article on Kernstown appeared in Volume II of the Century Series, and his fame was spread as the book found its way into small-town libraries and onto parlor tables in the final years of the century.

A soldier-historian, when all information about his own

regiment was exhausted, could turn to the battlefield careers of other units. Occasionally, when the regimental histories were in vogue, old East-West antipathies were forgotten and regiments wrote to each other with sales pitches for the books. McClure, who had been elected secretary of the Fourteenth Indiana Association, received a letter from a veteran of the 108th New York offering to sell copies of his new book to interested veterans for "$4 a copy to a club of 25 or more." The author enclosed a review from a Rochester, New York paper:

> *History of the 108th N.Y. Volunteers* is the title of a large, neatly bound and handsomely illustrated volume just issued by Private George H. Washburn of Company D. This work, which it has taken years of arduous toil to complete, is a complete history of the regiment from 1862-1864, together with a roster of the regiment, rebel oaths of allegiance, rebel passes, reminiscenses, life sketches of officers and members of the several companies, photographs and many excellent scenes of the principal battles. . . .
> [Included in the history] are such interesting features as Lincoln and the Union Commanders. . . Davis and the Confederate commanders. . . extracts from the diary of Captain Boyd, Incidents of the surrender, anniversary of the Battle of Antietam. . . annual reunions.[24]

Washburn said that his aim was to "give just a general glance at the services, privations and honors of the 108th regiment, and those who served in the same brigade and division. . . and to show briefly what a conspicuous and glorious part it took in the triumph of the Union Army."

Thus the veterans of the Fourteenth Indiana, like the other gray-haired, middle-aged men who had fought either to save or split the Union, went on quite consciously to build the reputation of their military units, to discuss past glory, and to analyze and reanalyze with reverence and great interest the bloody war which had sickened them when it was stark reality instead of nostalgic recollection. The reflection "it is well that war is so terrible, or else we should grow too fond of it" applies not only to generals standing on the edge of great battles deploying units of troops like toy soldiers; it also applies to veterans who have returned and who endlessly chew over past battles like dogs with savory bones.

The Fourteenth never buried its bones; in spite of family responsibilities and business worries in the fast-moving world to which they had returned, and national depressions and changes in government, the endless discussion of what went on in what battle kept the noble escutcheon shining.

But the most important cause of the continuation of regimental spirit through the veterans' older years went beyond reunions and monument building. The continuing interest in the regiment could not have existed if it were not for the deep personal ties which grew out of the comradeship of the war years and continued as a human network of support. As has been said, the regimental spirit of the Fourteenth was finally cemented at Antietam because of its immense personal impact and the interdependent action that it inspired. The men were unified there, and through the experiences that followed became closer than kinfolk in many cases. Emotions were amplified; a man had to hate intensely, but he could also love fervently.

Many of these personal relationships continued. The series of letters following is remarkable not only for its revelations of the continuing mystique of the regiment but also for its comments on the state and country across which the men of the regiment were scattered. The correspondence, much of it directed to McClure as secretary,[25] tells its own story and in doing so completes the chronicle of the Fourteenth Indiana.

June 21, 1887
Office of Cavins and Cavins
Attorneys and Counselors at Law

Nathan Kimball
Odgen, Utah
Dear General

I received your letter with suggestion in regard to my contemplated article in regard to Winchester, and am much obliged and will observe your suggestions. A short time before receiving your letter, my only son suddenly died of congestion of the lungs. He was practicing medicine in Pennsylvania, had graduated from Jefferson Medical College at Philadelphia and was a very promising young man. This sad dispensation of providence so overwhelmed me that I have had no heart to pursue my history of the 14th Indiana. But within the last week I have resumed it — and I will probably complete my article on Winchester. . . .

E. H. C. Cavins

July 20, 1892

Comrade

The 6th annual reunion of the 14th Regiment Indiana Volunteers will be held at Clinton, Vermillion County, Indiana September 1st and 2nd, 1892.

Comrades, come and share the welcome the home of Company I will give you.

Gen Kimball will be with us.

T. N. Lownsdale, Sec'y
St. Bernice, Indiana
W. D. Mull, President
W. P. Haskell, Vice Pres
J. L. Hays, Treas

The 14th Ind. Vols. in reunion at Bloomfield Ind August 19, 1896 are sorrowfully required to record the death of Comrade W. D. Mull of Co A of our Regt. He died at Rockville Indiana April 25, 1896 from a wound inflicted by an insane man upon a public street without any course of provocation.

The insane assassin at once took his own life. Comrade Mull was the Sheriff of Parke County at the time of his most unfortunate death and possessed the highest esteem of all of his fellow citizens. . . . Comrade Mull was severely wounded at the battle of Antietam Sept. 17, 1862, from which he was discharged. He recovered and was commissioned Lieut Col of the 149th Ind Vols with which he served to the close of the war. His "civil" life was as patriotically devoted to duty as his military career and all who knew him join in testifying to his eminent worth in all the elements which make him a good soldier and worthy citizen.

Resolved that the foregoing be published in our roll of honor and a copy be furnished to the descendent's family.

George Reily
David Beem

To General Nathan Kimball, Ogden, Utah
Dear General and Comrade:

The reunion of the 14th regiment Ind Vols assembled at Loogootee Ind August 21st 1895 sends you our heart felt sympathy for your sickness and suffering and regrets that you cannot be with us in this most interesting occasion. We have met at your old house among your old neighbors and friends before the war where you stirred the hearts of the young men and nerved their arms to deeds of heroism by your eloquent and patriotic public addresses at the outbreaking of the rebellion. You raised the first co that left this county and were elected its captain. . . promotions followed close and fast upon each other so that the Capt commanding a company of one hundred men at the commencement of the war became a major Gen commanding one of the most famous Divisions of the Army of the Cumberland.

You were most grievously wounded. . . your wound never healed but as soon as you could hobble you took to the field again. . . your conduct has been such that at the close of a most active and fruitful life, all good men will say of you, "Well done good and faithful servant" and your dutiful and loving comrades say in addition, accept our most earnest hopes for your restoration to health and happiness.

David E. Beem
George G. Reily
E. H. C. Cavins

McClure's good-looking and talented daughter Nannie, whom one of his regimental friends referred to as "charming," was married on October 22, 1896. (The marriage occurred the year that his cousin and comrade Henderson Simpson and his

wife parted and Simpson moved to Florida.) Several members of the Fourteenth must have been at the wedding because Nannie was marrying Brooks' nephew and Houghton's cousin John H. Niblack. It was a cause for a partified southern Indiana wedding, although McClure evidently grieved for the loss of this gem of the family.

His mourning must have been even more intense when Nannie died following surgery for complications from the birth of her third child in 1899. Cavins wrote to McClure:

My Dear Friend and Comrade:

Your letter of 21st has just been received. I saw Captain Beem yesterday and received a letter a few days ago from Maj Houghton.

All seem to think that it would be too sad an affair to have it [the reunion] at Vincennes this year and all that I have heard from are in favor of changing it. . . under the circumstances I am in favor of Terre Haute at the time of the State Encampment. . . .
E. H. C. Cavins

The reunions tied years and events all together—

September 16, 1905
The White River Bank
Wm. Houghton, President

John R. McClure
Vincennes

My Dear Comrade:

I have your letter of yesterday. Will be on hand Tuesday Morning all right — for Terre Haute and our Reunion. Just received a letter from Co Cavins saying his wife would go to Terre Haute Monday. Looks like we would have a pretty good attendance.

Heard from Myerhof. He and Eberhardt and Shouse will be on hand anyway. I am anticipating a good time. With best wishes and kind regards to old comrades and friends I remain
Very truly yours
Wm. Houghton

RR 1, Bruceville, Ind.
Jan 31, 1906

Comrade, Friend Mc[Clure]

I have become so lazy and cranky that I have not been able to get out much as far this winter and have almost lost touch of everything. . . . Brooks sent me word a day or two ago that he was coming down to shave me (he was in town at the time). I have a couple of letters from CHP and he writes as though he and his daughter are having the time of their lives — he has met a lot of Knox County people and has been to quite a lot of places and he writes me that he has gained 13 pounds and can eat everything that he wants to and enjoys his food better than for years. . . . CHP tells me some pretty big stories of what he has saw of the climate of the flowers and flower parade on New Year's day and of the people fishing from the pier at Pasadena. His wife was over here a few days ago, says that he is getting quite gay for man sixty odd years old. Did you get one of the photographs of our reunion at Terre Haute? I did and I think it is the best picture that we have ever had taken. . . . Brooks is coming down Friday or Saturday. What do you think of politics in Knox County. Respectfully your friend

T. B. Thompson

Evansville
June 27, 1908

Dear Friend and comrade John R. McClure

I have not heard a word from any one for a long time. I feel like that I would like to hear from some of the comrades from Vincennes. Is my friend Tom Thompson all right and yourself. Also from Joseph Roseman and Comrade Mart Johnson. John since I lost my wife I am all broke up and can't content myself any more. You know how it is to lose your best friend in the world. I am left alone in this world with no one within a thousands of miles of here to see. I want to see all the boys once more before I leave this world of ours. . . .

Yours truly
Solomon Gundrum

The Nut Nursery
Simpson Bros. Prop.
Ft. Myers, Fla.
March 1, 1908

Dear Cousin:

I have been intending to write you before but put it off from time to time. . . . Harry's baby took the whooping cough just after we arrived here but it got along fine and is about over the cough now.

Everybody takes it easy down here, just so they eat is about all they care for. They expect the niger to do all the work and he is as lazy as can be so there is but little done in the way of labor. A man with get up and go can do well here. Ray has done fine and has bright prospects for another year. Ray has five white men from Ind and each one is worth two or three nigers. Wish you could be here on Saturday to see the nigers come into town as they come in all kinds of rigs from an oxcart to a buggy. . . they pay nigers 75¢ a day but few of them will work on Saturday. Roy has three or four pretty good nigers and has finally got them to work until Saturday at noon. If a niger gets a little sausy to the whites he may look to get shot any time. They say if they don't do it the nigers would soon be so bad the whites could not do anything with them. . . . All the natives both white and black go out in fields to work without their breakfast and it is sent out in the fields to them about 8 o'clock. . . . They say there is 16 girls to one young man in this town. This is a dry town and Jacksonville 140 miles off is the nearest saloon. In Georgia the saloons are all wiped out and it is dry all over the state. There are a number of old confederate veterans here and only a few that do not seem to be reconstructed. . . .

Yours truly
H. Simpson

Mt. Vernon, Ohio
August 3rd, 1907

Comrade:

On Sept. 17 & 18, 1907, being the 45th anniversary of the Battle of Antietam, the surviving members and the widows of deceased Comrades of the 8th Ohio Infantry will assemble for the 43rd annual Reunion at the City of Elyria, Ohio. . . . The Post and Corps will furnish dinner and supper for all members and friends. . . . You are cordially invited to be present. . . .

> Fraternally yours,
> G. Daniels, Secretary

> David E. Beem
> Attorney at Law
> Spencer, Ind.
> August 7, 1908

John R. McClure

Vincennes, Indiana
Dear Sir and Comrade

Yours of the 6th inst. received. I note what you say in regard to changing the place of the reunion of the Fourteenth Indiana to Toledo. I think it is too late to make the change, even if it was desirable, which I doubt. It has been very generally given out that the reunion is to be here, and committees have been appointed to make arrangements. We are expecting to make preparations for a great time. . . this should not hinder any of the old boys from going to Toledo and attending the meeting there. . . . I have written to Cavins and Houghton.

> Yours truly in FP & L
> David E. Beem

> 1913
> Fiftieth Anniversary of the
> Battle of Gettysburg
> July 1, 2, 3, and 4, 1913

John R. McClure
Vincennes, Indiana

Dear John and Comrade:

I do not see why you can't make out your papers for Gettysburg. You say you were sick and with the wagon train. So you were present on the field of Gettysburg and joined us on the field. You do not swear falsely, if you make affidavid. You were on the field. The meaning of "field" means any where near, [you were] several miles from Gettysburg yet the fight there of Cavalry means the Gettysburg battle. All skirmishes in Virginia or on our way to Gettysburg or even after Gettysburg mean "field of Gettysburg."

> Your comrade
> N. D. Cox
> Commissioner for Indiana

> Washington, D.C.
> July 18, 1913

My Dear Comrade McClure

I want to congratulate you on your final successful escape from Gettysburg. You must certainly have had a very narrow escape. I am told that they chased you nearly to Cumberland and then from there home that when you reached home you was coatless, hatless and had but one shoe. I remember seeing men in that shape during the war but was surprised when I heard fifty years after the war that an old soldier had been compelled to face such trials and suffering as I am told you passed through in your second Battle of Gettysburg. . . . Now John it is about time to again think about Reunion and make arrangements. . . if the boys could select a date about the middle of Sept that would not conflict with anything else I am pretty certain I could be with you. I will be very sorrowful if I am unable to be with the boys because this is one of the meetings I look forward to with fond anticipation. . . .

> I am as ever
> James J. Shouse

> August 12, 1915
> Evansville, Ind.

John R. McClure

Dear Comrade:

. . . For the good of the Reunion you might get his honor Mayor House to make us a speech of welcome and if he desires he might say something about Col Coons, Capt. Patterson. . . and others. If you could get some church choir or male quartet to give us a song or two that would be agreeable. I feel that if we were by ourselves we could take up all the time in bringing up different movements and incidents and leave out the rude funny business. By doing so I think we

could get a good report in the papers. I wrote up our funny business
in our last Reunion for the *National Tribune* but they cut it all out. . . .

Yours
Charles H. Myerhof

The Spanish American War came and went then another,
larger war in Europe.

The White River Bank
William Houghton, Pres.
September 25, 1917

John R. McClure, Esq.
Vincennes, Indiana

Dear Comrade:

   Just received your letter also one of Captain Myerhoff written you
— sorry Charlie [Myerhoff] went off so soon. I think he will be sorry
when he thinks it over. Am sending yours and his letter to Beem — I
think he will think with me that Vincennes is the place and we will
not change — we will never have another Sullivan or Rockport
reunion — we are too few and the war absorbs all the interest.

Your comrade
Will Houghton

In Memoriam, Major William Houghton
August 11, 1918

   The esteemed soldier, citizen and friend passed to the life beyond,
aged 78 years, 9 months and 14 days. During the last twelve months
his health was impaired, but he continued at his work in his business,
in the County Council of Defense and his other affairs, yet it was
apparent that his strength was failing. On the 18th of July he was
called to his home by sickness of his wife. During the night he
became seriously ill. . . . He was stricken with a complication of
diseases attended with a degree of poisoning.

   The qualities of this thought and feeling continued apparent in
his closing days. The World War was greatly on his mind, and the

field of battle in his fancies flashed to view with many of the phases of the awful. . . . [Someone with Houghton at his deathbed said,] "You should have heard him! He seemed in vision at the head of his troops once more with dashing steed and waving sword and commanding voice. He rushes on. . . and beckons to his nephews Dale and Howard to fall in line. . . . His old Gibraltar Brigade has risen from the dead and is alive again as the Rainbow Division and on the battlefield beyond the Marne. . . to him it would seem Victory is crowning the ranks that are fighting for human freedom and he is ready to depart. . . . And so it was, that [he died]. . . the flag he loved so well formed a most fitting background to the arrangement of flowers and floral pieces. At the foot of the casket were his army relics and sword. On a card suspended from its handle, were inscribed these words "He drew his sword in defense of the flag in 1861. He sheathed it when the Union was restored."

David E. Beem, Attorney
Spencer, Indiana
August 22, 1919

John R. McClure
Vincennes, Indiana

Dear Comrade:

I received a letter from the son of Chas. H. Myerhof, from which I learn that he is too feeble in mind and body to look after the matter of the reunion of the 14th Indiana. . . . I am in receipt of a letter from the secretary of the association of the 59th Ind. which informs me that they expect to have a reunion at Bloomfield about the 25 Sept. and wish to have our reunion at Spencer say Sept. 17. . . I am willing to go to Bloomfield if thought best, however. . . . Let me hear from you by return mail.

Yours in F.C. and L.
David E. Beem

Venice, Calif.
Oct. 23, 1920

Comrade John and Sister Fannie:

We arrived home OK and our trip was made beautiful from the time we left until we returned and away down deep in our heart we said Oh God, what dear friends we have back in Indiana. Our minds run back to childhood days when we with you dear friends used to romp the hills around the old school house and have such grand times together and now when we look at each other, bent over, wrinkles in the face, hair white with many winters — you boys look braver, more sturdy and better than you did some 50 years ago. And you old gray haired gals look sweeter to me than you did 50 years ago and all together we were all happy when last we met at the depot in Vincennes. And oh I hope we will be permitted to meet again as we didn't have enough time together. And the sad part of it was to think that the day we arrived home Comrade Simpson whom we all loved had to lay down and die and I fear that others have answered the Last Roll Call by this time as some looked so feeble. . . . I guess that is all. I would be so glad to hear from you if you care to write. I forgot to tell you that my daughter took a Codak shot of "Colonel" Uncle Joe Roseman at the Monument — in giving a glowing description of the speeches made were John R. McClure, John Simpson, Abe Reel and "Colonel" Roseman. Well goodbye, give my love to all the friends, as ever

Abe S. Reel

Los Angeles, Cal.
September 24, 1921

Mr. John McClure
Secretary

Dear Comrade

Your invitation to attend the regular reunion of the Old Fourteenth Indiana Regiment at Gosport on Sept. 24 received. . . .

This year I am again deprived of the pleasure. Am just recovering from a severe spell of Bronchitis and extreme prostration, and while my soul and heart are with the dear old comrades, and would love to meet them once more, I feel unequal to the occasion. . . .

Fifty six years ago last July, the grand Old Regiment stacked arms for the last time in Indianapolis, disbanded the organization and said goodbye to army life, each of the old comrades proceeded to their several houses to assume the duties of civil life. This year today, Sept. 24 by the strong ties of fellowship the survivors of the old Regt. will meet together again to talk over. . . the grand old regiment as they did many times in the past around the campfire in front of a brave, courageous and misguided enemy.

May the valor, chivalry and history of the proud old regiment continue to shed its luster on its worn and tattered old colors, to animate and encourage all true and good citizens loyal to the cause of a United country.

Am sorry I can't be with you.

> Fraternally,
> E. E. Jenkins
> Company F

> Newport, Cal.
> Sept. 15, 1922

Mr. John R. McClure
Sec. of the 14th Indiana Reunion

Dear Sir

Your card of invitation to the reunion of the 14th Indiana received. How I do wish that I could be with you all for just that one day.

But I fell and broke my leg in January and have been confined to my bed and wheel chair since then. I will be with you in memory on that day at any rate.

If any of you boys should come out to California, be sure and look me up.

> Your comrade to the end
> W. F. Fickas

> Winfield, Kansas 9/18/22

Comrades of the old 14th

I cannot be with you today in person but I will be with you in spirit and my thoughts will be of you and your heroic endurance of the hardships of camp and on many a hard march and your courage and bravery on many a battlefield.

The fifty or more years that has past since you rendered these services to the government in time of its greatest need has not obliterated from my memory your many deeds. . . we few are survivors of the ravages of time — time is rapidly thinning our ranks and it will not be long till the last one will have answered the last roll call and as Tenison says we will all have "passed over the bar."

But the deeds, the valor of the men of the old 14th from 61 to 65 will live on and be cherished in the minds of our children and grandchildren long after we have answered the last roll call.

It sure would be a pleasure to me to meet with you today and enjoy a comrade handshake and the reminiscent stories of you comrades. . . . I am truly sorry to learn by the card. . . that this is likely to be the last reunion assemblage of the 14th. But I assume the ranks have thinned down to that point in the old 14. So comrades, the spirit of 61 to 65 is still alive in me and that my thoughts will be with you with a heart felt prayer for your enjoyment. . . .

Comrades I am 85 past, but able to get around quite actively for one of that age and expect to go to the National GAR Encampment at Des Moines, Iowa.

> Yours in F. C. and S.
> Ran. Anderson
> Company K

CIVIL WAR VETS ENJOYED REUNION HERE WEDNESDAY

The thirty-eighth annual reunion of the 59th regiment Indiana volunteers was held in Gosport Wednesday jointly with the 14th regiment.

Sixteen members of the 59th and nine members of the 14th with visitors to the number of seventeen registered in the Baptist Church when the morning session began at 9:30.

The morning session was given over to business sessions. . . and the decision to disband and hold no more reunions on the part of the 14th. This decision was pathetic and the sad faces of each of the members of the 14th at the close of the session showed that they realized the tragedy of such a decision. . . .

> *Gosport Reporter*
> September 22, 1922

"Reunion of the Fourteenth Indiana Volunteers at Gosport Indiana" (manuscript)
September 20, 1922

June 7th, 1861 at Camp Vigo near Terre Haute the Fourteenth, it being the first Regiment mustered into the service in the Civil War from Indiana for three years with 1,134 men and the beloved Nathan Kimball as Colonel, on the 5th day of July it left for Virginia where it received its baptism of blood. This regiment continued in service with the Army of the Potomac participating in all the great battles of that Army. . . of the 1,134 men who were mustered, there now survive less than half a hundred, and they are scattered over the country from the Atlantic to the Pacific.

For two score years survivors of this Regiment have been meeting in Annual reunions until now very few are here. Many memories, both precious and sad, crowd in and upon us today as we recall those far-off battle years and communion with our comrades in our several reunions. The glorious victories of the Fourteenth regiment are among the archives of our beloved country at the Capitols at Washington D.C. and Indianapolis to remain a perpetual memorial to its achievements.

In view of these lamentable facts it will be impractical to get enough numbers together to make another reunion worthwhile.

Therefore, be it resolved that the Reunion Association of the Fourteenth Indiana Regiment be dissolved, and that this be, and is hereby declared its last and final meeting.

> David Beem, President
> John R. McClure, Sec.

Despite the formal dissolving, the regiment, of course, would not really be disbanded until the last man was gone. Three months later McClure's wife died, and, sounding a little bit like Stonewall Jackson, he said, "I think it's time for me to pass over" and allowed himself to die of what started out to be a minor cold. David Beem followed the next year. Finally, in 1938 as Hitler was moving through Europe, the last veteran of the Fourteenth Indiana Volunteers died.[26] This was Isaac Crim, who had recently begun his memoirs with the words, "I first saw the light of day at Hindostan Falls, Martin County, Indiana in 1842," who had walked eight miles to join Company C, who went behind enemy lines to get Lieutenant Junod's body and who fought bravely at Cheat Mountain, Virginia, when he was only nineteen years old.

It is popular to downgrade the Victorians these days — to analyze patronizingly their imperialism, their Gilded Age hypocrisy, and their sexual inhibitions (Beem's proud "modesty"). But it was the ideals of those Victorians — faith in God, love of country, and belief in oneself — amplified by the incredible physical and spiritual demands of the American frontier, which produced exactly the kind of soldier necessary to fight the Civil War.

The spirit of 1861-65 was just about played out in America by 1910. With the generation of men who bore that spirit, America's frontier youth was dying. William McGuffey's books had little appeal for the new generation of the Jazz Age. Still, what McGuffey and all the rest of the frontier educational process had taught left its stamp. Americans are today, and probably always will be, stubborn, bold, and incorrigibly idealistic, lovers of democracy who sometimes seem to be the only ones in the world who believe that it will really work. They were this way when, rising out of the outposts of the eastern-seaboard frontier, they threw off the kings of Europe; they were even more this way when they refused to let the good dream die during the Civil War.

And of course regimental democracy, which was a result of the frontier process in action, accomplished a marvel when the war was over; it completed the Revolution that had only been begun by the patriots all the Civil War soldiers so revered. Blacksmiths had fought with bank presidents' sons from '61 to '65, and they would never settle for anything else but the reality of equality when they returned.

The pioneer spirit had its finest hour in the Civil War, just as its sun was beginning to go down; and its finest, clearest sunset light shone through the performance of the Western Civil War soldier. Even today as we look at him (and of course all of his cohorts from the Northern Army) in the camps around Vicksburg and at Falmouth, grizzled and flippantly smiling at the photographer, we are awed at whatever it was that kept them all going — and smiling. In the final analysis, the frontier wrought a splendid product. Surely French was right

when, after Antietam, he looked at the performance of the
Gibraltar Brigade and the other units in Lincoln's army and
said, "There never has been such material in any army."

1. *Indiana in the Civil War Era,* pp. 404-424.

2. Ibid., p. 557. The author quotes Gilbert, *Evansville and Vanderburg County, Indiana.* Also helpful is James Morlock, *The Evansville Story: A Cultural Interpretation* (Evansville, Indiana: Creative Press, 1956).

3. *The Evansville Story,* pp. 97-101.

4. *Indiana in the Civil War Era,* pp. 559-560.

5. U.S. Census of 1880, quoted in *Indiana in the Civil War Era,* p. 537.

6. *Houghton Memorial Booklet.*

7. *Brooks Memorial Booklet.*

8. *Vincennes Western Sun,* February 23, 1867. Honorable William E. Niblack, member of the House, had made inquiries in Washington.

9. Letters of Van Dyke, July 11, 23, and 29 and September 19, 1865.

10. *Journal of the 80th (81st, 82nd and 83rd) National Encampment of the Grand Army of the Republic* (Washington, D.C.: U.S. Government Printing Office).

11. *Houghton Memorial Booklet.*

12. *History of Evansville and Vanderburg County, Indiana,* p. 322.

13. Letter of Cavins to McClure, October 22, 1910.

14. Letter of O. W. Daniels, on the letterhead of Joe Hooker Post No. 21, Department of Ohio Grand Army of the Republic, 1908.

15. Letter of Oscar Rankin to John McClure, April 21, 1900.

16. *Dedication of the Soldiers' Monument by the Citizens of Knox County,* memorial booklet, October 8, 1914.

17. In the Indiana State Library.

18. *The Ninth New York Volunteers,* in the Vassar College Library, Poughkeepsie, New York.

19. Also in the library at Vassar College.

20. Edwards, *Brief Biography,* pp. 25-26.

21. In the Indiana State Library.

22. This exchange is also in Myerhof's booklet.

23. In the Nathan Kimball Papers, June 21, 1887.

24. Letter of George H. Mohlron to McClure, May 8, 1884.

25. The veterans' papers are in the author's possession as McClure's direct descendant.

26. Crim is buried at Green Hills Cemetery, Bedford, Indiana.

Colonel E. H. C. Cavins, of the Fourteenth's Greene County company, was a major when this photo was taken.

Officer presumed to be Thomas C. Bailey, First Lieutenant, Company C; and Adjutant, Company A.

Second Lieutenant John Stannis, Company C.

Private J. C. Willemon,
Company C.

Private J. Bowers,
Company G.

An unidentified member
of the Fourteenth.